# Communism and Democracy

History, debates and potentials

For Elaine

# Communism and Democracy

## History, debates and potentials

*Mike Makin-Waite*

Lawrence & Wishart
London 2017

British Library Cataloguing in Publication Data.
A catalogue record for this book is available from the British Library

ISBN 978-1-910448-76-2

Lawrence and Wishart Limited,
Central Books Building
Freshwater Road
Chadwell Heath
RM8 1RX

# Contents

# ACKNOWLEDGEMENTS AND DEDICATION

This book owes its inception to the late Phil Leeson. In the second half of the 1980s and early 1990s, I learned a great deal from discussions with members of an older generation of left-wingers I met through the North West District Committee of the British Communist Party. In these Phil was a calm, modest and influential voice. As communism collapsed, Phil and I were amongst those who believed that the tasks facing left-wingers did not involve rushing into new partisan commitments. Rather, we felt we needed to organise around the problem that there was not, currently, a viable model of socialism to offer.

The challenge was to review and redefine our co-ordinates. Questioning the fundamentals of the politics we had held to was part of this: a process at the same time demoralising and ambitious, exciting and unsettling. At first we hoped that our considerations and shaky campaigns might sustain the newly set up 'Democratic Left' as a consistently Eurocommunist organisation: we helped set up the North West structures of DL as the Communist Party of Great Britain was disbanded. But in the end DL was too organisationally weak and politically confused to survive: it had inherited a momentum of decline from the Communist Party, and most of its active members were either inexperienced or tired out, while many of us were disorientated and some of us faced in different political directions. DL quickly proved to be another false hope, itself unsustainable – other than in Scotland, where a fragile but valuable Democratic Left network still continues to promote radical, environmental and feminist politics.

Some of the jottings I made during conversations with Phil twenty-five years ago have been incorporated into the present work. My early sprawling drafts for the book gradually became more focused as a result of a great many thoughtful comments from David Purdy, Willie Thompson and Mike Tyldesley. I also benefited from further encouragement, pointers and warnings on particular draft chapters from Aidan Byrne, Derek Boothman, John Callaghan, Alison Gilchrist,

Deborah Grayson, Francis King, Ben McCall, Kevin Morgan, Mike Squires, Matt Worley and Jeff Yates.

Sally Davison and her colleagues at Lawrence and Wishart combined enthusiasm, patience and care through substantial editorial advice and in bringing the work to press. Both because of its history, and its commitment to contribute to future progressive radicalism, it is an honour to be published by L&W.

The usual disclaimers apply: sensible lines of argument have been suggested by others. All errors, imprecisions and questionable judgements are my own. No one named above necessarily agrees with any particular point or theme in this book.

In terms of personal support, thanks are due to Robin Solomon and Mike Squires for generous hospitality during visits to London for 'socialist history' meetings over the years.

Suggestions from my daughters Genevieve and Jessica, and observations from Elaine's children Tomas and Grace, have been particularly appreciated. And I have greatly valued conversations on some of the issues in the book with my father-in-law Ken Makin. I hope that his good sense has helped me tone down some of the wilder points I might otherwise have made.

My biggest thanks go to my wife Elaine, for her patience with my 'tip-tapping', her practicality, and her knowledge of what is really important.

# Introduction

## BACK TO THE FUTURE?

Much has changed since an ideologist of American power announced 'the end of history' in 1989. At the time, as Soviet communism stood on the brink of collapse, Francis Fukuyama's thesis that liberal capitalism now set the limits of all social possibility enjoyed wide influence, and was reluctantly accepted even by many who did not welcome it.[1]

Today, however, the landscape is full of new possibilities for radical social change.[2]

This is largely a response to developments in the intervening period of resurgent capitalism, which has seen an increase in poverty, misery and conflict, and an increasing danger of environmental disaster. The dominance and spread of neoliberal economics over the last quarter century has led to deepening inequality, and weakened the institutions of western democracy.

In Europe and the USA, some of the reactions to these problems have taken the form of right-wing populisms. But there are also encouraging signs on the left: left-wing candidates and parties have recently been winning wider support than has been the case for decades. There are new and promising forms of interaction between lively social movements and political organisations. Hundreds of thousands of young people hold to varied, lively and determined forms of politics that encompass an understanding of gender, race, sexuality and other aspects of identity as well as class. Their knowledge of the ways in which our complex and diverse sense of ourselves can be both the focus of oppressions and the basis of joy and pride offers hope for substantial improvements in the quality of our political and social life. Green parties are increasingly well established and confident; and recognition of the pressing need to address the ecological agenda is not limited to their members and voters. And, in and amongst these growing and varied possibilities, there has been some revival of interest in the values and potentials of communism.

A number of writers have made theoretical contributions to this development. They include the stimulating, provocative and inconsistent Slavoj Zizek, who promotes an abstract 'communist hypothesis';[3] the more thoughtful and committed Jodi Dean, who has stated the case for new forms of communist party organisation;[4] and Nick Srnicek and Alex Williams, whose joint work proposes long-term strategic efforts to develop a modern left hegemonic project, engaging closely with social and technological trends as the basis for inventing a possible future beyond neoliberalism.[5]

Such interventions suggest that debates about the nature of communism could become increasingly important over the coming years. Growing numbers of activists want to change the fundamental workings of society so as to meet ordinary people's needs, reverse or overcome current trends of social degradation, and avert the risk of environmental catastrophe. Only some of these identify themselves as thorough-going socialists pursuing a deep critique of capitalism, and arguing that system change is needed, not just reform. But insofar as they show any signs of succeeding, all such activists are likely to face 'accusations' of 'being Marxist', and of attempting to recreate twentieth-century communism.[6] It will not be possible to simply 'spring free' and 'leave behind' the legacy of this major historical movement. Those who oppose radical change will certainly not allow this. And, even if they were minded to do so, it is a responsible and useful thing for progressive people to assess communism's historical effort to transcend capitalism, and to draw appropriate lessons. For the foreseeable future, radical campaigners will need to be able to position themselves in relation to communism's record.

For these reasons, inventing a co-ordinated, resolute and effective anti-systemic movement for the future involves some looking backwards. In Lucio Magri's words, it means confronting, 'without reticence or censorship' the deterioration and ultimate failure of the revolutions of the twentieth century, and seeking to understand the underlying reasons for that failure, 'not only the particular historical conditions'; and on this basis then seeking 'to identify and value those teachings which the political history and theoretical traditions of communism can offer for analysis of the present and projection of the future'.[7]

This book offers a contribution to that work, through a critical consideration of aspects of the Marxist tradition; a look at some of the key moments in the history of the Soviet Union; and a discussion of developments in some of the communist parties that formed following the Russian revolution. These parties, inspired by Lenin and the Bolsheviks, were characterised at the time of their formation by a belief in the need for a ruptural break between the capitalist present and the socialist future, and by the idea that the working class, as the leading force in society, would be the agent to achieve this break. They also proposed the abandonment of old forms of 'bourgeois democracy', proposing instead that working-class representatives could directly rule society through 'soviets', or councils. Communists argued that bourgeois forms of democracy could not be vehicles for revolutionary change: they were, rather, blocks to pursuing the interests of the working class. One of the themes of this book is the development over subsequent decades of an understanding that, although this theory had apparently brought success in establishing the Soviet Union, there was in fact the need to bring a commitment to democracy back into strategies for radical change. Key moments in this shifting perception include the fundamental recasting of Comintern policies in the mid-1930s in response to the rise of fascism, and the development of Eurocommunism in the 1970s.

## LESSONS FROM LAST TIME?

Anyone proposing or being 'accused' of communism in our times faces some serious challenges. It is a politics overwhelmingly identified with the Soviet experience, and with the communist-run states put in place in Eastern Europe at the end of the second world war. All these collapsed in 1989, and this was also the time when China's leaders shifted their country's economy towards a distinctive form of capitalism. These developments marked the end of the 'short communist century': surely its political and economic models are dead and gone?

In any case, goes the argument, who would want to recover them? They were not positive examples. Although the Soviet Union did achieve rapid industrialisation in the 1930s, this came at the cost of great repression; and centralised state planning proved itself increasingly inefficient in the postwar period: it was not able to meet ordinary people's needs or desires. Furthermore, political culture in the communist states was oppressive and undemocratic.

From the early 1990s, recognition of these realities, even more than the simple defeat of the communist project, led to a period of great demoralisation and disorientation on the radical left and more widely. Tony Judt, who was a thoughtful opponent of Marxism, nevertheless recognised that the Soviet Union's downfall had 'undermined not just communism, but a whole progressive narrative of advance and collectivisation'.[8] And Russell Jacoby linked 'the collapse of the communist states' to 'something more difficult to pinpoint ... an incremental impoverishment of what might be called Western imagination'.[9] Communism's eclipse was just one expression of a reducing optimism about the possibility of ever shaping the world in line with the democratically agreed outcomes of reasoned consideration, with the aim of meeting shared human needs.

Social-democrats had also experienced serious decline during the rise of neoliberalism. This other main branch of socialism had come out of the same nineteenth century tradition as the communists, and when the Bolsheviks broke away from it they had kept the label, which thus came to represent the 'reformist' part of the socialist movement. For those who now declared themselves communists, social-democracy for a while became anathema. For their part, these non-revolutionary socialists focused their sights on achieving positive reforms that were possible *within* capitalist structures.

Before they were stopped by the neoliberal turn, European social-democrats formed governments that established important institutions and progressive arrangements, from the early 1930s in Sweden; in the 1940s, 1960s and 1970s in Britain; from the late 1960s in West Germany; and during the 1980s in France, Spain and Greece. Their achievements included welfare systems, health services, expanded access to education, and legislation to underpin workers' rights and to counter sex discrimination.

But since the 1980s social-democrats have been in increasing disarray: their tradition has been disorganised and pulled in different directions. Their very success in facilitating rising living standards and income growth for ordinary people played a role in laying the basis for the attitudinal shifts that ultimately undermined their appeal. Increasing numbers of aspirational workers came to identify with visions of individual success as promoted by the political right, and to see the market as the best way of delivering goods and services. Over time, most social-democrat leaders responded to this trend, and to wider changes in the economy and society, by themselves embracing neoliberalism, and becoming fully integrated members of the 'political class'.

Gaps then grew between the party leaderships and their 'traditional' constituencies. And this in turn both reflected and accelerated trends of disengagement from established politics. One consequence of the resulting disaffection has been the opening up of space for the populist and anti-establishment reactions that have taken right-wing or ethno-nationalist forms.

A sense of disconnection from mainstream politics has been reinforced for some radical and progressive people by the establishment's attitudes to issues such as the environmental crisis – a crisis which is the more serious for being so often presented as if its reality can be the subject of 'debate', or dismissed as a 'hoax'. Declining confidence in democracy partly results from the evident inability – or refusal – of governments to address such problems. The centuries-long ecological emergency into which we have now entered presents current and future generations with the costs and consequences of exploitative economic relations in dramatic forms that we have hardly begun to register.

Since the neoliberal financial crisis of 2007-8, coherence and direction have become even greater problems for social-democrats across Europe, as they have attempted to respond to the concerns that are animating right-wing populism; promote 'responsible' economics; and at the same time respond to a development that seemed unthinkable back in the 1990s – the renewal of the radical left.[10]

In Greece and the Netherlands, young parties with roots in social movements and Eurocommunism have recently been out-polling the 'old' social-democratic parties; in Spain, the new left party Podemos has had a spectacular rise. In Britain, the left has made a significant impact *within* the old social-democratic party itself, with Jeremy Corbyn being twice elected Labour leader, following campaigns in which grassroots activism, including through the Momentum network, has engaged new support for the party. This trend was further consolidated when the new Labour programme achieved increased support and seats in the 2017 general election. In France, Jean-Luc Melenchon's 2017 presidential campaign also evidenced scope for new left-wing alliances. In the first round of voting, his independent movement, backed by communists, attracted more than three times as many votes as the social-democratic candidate. (The Socialist Party candidate polled a mere 6.36 per cent of the vote, while Melenchon won 19.58 per cent, a figure that was within less than two percentage points of Le Pen's – though this received very little attention from the press.)

There is a growing sense that renewing the appeal of socialism requires the assertion of radical policies, and this is the broad context for emerging discussions on how Marxism could make a contribution to a renewed critique of capitalism; which aspects of communism's legacy might assist in working out how to bring an end to neoliberalism; and whether any of its political approaches suggest how system change could be brought about today: whether, in sum, lessons from twentieth-century communism could feed back into today's projects for positive social change and assist the current renewal of progressive politics.

In these discussions there are specific problems to consider. Perhaps the most important of these is the issue of democracy, an issue which is strongly associated with the dismal record of the Soviet Union in this matter, and with the politics of Leninism.

Other, related, problems include how to approach the issues generated by market economics. Celebrating the market has allowed capitalism to adapt to and shape consumer choices, and thus relate its economic workings to the values of democracy.

Left-wingers understand that market forces necessarily produce inequality, and take no account of social need. In fact, they function in ways which tend to make social need – and issues of ecological sustainability – disappear from economic consideration. But, as is now evident from the experience of twentieth-century communism, the ambition of controlling or superseding the market also produces major challenges about how to do that in ways which are efficient and effective – and democratic, so that the economy works to address people's agreed needs and desires.

## DEMOCRACY: A CONTESTED CONCEPT

Against this backdrop, this book explores relationships between twentieth-century communism and democracy. A common sense view might be that such a book need only be very short: there is no real 'relationship' to talk of. Communism's failure and defeat both resulted from and confirmed the movement's incompatibility with democracy.

But the evidence presented here recovers the history of communism's democratic and even liberal strands. These were hidden, buried and compromised by the regimes which most defined communism in power: Stalin's Russia in particular.

There were, however, other periods and places which showed the potential of combining an ambition to supersede capitalism with a commitment to democratic principles. Through the Popular Front of the 1930s, to 1968's Prague Spring and the Eurocommunism of the 1970s, the need for popular engagement and accountability as part of a politics for radical change has resurfaced over and over again inside the communist movement: in power in Czechoslovakia in 1968, with Alexander Dubcek; in opposition in Italy from the 1940s to the 1980s; running state structures in West Bengal from the late 1970s to 2011; in French local government, where communists have long been a strong and sustained presence; or in illegal underground operations in South Africa under apartheid and in many other repressive regimes. Communists in these parties have demonstrated again and again that it is perfectly possible to be at the same time radically left-wing *and* democratic.

Some of the debates discussed in this book also highlight the many limitations and contradictions that are inherent in current democratic arrangements. These are often shaped by the way they first emerged, alongside the development of capitalist economic systems. But democracy has always been an essentially and profoundly progressive cause. In its modern European forms, it developed with and from the French Revolution of 1789, which saw the entry of previously excluded masses of people into political and social life. Following this first revolution against the *ancien regime*, and the later growth of the socialist movement in the nineteenth century, emergent democracy combined the goals of extending political power to ordinary workers and peasants, and organising society so as to distribute resources on a fairer basis, in order to benefit those who were newly enfranchised.

Democrats emphasised the commonality of society, and sought to create a united people: democracy and modern notions of the nation developed in tandem. Democracy was not only concerned with mechanisms of political method and process, and ensuring rights for individuals: it also aimed at substantive results and promoted particular social relations and moral obligations. Rather than being primarily concerned with particular procedural details of decision-making, the radical nineteenth-century champions of democracy expressed convictions about the nature of sovereignty – of where power should lie. The view was that the state's legitimacy should rest on the whole community of people in a nation, and that, as a basis for this, there should be substantial social equality.[11]

As with many apparently straightforward concepts, definitions of democracy have changed dramatically in form and meaning over the years: what it signifies has 'floated', altered and been contested. In the years after the French Revolution

> democracy became in effect the regime name of the route towards equality, gracing whatever political institutions volunteered to shoulder the responsibility of pressing towards that elusive goal.[12]

Partly to limit such radicalism, 'liberal democracy' has defined itself through particular structures, rituals and practices: contested elections for public office between candidates of rival parties are at the heart of these.

The ongoing instability and plasticity of the concept of democracy comes from the way it combines different traditions: political liberalism, centred on the notion of individual freedoms and rights, and a push for popular sovereignty based on social equality. During the 1800s, these strands came together 'contingently', rather than necessarily. As industrial revolution led to the expansion of economies and populations, the concept was recovered and reworked from ancient Greece in order to name and manage the massive social process of ordinary people coming into political life. Democracy was partly their agenda, and partly the agenda by which the 'threat' they represented to established elites could be accommodated, handled, reduced, blocked and frustrated.

This history explains why it was that, during the late nineteenth century, democracy and the mass politics of socialism had an uneasy relationship, creating questions and confusions both for the powerful and those seeking enfranchisement. 'Enlightened', 'liberal', members of social groups who had held onto or gained a share of power through the 1800s sought to institute systems which would respond to, quieten and blunt the pressure for mass democracy, at the same time as preserving the rights of property owners, and making provision within the new systems for the already powerful and the proven expert. As John Dunn argues, 'the resulting liberal democracy established a joint idea which we have become entirely accustomed to: the concepts "go together"'. But, as Colin Crouch points out, this remains a coupling of two separate elements: democracy requires 'certain rough equalities' if there is to be a real capacity to affect political outcomes by all citizens. Liberalism, however, 'requires free, diverse and ample opportunities to affect those outcomes'.[13]

When this liberal principle is not combined with 'rough equalities', but operates instead in a context of significant and growing inequalities, it results in disproportionate influence for the rich and those already embedded in elite structures: democratic practice thus becomes hollowed out and less democratic. If, in spite of this, its name is continually and cynically linked to processes that serve the interests of the already powerful, the very idea of democracy then becomes discredited and diminished; and the risk of it being discarded altogether is all too real.

On this basis, socialists have often pushed against the limits of liberal democracy. They have sought to go beyond the kinds of political change offered in routine elections, where party representatives compete to run the established state at national and local levels. Communists – and many left-wing social democrats – have sought to use the existing state to implement radical politics and far-reaching social changes, including in the ways that the economy works. Some have further sought a transformation of the very relationship between state and civil society, or between politics and the economy.

In testing such limits, hostility from dominant and established forces has always been a real problem. Surveying the history of global politics and international relations from the 1940s to the 1980s, it is now possible to see that the fortunes and scope of the 'upstart' socialist countries – the Soviet Union, Eastern European states and China – were shaped and misshaped by the cold war. Imperialist powers were always dominant in this competition, even where socialist forces temporarily achieved success, as in Vietnam in the 1950s and 1970s. On the few occasions that Marxists achieved government positions in capitalist countries and began implementing changes in economic structures which would radically redistribute wealth and power, they faced repressive backlash.

This is evidenced only too well by the example of Chile in 1973, which is discussed in Chapter 13 below. For some leftists, the ruling class's preparedness to resort to violent counter-revolution as in Chile confirms that all bourgeois talk of democracy is in bad faith. It is a smokescreen and a trap: best to dispense with such distraction, and get on with pushing for working-class power 'by any means necessary'. But the record of twentieth-century communism confirms the importance of shaping and implementing radical change through democratic process.

## OVERVIEW

This book is organised into three parts. Part I traces the origins of socialism and its communist variant, and the ways that these emerged as political movements. Chapter 1 offers a brief overview and assessment of communism's record, as a way of introducing key themes. The chapters then follow a rough chronology, with Chapter 2 identifying some roots of socialism and communism in the Enlightenment and the French Revolution. The next three chapters track the emergence of Marxism and its influence within the growing socialist movement, and the ways in which these developments related to the growth of democracy and to liberalism. Chapter 6 considers debates within socialism during the quarter century before the Russian revolution of 1917.

Part II covers particular aspects of communist history. This is the biggest part of the book, but it is still necessarily selective.[14] Chapters 7 and 8 include a sketch of Lenin's leadership style, and the momentous events of 1917, and a brief account of the early years and complex internationalism of the Comintern; Chapter 9 offers an assessment of Stalinism; Chapter 10 describes the Popular Front politics of the mid-1930s; and Chapters 11 and 12 turn on two key years in the history of the left after the second world war: 1956 and 1968. Chapter 13 considers the coup which overthrew an elected government in Chile in 1973 and brought Pinochet to power; while Chapter 14 gives detailed consideration to Eurocommunism, which was partly informed by lessons from Chile. Chapter 15 covers the demise of the twentieth-century communist movement and indicates how this relates to the rise of neoliberalism.

Part III consists of three chapters offering suggestions about the lessons of communism's history for rethinking socialism and radical politics today. This part of the book draws out themes which were developed by communists in opposition in Italy, France, Spain, Britain and elsewhere, who spent a long time between the 1950s and the 1980s thinking about the problems of communism, and who were also informed by critiques of social democracy. Their analyses and debates still offer useful perspectives on how radicals might pursue a long-term 'war of position' in order to promote successful progressive alliances.[15]

In this way, these closing chapters aim to relate insights from the book's historical sections to some current challenges and debates. Chapter 16 highlights the most fundamental agenda which needs to be addressed in reshaping progressive politics – ecology. Chapter 17 sketches key aspects of left developments since the 1990s. And the final chapter attempts to look forward, registering the terrible risks that lie ahead, but at the same time affirming more positive prospects.

The overall argument of the book is that it is crucial to integrate democratic principles and practice into projects for radical change. This is not because the current powers-that-be insist that things have to be 'democratic', in their limited sense of the word; nor because 'democracy' is a 'nice to have'. It is because democracy is absolutely indispensable to progressive radicalism. You cannot sustain progressive radical change without achieving it in democratic ways; and you cannot have consistent democracy without radically changing today's social and economic settlements.

## NOTES

1. Francis Fukuyama, 'The End of History', *The National Interest*, summer 1989, developed in book form as *The End of History and the Last Man*, Simon and Schuster, New York 1992.
2. 'Radical' is a word that can be used in a number of different ways. It is most often used in this book as short-hand for political efforts and ambitions which aim at 'progressive' change through addressing the roots of problems. Radicals approach crises not as things to be solved on their own terms: they are to be addressed, instead, through changing the conditions which gave rise to them.
3. Slavoj Zizek, *In Defense of Lost Causes*, Verso, London 2009; Slavoj Zizek, *First As Tragedy, Then As Farce*, Verso, London 2009; Costas Douzinas and Slavoj Zizek (eds), *The Idea of Communism*, Verso, London 2010; and Slavoj Zizek (ed), *The Idea of Communism 2: the New York conference*, Verso, London 2013.

4. Jodi Dean, *Crowds and Party*, Verso, London 2016.
5. Nick Srnicek and Alex Williams, *Inventing the Future*, Verso, London 2015.
6. Even relatively modest reform proposals provoke the supposedly insulting epithet. Thomas Piketty's best-selling 2014 book *Capital in the 21st Century* presented well-grounded arguments for redistribution of wealth through internationally enforced taxes. Some on the right, particularly in America, were apoplectic, describing it, horror of horrors, as 'neo-Marxist'. Thinkers around New Labour were, however, relieved to note that 'despite his book's allusion to Marx, [Piketty] is a mainstream social-democrat, not a revolutionary socialist': editorial, *New Statesman*, 9 May 2014. Others recently accused of 'Marxism' in sections of the media include Barack Obama in respect of his health care reforms as US President, and the Labour Party's John McDonnell during the 2017 general election campaign.
7. Lucio Magri, 'Parting Words', *New Left Review*, January – February 2005.
8. Tony Judt, private email sent to Ian Buruma in 2011, quoted by Geoffrey Wheatcroft, *Times Literary Supplement*, 5 April 2013.
9. Russell Jacoby, *Picture Imperfect*, Columbia University Press, New York 2005, Chapter 1.
10. In 2008, after the collapse of the financial system, the Conservative Party managed to recast the problem of irresponsible bank lending and inadequate regulation 'as a problem of sovereign debt, the remedy for which was presented as austerity'. Pat Devine, 'The Greek crisis and the crisis of the Euro', *Perspectives*, Democratic Left Scotland, Dundee, summer 2015.
11. An alternative conception of democracy, in some ways consistent and complementary to the French model, but in other ways in tension with it, was constructed retrospectively around the political system established in the early United States of America. This emphasised individual rights and freedom from oppression, and mechanisms of checks and balances in the legislative process. It aimed at 'an equality of standing, and a comprehensive rejection of all overt forms of political condescension'. John Dunn, *Setting the People Free*, Atlantic Books, London 2005, p126.
12. Ibid, p152.
13. Colin Crouch, *Coping with Post-democracy*, Fabian Society, London 2000, p10.
14. The key focus is on the relationship between the history of the Soviet Union and Europe, and particularly on the politics of Western Europe. To have included adequate material on other countries would have multiplied the length of the book beyond any sensible limit.
15. For an explanation of the concept of 'war of position' see Chapter 10.

# 1. The record of communism

## THE ELECTRIC SENSE

Communism can be understood as an attempt to realise the promise of modernity. It offered a heady and resolute ambition to rework the world. Its transformative politics would overcome the inherent tendencies of capitalism towards waste and barbarism. For the radical socialists who established communist parties after 1917, the dislocations and betrayals of the 1914-18 war had proved the need for break and renewal. Decisive action should be taken to close one era and open another. As Perry Anderson describes it, the revolutionaries had 'an electric sense of the present as fraught with a momentous future'.[1]

Communism was an exciting, serious movement: it attracted, engaged and developed hundreds of thousands of the most positively minded, moral, selfless and talented members of successive political generations. For some, communism was a way to rebel; for others, a way to conform (and for still others it proved the vehicle to do both). But for all of the movement's adherents, becoming communist expressed *ambition*. They chased the potentials of order and human happiness that science and social progress had projected.

Over seven decades, and in many countries, communism improved living standards and increased people's sense of dignity, both directly and indirectly. In government they drove through programmes of modernisation, economic development and industrialisation, and they also supported people across the continents who were working for popular rights and national liberation and the overthrow of imperialist rule. Communists in power established welfare, healthcare and education provision at levels unavailable in other parts of the developing world. They shaped and fed a range of progressive governments, positive social movements and democratic organisations, giving hundreds of millions the vision and hope of a much better world.

Because of the specificities of local context, however, these efforts to deliver on the positive potential of modernity varied considerably. Whilst the whole movement drew their approach and method from a shared canon, rooted in selective readings of Karl Marx and some of his followers, each developed in particular social and historical circumstances. The ideas and principles which animated communism were taken up and given concrete expression in many different ways. Furthermore, there were major tensions, fault-lines and differing impulses within and between some of these diverse attempts (though perhaps the most marked differences were those between communist parties in power and those who remained in opposition).

Comparing the strategies and tactics of different parties and groupings, in different countries, throws up examples of approaches which are not only various, but sometimes diametrically opposed.[2] For example, as explored later, policy differences between the various strands of opinion *within* the Russian communist party in the mid-1920s were greater than the gaps which, most of the time, separate mainstream political parties in Europe today.

Communist approaches could take the form of sectarian self-assertion and abrupt impatience with anyone not in support of the 'line'; but they could also mean patient alliance-building, based on genuine interest in and respect for differences of perspective and values. Some communists expressed contempt for democratic values and exhibited a preparedness to override them, or to spout them cynically, in bad faith, for short-term tactical reasons; others showed a strong and sustained commitment to the value of democracy, combined with a deep thoughtfulness about its real meaning. Communism could involve 'extremist' opposition to current settlements and legislation, with a preparedness to act illegally, including through terrorism; but it could also involve a realistic recognition of the limits to social change, and a concern to advance through steady steps which took account of current possibilities, combined with full respect for the rule of law. It could be expressed in the morals and methods of the police officer, but also in the values and cunning of the street fighter; in the orderly habits of the bureaucrat, but also through the impulses of the iconoclast. It could mean opposition to every expression of nationalism, or the cultivation and promotion of a variety of forms of nationalism; support for the rights of minorities and vigorous defence against discrimination; but also blunt efforts to forcibly integrate subaltern groups on the terms of the majority – or sometimes the dominant minority (including campaigns to 'modernise' the position of Muslims, from the southern soviet republics in the 1920s to Bulgaria and Afghanistan in the 1980s). These contradictions were in many ways shaped by the interplays and tensions between an approach that on the one hand sought to facilitate liberation and self-determination but on the other sought to control society.

Because of this, perhaps we should talk of *communisms*, rather than *communism*, so as to emphasise the movement's variety. It is certainly a myth that communism was a monolithic, one-bloc entity, entirely centrally controlled and directed from Moscow. Even before the major divergence between Soviet and Chinese variants evident from the early 1960s, a diverse range of positions and cultures always existed within communism. After the second world war, the cold war counter-position of 'pluralism' to 'communism' tended to obscure the ways that communism was itself plural. Significant debates and controversies animated the movement when degrees of democracy were possible or allowed, and shaped it through subterranean activity and absences when democratic spaces were closed down.

Communism's divisions formed around shared assumptions, aims and language; and the common commitment to discipline and the benefits of unity in action meant that disputes were always about establishing the correct approach for *all* comrades. Resulting disagreements were continual, serious and consequential.

From the 1940s to the 1980s, around one third of the world's population lived in countries run by communist parties.[3] There were 'non-ruling' parties in nearly every other country. From Italy to South Africa, and from India to Chile, large communist organisations played important roles in legal or illegal opposition to governments and regimes, ran local municipalities and regional governmental structures, and shaped social movements. Even where parties were a small, marginal and somewhat exotic presence in their national political scenes – as in Britain and the United States – they generated significant campaigns and cultural activities which led to real social progress. Through work in wider movements, trade unions and research units, communists informed a wide range of government initiatives, such as the nationalisation programmes in Britain at the end of the second world war.

Successive moments of social crisis and political optimism fed the renewal and momentum of the movement, bringing in large new cohorts of young people who were committed to communism's founding ideals and sought to remake and realise them in their own times, from the 1930s to the 1970s. But although communism attracted tens of thousands, sometimes hundreds of thousands, of supporters in nations across the world, the movement was never able to convince most people – other than in a few locales and for short periods – that the cause was really the best way to secure and advance their interests.

Unable to establish itself on a robust democratic basis, state communism warped, became perverse, and promoted immoral, duplicitous and patriarchal leaders. Pretending that the political parties that they had taken over were identical with the unified interests of 'the working class', these men made victims of vast numbers of ordinary people – and of their own comrades – thus alienating most of communism's potential supporters. Communism generated regimes and organisations which were vicious, criminal, cruel, inhuman and murderous, as well as inefficient and wasteful. The movement's promise of a fair and equal society was corrupted, and these values were subsequently claimed by regimes that were all too often authoritarian and repressive. In many countries, communism's positive vision lived on as a cruel joke in the face of 'actually existing socialism', and its cynical abuse by dishonest, self-serving elites. Democratic communists were thus confronted with disabling ethical dilemmas, and intractable political and theoretical challenges.

These serious defects were exacerbated and exploited by the opponents of communism in the capitalist world. The capitalist wealthy recognised that they were up against a threat that was much greater than that of mere competition: Marxists in power were an existential threat to their interests. They therefore, from the beginning, promoted anti-communism in all its varied forms: they were energetic, intransigent, sometimes sophisticated, often blunt – and all too often murderous.

At the end of the 1980s, state communism in the Soviet Union and Europe collapsed amidst the interplay of effective oppositions and its own self-defeating flaws. The movement proved unable to overcome and transcend capitalism. This profit-based system still continues to maintain its workings, through adaptation and renewal, in spite of its inbuilt and gross inability to deliver on its promises, its wastefulness, unfairness, frequent systemic crises, inherent tendencies to create inequality and reward oppression, the dishonesty and shallowness it promotes in politics and culture, and its degradation of our environment – a problem which has now become a crisis.

But the rival 'possibility' of communism left the stage having proved even less capable of realising the ambitions it had set for itself. Having long claimed to be a form of society superior to and historically beyond capitalism, it floundered and failed in all the areas most central to its effort: its internationalism; its attempt to develop non-capitalist economies; and its democracy.

## FUNDAMENTAL DIFFICULTIES

Communists promoted a strong internationalism, emphasising the common class interest shared by workers of warring nations. According to a familiar critique, over time the Comintern and its constituent parties were corrupted by Stalinism. Although never entirely or simply 'subordinate to Moscow', the national parties within the Comintern were increasingly required to act in line with the Soviet Union's interests: 'internationalism' came to be redefined as communists everywhere needing to promote loyalty to the first socialist state.

This analysis leaves out some of the more positive achievements of communist internationalism. The existence of the Soviet Union and related powers as both moral inspiration and as sources of material and, sometimes, military support, gave resources and support to many left-nationalist movements, from the foundation of the Third International right up until the movement's end. Marxists put down strong roots in many oppressed nations by demonstrating that bourgeois politicians could often be hypocritical in their advocacy of limited national rights. They showed how the market economy repeatedly spelled crude exploitation of national resources and labour.

But in the end the varied and complex internationalism of communism never did establish a world politics: the Sino-Soviet split of the 1960s was in large part a reaction against Russian chauvinism, an assertion of Chinese national autonomy. Between 1989 and 1991, nationalist mobilisations fuelled the bloody breakup of Yugoslavia, and 'peripheral' states reacted against centres. Old territorial rivalries re-emerged. Archaic nationalisms were recovered or invented.

Supposedly 'buried' issues resurfaced from among those affected by Stalin's forced population shifts.

These contradictions and disputes around nationalism and internationalism were disabling enough for communism. But it faced even more fundamental difficulties in the sphere of economics.

Marxists had rejected capitalism as an exploitative system motored by the pursuit of private profit, necessarily in conflict with the satisfaction of human needs, entirely unsustainable, and urgently needing to be replaced. And here communists made the largest claims for their own politics: the boast was that they would establish alternative systems, superior to wasteful capitalism. They were in favour of economic growth, to be sure, and limited support could be afforded to the bourgeoisie where they promoted development. But under capitalism, such growth was limited and distorted by the imperative to generate ever higher returns to a minority interest: private investors. In that anarchic system, crises, creating material hardship and stress, were recurrent. Marxists' optimistic vision was that, under communism, the progressive forces of science and technology would no longer be impeded but could be applied to the building of a society of abundance for the many, not just the few.

The problems communists experienced in trying to develop forms of economic management and development which superseded the profit motive and the market were therefore particularly serious. Whilst they did establish a range of economic systems that were characterised by the absence or near absence of private property, and within which central planning was the main tool for boosting production, distributing on the basis of (a version of) fairness and equality and providing systems of welfare, none of these systems could be sustained.

This problem was matched by another. As Alec Nove has argued, wherever it was established, the functional logic of centralised planning turned out to fit far too easily 'into the practice of centralised despotism'.[4] But effective and sustainable economic planning could only have worked with the active engagement of producers and consumers. The failure of communist governments to establish and extend democratic rights thus provides the key explanation as to why they lost the cold war. The absence of democratic practice in communism meant that advocates of capitalism, at least in the West (other than in periods of fascism or dictatorship) could equate democracy with participation in a market economy, along with the range of individual and associational rights supposedly consistent with, even dependent upon, the market.

## SOMETHING NEW UNDER THE SUN

To focus only on failings, contradictions and difficulties would, however, be unbalanced. Communism's record includes many positive achievements. The denial of these achievements by opponents of progressive social change is aimed at discrediting the wider left. Some critics promote the proposition that socialism equals Gulag, always, inevitably.[5] For this reason it continues to be important to counter reactionary interpretations of communism. As the historian E.H. Carr argued:

> one need hardly dwell on the negative consequences of the [Russian] revolution ... the danger is not that we shall draw a veil over the enormous blots on the record of the revolution, over its cost in human suffering, over the crimes committed in its name. The danger is that we shall be tempted to forget it altogether, and to pass over in silence its immense achievements.[6]

The balanced judgement must be that twentieth-century communism was a failed modernist project in the course of which many positives were achieved. There were multiple 'victories-in-defeat'. Some of these were military – from the battle of Stalingrad in winter 1942-3, when Soviet forces turned the tide and began the effective fightback against Hitler's Nazis, to the defeat of the US-backed South Vietnam regime in Saigon in 1975, when popular Vietnamese forces defeated American military might. But most were moral and social successes – the expansion of education and welfare, and the promotion of optimism and confidence for ordinary people. As Robin Blackburn has argued: 'communism failed as a project for a different kind of society ... [but] as a movement it was by no means always contemptible'.[7]

To be somewhat more upbeat: for decade upon decade, the movement mobilised millions for reform within existing systems by linking successes on immediate issues to a positive vision of the future of human society. In the words of Francis Spufford, the Soviet Union's existence and achievements stood as 'proof positive that the old order of things is shiftable, that there can be novelty under the sun'.[8] The

Soviet Union also directly resourced movements for genuine liberation and democracy, positively influencing anti-colonial and anti-imperialist forces.[9] Moreover, the achievements of some of the activists who carried on attempting to uphold the tradition into the twenty-first century are evidence of communism's potential as a democratising force in very difficult circumstances, for example in South Africa through to the end of apartheid and into the decades that followed, and in Nepal in the years around 2007.

Communism provided the basis for more advantageous social welfare and wages settlements than would otherwise have ever been feasible for masses of people emerging from feudal arrangements in countries such as Russia, Romania and Bulgaria. Post-war redistribution of land in the capitalist economies of Japan, Taiwan and South Korea can be seen as a direct response to 'the communist threat'. Even indirectly, the social pressure of the existence of the Soviet Union and the wider socialist world served as a lever to the successes of social-democracy in Western Europe, and democratising and inclusive politics in North America.

Such balance-sheets, and efforts to sort out achievements from problems, may be taken to suggest that future efforts at progressive radical change can move forward by 'choosing' only the welcome resources. Not so. There will never be perfect or ideal conditions for solely and straightforwardly positive steps. This was all too evidently the case with twentieth-century communism: its proud achievements and shameful crimes were related, wired together, mixed up and interlinked. The 'monstrous failure' was, at the same time, 'the hope of the world'.

Nor can lessons from the movement's contradictory record be directly lifted and applied to current and foreseeable challenges. Any account of a major social and political movement which incorporates more than a few concrete historical details shows that it cannot be re-enacted: its choices can no longer be revisited. Nevertheless, themes emerge in the following chapters which do repay reflection today.

Communists wrestled with different kinds of difficulty on issues of democracy. There was a category of objective difficulties: the conditions in which, and oppositions against which, they needed to push their politics. A second category resulted from a subjective lack, resulting from weaknesses, contradictions and gaps in Marxist conceptions of democracy, and from the culture of the movement. Given this, and given liberal democracy's apparent uselessness as a vehicle for the radical and thorough-going economic and social changes they sought, communists faced a recurring decision about how to respond. When difficulties developed in pushing the project forward, the choice often had to be made between working to establish an expanded conception of democracy, or pressing ahead and rejecting its ethos and practice.

This was never an entirely free choice. Political agents are free to choose, but not to choose the limits within which that choice is shaped. Too often, urgent pressures of war, social division, the enemy's agenda, and the need to achieve economic targets, seemed to justify pushes towards the goal without putting in the necessary work to establish, test and expand popular support.

In spite of this problem in communist political culture, every decade between 1917 and 1989 saw some communists seeking to 'recover' and reapply the democratic content and impulse at the heart of the politics. Through the Popular Front of the 1930s, to 1968's Prague Spring, and 1970s Eurocommunism, the need to promote democratic values and accountability as part of radical change kept re-emerging and 'coming back'. This was not because democracy is some 'essential' presence, always there, which keeps 'breaking through'. It was because the construction and maintenance of democratic processes is a necessary precondition for the implementation of socialist principles.[10]

## NOTES

1. Perry Anderson, *The Origins of Postmodernity*, Verso, London 1998, p12.
2. As Robert A Gorman comments, there was ample room for 'divergent, often conflicting, opinions regarding the social and political roles of the communist party, apt strategies for revolutionary national workers' parties, and the quality of political life in socialism': *Biographical Dictionary of Marxism*, Mansell Publishing, London 1986, p10. The understandable need to sift and reduce the complexity of the field has led taxonomists to adopt simple, often binary distinctions: historical materialism/dialectical materialism; Marxism/neo-Marxism; Leninism/Western Marxism; official communism/reform communism; Stalinism/Trotskyism. Useful to some degree, when used with care, such distinctions run the risk of suggesting greater homogeneity within any one 'side' than is ever really the case, and of downplaying the extent to which some thinkers on each 'side' of the 'divide' would still agree with key tenets proposed by some of those on the other 'side'.

3. In 1982, for example, there were twenty-two countries run by communist parties, counting the USSR with all its constituent republics as just one country: Afghanistan (16.8 million inhabitants in 1982, according to the World Bank's *World Development Report 1984*); Albania (2.9); Angola (8.0); Bulgaria (8.9); Kampuchea (8.4 in 1977, 1982 figure not available, as a result of the murderous Pol Pot regime); China (1,008.2); Cuba (9.8); Czechoslovakia (15.4); Ethiopia (32.9); German Democratic Republic (16.7); Hungary (10.7); Laos (3.6); Madagascar (9.2); Mongolia (1.8); Mozambique (12.9); North Korea (18.7); Poland (36.2); Romania (22.5); South Yemen (2.0); Soviet Union (270.0); Vietnam (57.0); Yugoslavia (22.6). Total: 1,586.8 million people. According to Eric Hobsbawm, the 'socialist sector of the globe' had substantially taken shape by 1950. 'Thanks to the enormous numbers of the Chinese people, it ... included about one third of the world's population, though the average size of the socialist states other than China, the USSR and [later] Vietnam was not particularly large': *Age of Extremes*, Michael Joseph, London 1994, p373. In terms of the strength of its parties, communism probably claimed its greatest number of adherents during the 1970s: the same decade in which trade unions in the OECD countries reached their highest levels of affiliation.

4. Alec Nove, *The Economics of Feasible Socialism*, Allen and Unwin, London 1983, pix.

5. GULAG was the acronym of the agency which oversaw the prison camps, penal colonies and settlements of forced labourers in the Soviet Union.

6. E.H. Carr interview, *New Left Review*, September-October 1978.

7. Robin Blackburn in Blackburn (ed), *After the Fall*, Verso, London 1991, pxiv.

8. Francis Spufford, 'Red Plenty', *The Guardian*, 6 August 2010.

9. 'While the West offered only pious statements about apartheid's evils, the Soviet Union gave practical support' [to the African National Congress]. Ronnie Kasrils, *'Armed and Dangerous'*, Heinemann Educational, Oxford 1993, p82.

10. Warning against the consequences of the Bolsheviks establishing a one-party state, Rosa Luxemburg argued for the importance of democratic practice on the basis that the 'elimination of democracy ... stops up the very living source from which alone can come correction of all the innate shortcomings of social institutions'. 'The Russian Revolution' *Reform or revolution and other writings*, Dover Publications, New York 2006 [1918], p210.

# 2. Enlightenment and revolution

## ENLIGHTENMENT OUTLOOKS: AMBITION AND OPTIMISM

Where did the communist movement come from? In immediate terms, it resulted from a split in the wider socialist tradition, which had developed in Europe during the second half of the nineteenth century. Socialists had developed their politics in the context of, and in response to, nineteenth-century economic growth, technological advance, new industries, growing populations and urbanisation. Their increasingly confident and reflective movement argued that the progress that had been made since the 1700s could be harnessed and channelled so that it met the needs of all ordinary people.

But such notions do not simply appear: socialists in the nineteenth century were drawing heavily on themes that had emerged in the European Enlightenment.

During the seventeeth and eighteenth centuries, a range of discoveries, theories and creative impulses had cross-fertilised each other in the sciences, the arts and philosophy. This period of Enlightenment generated inter-related attitudes to nature and society, and the sharing and application of knowledge. There was a growing commitment to the principles and power of rationality; opposition to superstition; insistence on the importance of evidenced fact and careful observation; scepticism about received wisdom and established authority; the opening up of new areas and subjects for inquiry and debate; and a concern to be systematic, consistent and methodical during scientific investigation, and in reasoning about social issues. These Enlightenment ideas provided the seedbed of ideas from which socialism and then its communist variant would eventually grow, and it is therefore worth taking a moment to explore some of the lines of thought that were most significant for the development of socialism.

A belief in objective truth, which stood independently of the observer, became central to philosophical and social thought. The

German philosopher Immanuel Kant distinguished between two orders of reality – the 'phenomenal' and the 'noumenal'. This contrast between things *as they are in themselves* and things *as they appear to us* confirmed the importance of investigating the true character of both natural and social reality, rather than taking things 'at face value'.

Within the rich cross-cutting mix of Enlightenment thought, religious belief also became the subject of dispute and debate. This does not mean that there was an Enlightenment campaign against religion: rationally structured arguments were often used to confirm a belief in God. Many of those making major scientific discoveries were devout Christians, whose work built on the unfairly demeaned work which had been carried out under Church sponsorship during the Middle ages. As Robert Musil wrote many years ago, the first of the men who established the modern approach to building knowledge based on reason, 'Galileo, Copernicus, Newton, and their intellectual and spiritual comrades', were still altogether religious: 'their methods were not intended to inspire a defection from the church, but rather meant to flow back, someday, into reinforcing orthodox belief'.[1]

Other variations of Enlightenment thought tended towards pantheism or atheism. In the Netherlands, Baruch Spinoza systematised ideas from 'heretical' Protestant currents, as well as rejecting and reworking insights from his Judaic experience. Spinoza's concept of 'totality' means there is no God in the sense of something existing outside what there is: no transcendent supernatural deity, distinct from nature and independent of its processes. If there is 'God', he or it is immanent within everything that exists. In spite of the vilification he experienced for putting forward such arguments, this was by no means a recipe for immorality. Spinoza's simple maxims gave guidance to many followers: 'love your fellows and treat them with justice and charity'. His approach to social disputes was 'not to ridicule, not to lament or execrate, but to understand'. Today's 'new atheists' such as Richard Dawkins and A.C. Grayling pit their concepts of Enlightenment, rationality and atheism against religion, irrationality and obscurantism. But very few Enlightenment figures themselves rejected religion in any thorough-going way, or adopted atheism.

In what was one of the most important developments for the growth of socialist ideas, important thinkers – consciously or not – took over and recast notions of salvation and redemption, turning them from religious notions into goals for human society. They renewed 'the old and maligned and magnificent certainty' that 'human beings deserve to be saved'.[2]

But whether it was promoting or critiquing religious belief, the effect of Enlightenment thought was to undermine those who defended their worldly power and privilege by claiming 'divine right'. The development of secularism as the framework for managing the separation – and interaction – of religion and politics was an important development, and provided a context for scientific understanding and endeavour.

Particular historical episodes provided the impetus for a further linking of scientific thought, scepticism about religion and a commitment to overcoming the destructive character of certain natural events. The Lisbon earthquake of 1755, which killed 40,000 people, shook the earth in more than the usual ways. Through the newspapers and publications then becoming more widely accessible, the French writer Voltaire and other critics of religion suggested that the earthquake contradicted such established notions as the idea that 'virtuous' people are routinely rewarded, and 'sinners' punished. Resulting debates resourced new ambitions to tame nature. The belief grew that the context of human life could be planned and designed, and that the history of catastrophe could come to an end.

One can trace the beginnings of a modern approach to ecological issues here. There was an emphasis on the extent to which catastrophes resulted from particular kinds of social organisation and practice, not from the simple relationship between 'man' and 'nature'. New forms of relationship with 'nature' could result in perils being understood and managed.

Enlightenment rationality – a web of assumptions and views about the character of truth, reason, meaning, value and identity – took deep hold in Western culture. It became the dominant 'social imaginary'; or, rather, a varied and sometimes competing series of social imaginaries. The French *philosophes* urged the need to apply reason to every problem, creating space to pursue the truth without the threat of sanction for violating established ideas. This approach went along with the spread of individuality, and a conception of people as independent moral actors, entirely capable of choosing and determining their own path in life. As bourgeois society developed, this notion of individuality was projected onto institutions and enterprises: economic, political, and cultural. The assumption built up that the rational and healthy functioning of society would come about through competition and interaction between these distinct units. The very notion of social progress developed alongside a culture which validated the autonomy of the individual.

The Swiss-born French philosopher Jean-Jacques Rousseau helped define a modern sensibility, emphasising the centrality of personal experience, establishing key elements of humanitarianism, and showing that civilisation could be exploitative and corrupt. According to Willie Thompson, Rousseau differed from some other Enlightenment figures: he was sceptical of the notion of progress, and argued that the triumph of culture over nature had been a disaster rather than a blessing for mankind.[3] Such themes fed into individualist Romanticism, as well as later informing Friedrich Nietzsche's unsettling insights, which reveal the dynamics of oppression, desires for revenge, and self-delusion shaping traditional ethical injunctions. Through its astringent critique of modern conceptions of progress, Nietzsche's thought generates a range of fundamental challenges for liberal and socialist values.

Nevertheless, one of Rousseau's key convictions was that humans were 'naturally equal'. This was a crucial step towards the radical egalitarianism of socialism, which also developed Rousseau's suspicions that 'social order' serves to protect the privileges of the powerful, and that 'justice' in a divided society is a tool of oppression. Rousseau also advocated a transformation of political institutions and educational practices, and believed that both riches and poverty were obstacles to virtue.

The Neapolitan thinker Giambattista Vico conceived of change as a primarily social phenomenon, its possibilities resulting from human relationships and behaviour. Although the Enlightenment was sometimes conceived in terms of a return to an imagined classical 'golden age', a belief in 'progress' became influential. The French constitutionalist Nicolas de Condorcet argued that men, acting on the basis of science, could shape the progress that was already assured by history. Ideas could be applied to accelerate change: growing networks of intellectuals encouraged the notion of a unified human race moving towards an all-encompassing civil society founded on justice, and incorporating and expressing individual freedom.

Precursors of socialist politics drew on such resources as Kant's vision of rational progress toward the goal of a 'universal cosmopolitan condition' in order to promote influential theories about the advance of human knowledge, culture and civilisation. The pioneering sociologist Auguste Comte believed that observing, recording and systematically analysing facts would lead to people acquiring such a total and thorough knowledge about nature and society that they would be able to order them both. Precision would replace metaphysics, planning would resolve social conflicts, truth would replace subjectivity, and all the mysteries of human psychology and emotion would be explained by empirical knowledge.

Over time the outlooks and principles advanced by these thinkers became widespread. There was increasing optimism about the possible results of applying scientific knowledge. It was understood that current science was incomplete, and this generated a progressive culture of competition which drove individuals to claim 'discoveries' and seek to invent new things. An increasingly democratic spirit led ordinary people to question the norms and practices of their societies, and the vested interests which these often reflected.

These developments both expressed and accelerated great advances in European culture. There were moves towards universal education for children. Modern conceptions of law were established, aiming to separate the setting of rules by which all are governed from the way the already privileged and powerful worked to maintain their position. There were moves towards the orderly organisation of the state and systems of governance. Through the social shifts which took place from the end of the eighteenth century, large numbers of ordinary people came to be seen and to see themselves as both the subject and agency of politics – the key content of the modern democratic impulse.

Sometimes taken up by modernising rulers and political leaders and sometimes suppressed, the advancing cause of reason reflected and inspired opposition to tyranny, and resistance to the oppressions and restrictions of established power. Fuelling and fuelled by assertive social movements, a popular sense grew that history involved progress: stages leading from one to the next, in which both nature and social life would be ordered by sensible people acting maturely and in the general interest. As Eric Hobsbawm noted, increasing numbers of people believed that human history was 'an ascent, rather than a decline or an undulating movement about a level trend':

> They could observe that man's scientific knowledge and technical control over nature increased daily. They believed that human

society and individual man could be perfected by the same application of reason, and were destined to be so perfected by history.[4]

## BOURGEOIS REVOLUTION IN FRANCE

As these contours of political modernism took shape, the sense emerged that the state and the economy could and should be organised rationally. Ambitious philosophers and administrators saw that they could change or construct social institutions to work towards pre-planned goals. 'Reason' became the tool for overturning foolishly established and sustained traditions, and generated the politics of liberalism. This stood against superstition and intolerance, and promoted the rights of free individuals as a primary social value.

During the latter part of the eighteenth century, the values, ideas and practices pioneered by relatively small circles became generalised through universities, academies, salons and Masonic lodges, and through varied cultural forms – publishing, theatre, literature, painting, music and the sciences. The increasingly strong bourgeoisie began to call for restrictions on the power of the monarchy. These movements led, in their clearest form, to the French Revolution. The novelist Hilary Mantel catches how this major event was 'shaped by a groundswell of popular desire':

> to anyone with a political consciousness, it must have seemed as if history had speeded up. The slow centuries had dragged by, punctuated by oddly regressive peasants' revolts; then there was the summer of 1789.[5]

Age-old patterns of deference, custom, authority and hierarchy had been undermined by multiple social changes: demographic growth; increasing administrative rationality; growing secularisation; rising living standards; as well as the tendency of the elites to cut themselves off, physically and psychologically, from popular concerns, habits and beliefs, in ways which made it possible to position the royalist aristocracy as 'the enemy' of the nation.

In the context of multiple social pressures and disturbances, in May 1789 the French king convened a meeting of the 'Estates General' of France, intending that this would decide to increase taxation so as to help stabilise his position. After a series of disputes over democratic process, the 'Third Estate', of commoners, proclaimed a national assembly, and called for a new constitution. Though he had stated his agreement to this demand, Louis XVI then mobilised troops to suppress popular power. On 14 July there followed a preventive insurrection in Paris: a crowd of citizens seized the Bastille prison, a symbol of royal tyranny. This was the beginning of the revolution. Dramatic developments over the next few years included the official declaration that feudalism was abolished; widespread participation in a new, democratic, political culture; the nationalisation and distribution of land which had been previously owned by the church; invasion of the country by counter-revolutionary foreign powers; the execution of the king; and a series of political disputes between emerging political parties and factions, all accompanied by serious bloodletting. During this period there were major disputes and social struggles over radical policies, including debates about government control of prices, the abolition of slavery in the French Caribbean colonies, heavy taxation of the rich, programmes of national assistance for the poor and disabled, and plans for free and compulsory education.

Through all this, '1789' gave millions of ordinary people the sense that their lives could be changed as a direct result of their own involvement in campaigns, demonstrations, actions: *politics*. Willie Thompson defines the French Revolution as 'the first attempt in Europe, probably anywhere, to remould socio-political institutions in a systematic fashion'. There was an attempt to design a society that was more in accordance with secular notions of human welfare, and to regard all inhabitants of the nation, at least in principle, as citizens of equal social worth. As he comments, 'in this respect it initiated a process which has never ceased'.[6]

In instituting the modern conception of democracy, the French Revolution pushed the concepts of social and economic equality further than any other previous politics. For Marxists, this was the first bourgeois revolution: it signalled the beginning of the political displacement of the old aristocratic order by the rising bourgeois class. As Marx would write in *The Holy Family* in 1844, it 'brought forth ideas which led beyond the ideas of the entire old-world system'. This explains why concepts drawn from 1789 have served as key political reference points down to the present time: 'the nation'; 'the people'; 'left-wing'; 'right-wing'.

These notions and standpoints were produced by extremely contested and dramatic oppositions about the way the revolution should be developed, including disputes that sent hundreds to the guillotine. In spite of the many problems, not least of which was the violence that was engendered during the revolutionary process, the revolution established a field of political impulses; it established a whole new set of historical possibilities and a new framework for thinking about politics and society. Or, as Stathis Kouvelakis has put it, it was 'the founding moment in which the cluster of questions, conflicts and historical tendencies called "modernity" first emerged'.[7] These elements provided the raw materials which have ever since been combined in different forms, with different levels of ease and success, in various attempts to reconfigure political and social settlements.

The main social and political consequence of the French Revolution was to complete the process whereby 'the estates were transformed into social classes, i.e. the class distinctions in civil society became merely social differences in private life of no significance in political life'.[8] In legal terms, institutionalised inequality was abolished. Establishing the formal political equality of all citizens of the nation was the key content of the bourgeois revolution. This move was at first incomplete in many ways, including in its exclusion of women. Even today, after the extension of the vote to more and more people, and the growth in the number of countries with some form of representative democratic system, there are still many practical barriers to the full participation of all people in bourgeois democracy, and many disputes over the ways those systems should work. All this continues to generate justified democratic demands.

But even if the bourgeois democratic revolution were to be fully and completely realised throughout the world, a fundamental problem would remain. This was a revolution which left economic inequality in place.

By shifting economic inequality into the sphere of private rights, and by defining these in a way which protected them from political interference, the bourgeois revolution institutionalised and legalised new forms of inequality, which in some ways went even deeper than feudal inequality. At least in feudalism basic political and economic structures corresponded very closely and transparently. As Lucio Colletti put it, 'socio-economic distinctions (serf and lord) were also political distinctions (subject and sovereign)'.[9] Problems of inequality could be seen for what they were: the results of some people exercising dominance over others. In bourgeois democracies, apparent political equality would often obscure the reality and nature of economic inequality.

Nevertheless, in the confluence and eddy of the different stances and visions generated by the French Revolution, something recognisable as communist politics emerged. In 1795, some followers of the executed revolutionary leader Maximilien Robespierre and of the agitator Gracchus Babeuf attempted to overcome their divisions with a view to pursuing the revolution until 'genuine equality' had been obtained. The demands for economic equality which first appeared in the *Manifesto of Equals* were expressed in terms which would not have been out of place in any twentieth-century communist argument. At the time, however, this proto-communism was little more than an intellectual current.[10] For it to become a consequential movement there was a need for a significant social force capable of challenging the bourgeoisie, and whose constituents could, at least potentially, see that they had an interest in adopting communist policies.

Industrialisation gave rise to such a social force – the working class or 'proletariat', whose only meaningful possession was their ability to work. Trends fed each other: the growth of industry; a sense that the present was speeding up into a potentially much better future; and the development of a class-conscious labour movement. Economic growth and rapid urbanisation across many European countries led to a great increase in the numbers of people who believed that the future would be different – and better – than the past.

The revolutionary, progressive liberal bourgeoisie was transforming the economy, opening up new paths of growth and development, and taking apart the old 'society of orders'. Depending on and at the same time exploiting the growing class of wage labourers, their social project brought into focus the promise of modernity. This was the prospect that scientific and technological progress, with its tools, harnessing of power, techniques of automation and computation, could lead to freedom from want and hardship. The industrial revolution could be extended and generalised: it seemed that the technical know-how was at hand to develop production and use resources systematically. Surely, before long, it would be possible to abolish poverty and want?

This outlook fed through into widespread enthusiasm for technology in the mid to late nineteenth century, with socialists and many others imagining the social good that would come from the extension of electricity, communal living arrangements and the use of myriad gadgets and labour saving inventions in everyday life. The awesome dynamism of the capitalist economy suggested that, for the first time in human history, all material needs could be satisfied. People might move on from the millennia in which most of them had suffered, rather than benefited, from social arrangements. The 'rational mastery' of nature and society, through the application of science, would have great results. General abundance would bring an end to competition over scarce resources, and to the divisive politics that result from needing to make mutually exclusive choices. A vision emerged of people living together in ways which moved beyond the back-breaking toil and oppression that result from acquisitive behaviour. People could be as nearly all of us would like ourselves to be: brilliant, rational, socialised and humane. Individual self-realisation and cultural expression would be increasingly possible, once people were free from the division of labour. Two ambitious young German intellectuals foresaw that life could be arranged so that:

> ... nobody has one exclusive sphere of activity but each can become accomplished in any branch he wishes, society regulates the general production and thus makes it possible for me to do one thing today and another tomorrow, to hunt in the morning, to fish in the afternoon, rear cattle in the evening, criticise after dinner, just as I have a mind, without ever becoming hunter, fisherman, herdsman or critic.[11]

The political vision set out here is one in which problems of incentive, discipline and motivation could vanish. As Gregory Claeys argues, it both presupposes and describes a 'psychological revolution' that would follow the political success of the working class:

> the alteration of the economic relations would lead to the birth of a new species, capable of harmoniously interacting with others ... the differences between the countryside and the cities would be diluted, and people would be able to assert themselves as spontaneous, voluntary and eclectic workers; this transformation of the way man faces work would be reflected in a myriad of harmonious relationships with other men and women and with nature itself.[12]

Self-conscious, rational agency on the part of individuals and small groups would combine with social integration. Cohesion would not come at the price of subordination of particular groups or individuals. Human diversity would be the basis for celebration of difference, rather than used to cause division. Leadership would operate without strict organisational hierarchies of status, tenure and rank. Scientific and rational progress could build ever more peaceable and humane societies. As the German poet Bertolt Brecht was to say of the communist project which expressed this vision: how can something so simple be so difficult?

## NOTES

1. Robert Musil, 'The Religious Spirit, Modernism and Metaphysics', *Precision and Soul*, University of Chicago Press, Chicago IL 1990 [1912], p21.
2. Roberto Bolano, *Between Parentheses*, Picador, London 2012, p170.
3. See Willie Thompson, *Work, Sex and Power*, Pluto Press, London 2015, p223.
4. Eric Hobsbawm, *The Age of Revolution*, Weidenfeld and Nicholson, London 1975, pp234-35.
5. Hilary Mantel, 'If you'd seen his green eyes', *London Review of Books*, 20 April 2006.
6. Willie Thompson, *The Long Death of British Labourism*, Pluto Press London 1993, p2.
7. Stathis Kouvelakis, *Philosophy and Revolution*, Verso, London 2003, p 2.
8. Karl Marx, *Critique of Hegel's Doctrine of the State*, [1843].
9. Lucio Colletti, introduction to Karl Marx, *Early Writings*, Penguin Books, Harmondsworth 1975, p 34.
10. Nevertheless, as Eric Hobsbawm wrote: 'the unbroken history of communism as a modern social movement begins [with this moment] on the left-wing of the French Revolution. A direct line of descent links Babeuf's Conspiracy of the Equals through Buonarroti with Blanqui's revolutionary societies of the 1830s'. These in turn generated members for the 'League of the Just', which became the Communist League: *How to Change the World*, Little, Brown, London 2011, p22.
11. Karl Marx and Friedrich Engels, *The German Ideology*, International Publishers, New York 2004 [1846], p 53. Mike Tyldesley jokes with his students that this quote makes communism sound like an upper-crust weekend house party: dialectical materialism meets Downton Abbey. But the description of personal freedom to come is intended to assert that we should not be defined and limited by the jobs we have to do in capitalism's wage labour system. However this vision does of course betray the writer's

own background and unconscious aspirations. On BBC Four's 'Genius of the Modern World', 16 June 2016, Terrell Carver stated that scrutiny of the original manuscript shows that it was Engels who penned the vision of hunting, fishing and cattle-rearing. 'Criticising after dinner' was a comment scribbled in the margin by Marx with, Carver. suggests, sarcastic intent.

12. Gregory Claeys, 'Preface', *The Cambridge Companion to Utopian Literature*, Cambridge University Press, Cambridge 2010.

# 3. 'An extraordinary brainwave': the emergence of Marxism

By the early 1840s, members of radical intellectual circles across Europe were campaigning on issues of progress, equality and social justice. One of these was Karl Marx, who had been the young editor of a liberal newspaper in Germany before it closed after the intervention of the Prussian government. But censorship in his native Rhineland had no power to prevent Marx's critical involvement in philosophy and politics, and around this time he began to combine and extend some of the key insights of his age in a dramatic and consequential way.

One of Marx's starting-points was scientific rationalism, which built on the philosophical insights of Kant. The astronomer Johannes Kepler had established that images we 'see' are only indirectly linked to reality: we do not see the thing 'as it is'. As Terry Eagleton explains, our understanding is thus recognised as anchored in perception, but at the same time put into question:

> It looks as though the sun is coming up, but actually the earth is going down. A rift opens up between how things are and how we experience them. Since this is a rift inherent in reality itself, our experience of the world is bound to be a matter of misrecognition as well as knowledge.[1]

This insight that things are not necessarily as they seem combined in Marx's thinking with a theory of how things change. This drew heavily on the work of the German philosopher Georg Hegel. One of Hegel's founding notions – developing but critiquing Spinoza – was that of 'totality': phenomena do not exist in isolation but are formed and structured through the network of relations that constitute and position them. And he combined this sense of an overall unity in existence with the idea of a progressive movement of history. This was conceived as a gradual unfolding of human knowledge and comprehension through the conflict and interplay of differing ideas.

Hegel's 'dialectical viewpoint' stressed internal development and qualitative change. Things could transform themselves, morphing from being one thing to become another, not through the intervention of an 'other', but as a result of the working-out of inherent contradictions and potentialities. He sought to resolve the ever-widening gaps – 'antinomies' – between subject and object in modern culture. Working within and developing the German idealist tradition, he saw history as the progressive development of 'embodied Mind': each stage generated its successor from the seeds of its own dissolution. Hegel therefore approved of the French Revolution, at least in its early stages, as the necessary removal of an aristocratic system which had been progressive in its day, but whose contradictions had then rendered it redundant. In this he differed from more simplistic supporters of the revolution, who tended to regard the aristocracy as having always been pernicious.[2]

Hegel supported the established political order of his day, however, and in reacting against this, a Left-Hegelian school of younger philosophers and activists promoted the theory of historical progress, while simultaneously being critical of the conservative implications of idealist thinking. Radical Left-Hegelians developed the view that the 'antinomies' which concerned them reflected problems in political and economic arrangements. These needed to be transcended, not by philosophical enquiry but by social revolution.[3]

As part of this milieu, the young Marx was stimulated by the 'humanism' of the German philosopher Ludwig Feuerbach, whose insight was that 'God did not make man: man makes God'. This made him a key figure for Left-Hegelians: state and religion were tightly connected in the Prussian state and this made atheism a vehicle of radical political criticism. For Feuerbach – though he regarded religion as a necessary phase in human evolution – religion was a form of collective illusion, an outward projection of humans' inward nature. Religion represented an 'inverted world', but in passing through it humanity's powers could be developed to their full extent. This was not a rejection of religion's value or importance. Feuerbach aimed to show that religion contained truths which, when fully thought through, could lead beyond religion to the post-religious state which he called 'humanism'.

Participation in these Left-Hegelian debates led Marx to a thorough-going and radical rejection of philosophical idealism. But there are certainly other possible routes to the political conclusions that flow from Marxism. Christian liberation theology and left-wing articulations of Islam show that commitment to achieving social justice through class struggle can also be combined with a motivating religious belief.[4]

As Alberto Toscano has argued, Marx's early writings can be understood in terms of his developing realisation that attacking religion does not offer a solution for the emancipation of human reason (and can be a diversion from this aim). As he argues, 'the slogan encapsulating Marx's intervention into the fraught 1840s debate over religion and politics is "from the criticism of Heaven to the criticism of Earth"'.[5]

What was fundamental to the emergence of Marxism was not so much the critique of religion itself, but Marx's critique of the critique of religion. His insight was that religion, and philosophical understandings more generally, are social problems conceived in abstract form. This generated methodological approaches which Marx then applied to fields he regarded as far more significant than religion.

## AN ARTICLE BY ENGELS

At this point a new collaborative relationship assisted a shift in Marx's focus. Partly inspired by his first encounters with Engels, he now started to reflect on the material relations of production, and to begin reading works of political economy. For Marx this was the key to grasping the relationships between ideas and the material world: the task was to find ways to change the world rather than simply to interpret it, as he famously concluded in his theses on Feuerbach. He had what Jonathan Rée described as 'an extraordinary brainwave': he realised that Feuerbach's critique of religion and theology could be 'read across', extended and applied to capitalism.[6]

Suddenly, the real significance and usefulness of Feuerbach became the appliance of his approaches not just to the pursuance of atheism, but to the criticism of economics and politics. Feuerbach had derived a vision of a post-religious condition from his critique of theology. Marx now set himself the task of deriving a vision of a post-capitalist condition from a critique of political economy. Marx's writings from the mid-1840s notes sketch out a heady mix of economic criticism,

scathing attacks on bourgeois society and glimpses of a world transformed. The capitalist market, Marx began to think, was – like religion
– an 'inverted world', where humanity 'alienated' its own powers and
enslaved itself to them as if they were alien and even hostile to it.[7]
Whereas Hegel had seen alienation as a problem of objects of thought
not being comprehended, Marx now saw that it resulted from social
contradictions and divisions. For Hegel, thinkers could overcome
alienation through comprehension of what really is: for Marx, 'this
method leaves the world exactly as it was before, tacking a certificate
of rationality onto every form of oppression'.[8] Alienation cannot be
overcome through such 'philosophy': the need is to change the world.

Though political economy was to become his main focus, Marx's
radicalised application of Left-Hegelian thinking could be effectively
extended to every other social and political issue. It generated the theoretical foundations for the 'opinion' that some of his friends had already
arrived at: that mere political change was insufficient, and that a social
revolution which made productive property a shared resource and delivered substantial equality between people was the only social settlement
in line with their principles. It also provided the instruments to show
that the dominant way of looking at the world in any given society is
reflective of the dominance of a particular class order and its way of
understanding the world. As John Lanchester puts it, 'its apparently
neutral set of ideas ... are then taken as givens of the natural order'.[9]

The relationship between Marx and Engels was cemented in
summer 1844, during a ten-day visit by Engels to Paris, where Marx
was living in exile, and it became central to the rest of their lives and
work. As well as their intellectual collaboration, Engels went on to
provide sustained financial support to Marx; he subbed him for years
whilst working in the family firm in Manchester, and eventually
moved to London to further develop their close political collaboration.

Marx's thought draws on a rich variety of European disciplines, and
can be seen as a particularly radical but integral part of Enlightenment
rationality. The nineteenth-century popularity of scientific methods
of enquiry, including Charles Darwin's identification of the evolution of species through natural selection, provided context and
resource. Marx studied the work of bourgeois historians of the French
Revolution, from whom he drew the significance of social conflict; he
read the works of British economists, which highlighted class antagonism; and the French anarchist Pierre Joseph Proudhon inspired Marx

by proclaiming the modern proletariat to be the only real revolutionary class. He was also deeply interested in radical democratic movements such as the English Chartists.

Other assailants of the social order enriched Marx's outlook through their ruthless attacks on liberal hypocrisies, and their lively, scathing polemics. The reckless French revolutionary (Louis) Auguste Blanqui, and eccentric utopian socialists including Henri de Saint-Simon and Charles Fourier, all made their contribution: Blanqui insisted on the need for revolutionary dictatorship, while Saint-Simon and Fourier were imaginative advocates of socialist possibilities, including through the development and application of technology. In their different ways, these thinkers envisaged a positive future through fundamental changes in the very foundations of existing capitalist society; the abolition of classes; and the transformation of the state so that instead of being an instrument of class oppression it would become a mere technical tool to co-ordinate and administer production and the fair distribution of resources.

Marx's work developed in dialogue (often polemics) with other thinkers. It should not be seen as a unified and complete whole, a ready-made system, the truth of which is simply to be asserted and applied. It models an open method of analysis, an enquiring approach, open to adjustment and correction. Though striving for consistency, Marx did not conceive of his work as an all-inclusive 'philosophy', and there were indeed significant inconsistencies, gaps and reversals of position in his writings.

## THE PROBLEM OF IDEOLOGY – NOW YOU SEE IT ...

One starting-point for Marx was the idea that the make-up of social phenomena is not immediately apparent. The essence of things is not clearly given by what they seem to be, and truth and experience are not the same thing. The gap between appearance and reality is precisely what generates the need for science and critical thinking. Or, as Terry Eagleton has it, 'the laws that govern men's and women's behaviour are bound to be opaque to them':

> All the vital social processes ... go on behind the backs of the agents involved. There is a social unconscious as well as a psychical one, which is why people can be exploited without knowing it.[10]

This problem – the problem of ideology – shapes our day-to-day experience. Conscious thoughts and evidenced arguments are only part of the way we understand the world around us. There is often a massive distance between what we understand ourselves to be doing, and what we actually are doing, in terms of its social effect. Capitalism consolidates itself, as the Hungarian Marxist Georg Lukacs identified in the 1920s, through 'reification'. Ideology is not something disembodied, floating above reality. It takes material form, and it extends its confusions and mismatches into our consciousnesses. We perceive the world through the 'frames' that social arrangements generate and promote – in the media, through political discourse, the day-to-day language we use, and the actual things and experience of life.

A common reaction to this analysis of ideology is that it is patronising and demeaning: people are talked of as if they are not in control of what they are doing, and thus made to appear powerless. They apparently do not understand their own behaviour – they are the stupid and passive victims of indoctrination. Many people have understandably kicked back against the arrogance of Marxists who have believed that their 'analysis' means that they, uniquely, have understood the 'real meaning' of developments and the 'real interests' of people, and that anyone in disagreement is, self-evidently, suffering from 'false consciousness'. There is clearly a line from this way of thinking to anti-democratic practice and oppressive direction: 'they don't know what is good for them, so we will decide for them'.[11]

In fact, of course, ideology cannot be reduced to a slogan which gives those who use it the right to decide what other people's real interests are. What could be more ideological or self-deluding than that view?

But this is not to deny that, as systems of mystification inherent in the social world – not just as misinterpretations floating above it – ideologies do hold us and shape our understandings. The aim of critical thinking is to try to understand how these ideologies operate and shape us, but no-one can live outside them. Ideology is not an illusion masking the real state of things; it is a social construct which shapes our reality. Its power results from being embodied in and promoted by our everyday practices, and by the ways dominant social forces shape our existence, in spite of our conscious wishes.

As Renata Salecl puts it:

we don't notice the forms in which our lives are constructed. Society functions as something obvious, something given, almost natural. In order to understand the hidden imperatives, the codes of being ... we need to remove the veil of obviousness and given-ness. Only then do we notice the bizarre but highly ordered logic that we obey, unthinkingly, in our everyday lives.[12]

We can accept 'removing the veil' as a useful metaphor, whilst recognising that Salecl is not simplistically suggesting that there is a 'reality', easy to see, once the cover of ideology is lifted, as if seeing things as they 'really are' is possible through a kind of peek-a-boo. The fantasy that we can somehow fully escape from ideology is itself ideological. Nevertheless, the experience of social dislocation can enable us to notice the gaps in reality which ideologies fill and manage: and through our capacity for critical thinking (including through art and culture) we can understand and critique ideologies in ways which enable social change.

## MARX'S WORK: 'WHERE VALUE COMES FROM'

This was the task Marx now set about, through writing pamphlets, books (both published and unfinished), varied journalism and voluminous correspondence, as well as engaging in a range of political projects. Through shifting networks of intermittent followers, amongst whom Engels was the only constant, he began to promote a programme for establishing the social and economic conditions which would allow the realisation and full generalisation of the principles which are stated by liberal democracy, but which are not realisable or generalisable on the terrain of capitalism: the system which, in the last resort, the bourgeoisie defends in spite of any liberal scruples. Thus Marxism can be seen as emerging as a radical version of the Enlightenment tradition of rational thinking, energetically applying the resultant social and economic understanding to practical politics. As Herbert Marcuse would later note, its radicalism partly consisted in rejecting the view that civilisation had already and finally established the institutions and relationships within whose framework humanity could realise its nature, unfold its potentialities and fulfil its needs.[13]

Marx railed against the current economic system's cruel contradictions:

machinery, gifted with the wonderful power of shortening and fructifying human labour, we behold starving and overworking it. The new-fangled sources of wealth, by some strange weird spell, are turned into sources of want.[14]

In seeking to make sense of these 'weird' mysteries, Marx recognised the class struggle as the key moving force in the development of society. The political conclusion he drew meant that he would not promote positions on behalf of 'humanity' or 'society' as a whole. For him, the possibility of understanding in a situation of class division and conflict depended on having a particular viewpoint within the situation, and owning the responsibilities that flowed from that. In matters of society and politics, truth does not look down on real life from above. Truth takes sides.

Marx took sides in the class struggle, pushing the interests of one class on the basis that it would become universal. As Chris Arthur writes in his introduction to *The German Ideology* (which Marx and Engels wrote in 1845):

> Because the situation of the proletariat is so desperate that it has nothing to lose by revolution, it has no special interests in the existing order to protect. Therefore it can only free itself by establishing universal freedom, by overthrowing all existing bases of oppression.[15]

This outlook was to take material form in the socialist movement, and in the parties and governments later formed through communism. But we should note that this is a theoretical conceptualisation rather than a precise prescription for action: the view is that the proletariat, as it develops, will be the radical 'negation of capitalism', leading to the end of the economic system and the classes which it generates.[16] Marxism gave a theoretical form to the confident sense that was emerging in socialism more generally, that workers could themselves run industry and society. It can also be seen as reflecting the rapidly increasing social weight of the industrial working class.

Marx's great contribution to the socialist movement was to provide it with a systematic theory of political economy. One key insight was that the normative claims of modern economics were specific to the society which had generated them: they were not universal or applicable to all times. Civilisation has taken many different forms and gone through all kinds of developments: economic categories and their significance had varied and changed accordingly.[17] Bourgeois political economy was therefore a pseudo-science, covering up central facts about the subject which it appears to 'study': the exploitation at the heart of the system, and the inefficiencies and miseries which spring from this.

For Marx, key questions were the source of value, the nature of commodities, and what money is. As John Lanchester comments, these were very simple questions, but not ones that had been asked with such clarity before.[18] Marx's labour theory of value pinpointed how surplus value was expropriated from employees by capitalist employers. The formal 'economic freedom' celebrated in bourgeois legality obscures the exploitative relationships that keep society unequal. As Jean-Paul Sartre later summarised it:

> the swindle of capitalist exploitation is based on a contract ... it is, formally, a reciprocal relation; it is a free exchange between two men ... it is just that one of them pretends not to notice that the other is forced by the constraint of need to sell himself as a material object. The clear conscience of the employer is based entirely on that moment of exchange in which the wage-labourer appears to offer his labour-power in complete freedom.[19]

Marx's work identified inescapable tendencies towards economic breakdown in capitalism: the distorting effects of the drive for profit in the shaping of the development of mechanisation; the likelihood of market expansion reaching its limits; tendencies towards monopoly; the system's decreasing ability to recover from slumps; the tendency of the rate of profit to fall. As Pat Devine and his co-authors have reflected:

> the major achievement of Karl Marx was a perceptive analysis of a social system in which the increasing scale of commodity production led towards an increasing concentration of property ownership. This was a highly dynamic but also destructive process, which led to recurrent economic and social crises. Marx also showed how capitalist production turns social relations into commodities and human beings into things.[20]

The ambition which flowed from this analysis was to conquer political power in order to achieve economic freedom.

## INTO PRACTICE: INTERNATIONAL SOCIALISM

Marxism developed through connecting to, reflecting on and learning from the development of the European labour movement. This was shaped by a variety of traditions, and different political and social cultures. Some of these played out in the International Working Men's Association (IWMA) which was set up in 1864 (and whose founding conference Marx attended); this operated with varying degrees of coherence and success until 1876, when splits led to its effective dissolution. Some of the disputes and intrigues which shaped the Association (which later became known as the First International) reflected the different aims and agendas of its constituent parts: trade unionists, revolutionary and reformist intellectuals, anarchists, enthusiasts for self-sufficiency and espousers of retributive violence. The International's culture was shaped by trade union organisations, secret conspiracies of small groups and journalistic networks: it did not resemble the mass socialist parties that were yet to come.

But it was by no means a fragile organisation. It had significant influence in British trade unions. In Paris, by 1870, it had 50,000 members. Its communications networks overcame the isolation experienced by those struggling separately for their rights and interests, and it facilitated strike support and solidarity for workers' movements across European borders. The sense that working-class people were becoming a majority force in society, coupled with optimism about technical innovation and the advance of democracy, generated the view that socialism's chance to shape the future would soon come.

Marx and Engels spent the late 1860s working to secure acceptance of their perspectives within the International. This increasingly meant disputes with anarchists. Proudhon argued that society should be organised on the basis of mutual co-operation, so that the state – and modern banking systems – would be unnecessary. Mikhail Bakunin, a Russian anarchist with a strong following in Italy and Spain, distinguished 'political revolution', which aimed to wield state power as a weapon of the dispossessed, from 'social revolution'. His vision was about 'breaking' rather than 'taking' state power, and he was against the working class setting up its own political authority.

The Paris Commune of 1871 was a key moment for the International. The Commune was a revolutionary government set up by popular forces, and though it was short-lived (lasting from March to May), it offered a new model for popular self-government. As Gareth Stedman Jones pithily summarises, it combined and concentrated within one word the idea of national defence, of local democracy, and of revolution.[21] The Commune was the first initiator of many progressive practices, from the invention of the crèche system to the introduction of collective decision-making into factories and workshops. The modern agenda of women's rights was also promoted.

Such things could not be allowed to develop! The Commune was suppressed with extraordinary brutality in May 1871. French government troops killed over 20,000 communards during a few bloody weeks. Many more were imprisoned and deported half-way around the world.

Marx concluded that the need was to constitute large and legal working-class parties in each country as the necessary foundation of socialist revolution.[22] This perspective developed his established view that successful working-class struggles would take the form of open, democratic movements – not underground conspiracies of minorities preparing to seize power on behalf of 'the people'. But Marx's arguments for mass parties alienated those revolutionaries who wanted to dismantle the state and run things through decentralised workers' councils and small communes, rather than through gaining political control of an already established centralised state. In 1872, tired of wasting their energy in time-consuming intrigues, Marx and Engels succeeded in transferring the International's General Council to New York. American developments had been significant for the IWMA, and Marx had promoted support for the north during the civil war. But the organisation did not take hold in the United States, and petered out in 1876.

Its influence, though, continued. Marx and his collaborators had popularised the independent organisation of working class forces on the basis of a socially transformative programme. They had suggested how a partisan political party could serve as a bank of rage, a purposeful machine for storing the justified angers and resentments of the proletariat, for translation and release as effective, determined and consequential expression at a later stage: pay-back, reckoning and resolution. This vision would shape the next period of international labour movement organisation.

## COMMUNISM'S ENLIGHTENMENT ROOTS

Although those threatened by its influence have never ceased to present it as an aberration, the work of Marx and Engels was no deviation from mainstream rational, scientific culture. The uncompromising form of socialism which would be developed by their followers expressed a tradition: communism was the most serious and systematic attempt there has yet been to develop effective and consistent politics, and to produce consciously sought social outcomes from Enlightenment thinking.

Communism *was* an iconoclastic movement. But its revolutionary impulses were always driven by angers against unfair conditions, deep-rooted problems and immediate oppressions resulting from capitalist society. They were shaped by righteous desire for vengeance and justice. But this was not a *negative* agenda. Most of those who wanted to 'turn the world upside down' did so because they wanted it the right way up. Far from being about 'ripping things apart', the movement's key ambition was to recover, re-establish and realise promises and hopes that had built up over centuries of cultural and scientific progress, and to do this in a form that would benefit all. As for any reputation for promoting chaos, one of the key Soviet leaders would insist in the early 1960s that 'communism is an orderly, organised society'.[23]

Key Enlightenment themes would shape communism's attempt to realise the promise of modernity: the application of rational and scientific principles to social problems; the aspiration to a better, if not to a perfect society; a sense that society worked in line with laws analogous to the laws of nature, which could be known and 'mastered' in the interests of humanity; the idea that individual people should be seen, and used, as social tools for long-term progress; and the meaning of progress itself.

Many of communism's strengths and weaknesses resulted from its particular 'take' on ambitions to re-order society 'scientifically'. For this reason, assessing communism's record leads to a consideration of the extent to which its failures point to problems about the Enlightenment more generally. Critical assessment of the communist movement also implies critical assessment of those aspects of the wider culture that it drew on. The question arises of whether communism's demise in the late twentieth century was a symptom, or expression, of a wider crisis in confidence about the possibility of shaping the world to better meet humanity's needs.

Recent invocations of Enlightenment thought have shown little consideration for such nuances. A number of social commentators who have seen themselves as heirs to this tradition have resorted to crude use of the 'Enlightenment' weapon in polemical argument, including in favour of 'science', against religious belief; and in favour of 'progress' and production, against people with concerns about the environmental crisis.[24] It does no service to the cause of Enlightenment values that many of its contemporary self-appointed partisans have so little conception of the complexities of its origins and evolution.

In fact, the Enlightenment was dynamic and multi-layered, fizzing with conflicting tendencies; it gave rise to major debates along lines that are irreducible to any notion of consensus. The ideas focused and promoted through the Enlightenment are sometimes spoken of as if they fit neatly together: democracy, liberalism, individualism. But there are inevitable and important tensions between and within such concepts. And it was around such contradictions and the potential confusions they generated that the space emerged for socialist intentions.

## NOTES

1. Terry Eagleton, 'Lend me a fiver', *London Review of Books*, 23 June 2005.
2. See Willie Thompson, *Postmodernism and History*, Palgrave Macmillan, Basingstoke 2004, pp110-11.
3. See Andrew Feenberg, *The Philosophy of Praxis*, Verso, London 2014, p4.
4. In nineteenth-century Germany, a radical critique of religion led many young intellectuals to communism. By contrast, 'the religious interpretation of socialism and the conception of a new epoch as the fulfilment of the true content of Christianity were ... current coin in the French socialism of the 1830s and 1840s'. Leszek Kolakowski, *Main Currents of Marxism*, WW Norton and company, New York 2004, p73. More generally, Christianity has been crucial to western traditions of radical egalitarianism.
5. Alberto Toscano, *Fanaticism*, Verso, London 2010, pp178-9.
6. Jonathan Rée, 2005, material posted on www.open.edu/openlearn/history-the-arts/culture/philosophy/marx-biography?in_menu=12747. Accessed 22 December 2015.

7. Although some later theorists, such as the French communist Louis Althusser, believed there was a strong 'break' between the 'early' and the 'late' Marx, insights from this period fundamentally shaped Marx's mature work on political economy. In the Volume One, Chapter One section of *Capital* [1867], 'on the fetishism of commodities and the secret thereof', Marx states that: 'there is a definite social relation between men, that assumes, in their eyes, the fantastic form of a relation between things … to find an analogy, we must have recourse to the mist-enveloped regions of the religious world. In that world the productions of the human brain appear as independent beings endowed with life, and entering into relation both with one another and the human race. So it is in the world of commodities with the products of men's hands'.

8. Feenberg, op cit, p34.

9. John Lanchester, 'Marx at 193', *London Review of Books*, 5 April 2012.

10. Terry Eagleton, 'Lend me a fiver', *London Review of Books*, 23 June 2005.

11. It is the conclusion in this statement – 'so we will decide for them' – that is particularly objectionable. People may well be mistaken about what is good for them. They may, for example, be swayed by social and psychological forces such as advertising, addiction, habituation and peer-group pressure. This problem generates political distinctions between 'needs' and 'wants'.

12. Renata Salecl, *The Tyranny of Choice*, Profile Books, London 2010, pp9-10.

13. Herbert Marcuse, *Soviet Marxism*, Penguin Books, Harmondsworth 1971 [1957], p164.

14. Karl Marx, 'On the Anniversary of the *People's Paper*', [1856].

15. C.J. Arthur, 'Editor's Introduction', Karl Marx and Friedrich Engels, *The German Ideology*, Lawrence and Wishart, London 1991 [1970], p14.

16. This conceptualisation established an unfortunate practice of conceiving of 'the working class' as an already-formed subject, which simply needed to be represented. One outcome of this approach was that, under Stalinism, when the class did not act as its self-appointed representatives expected, it was so much the worse for the class.

17. As Moses Finley put it in *The Ancient Economy*, University of California Press, London 1973, p 147: 'technical progress, economic growth, productivity, even efficiency, have not been significant goals since the beginning of time. So long as an acceptable lifestyle could be maintained, however that was defined, other values held the stage'.

18. John Lanchester, 'Marx at 193' *London Review of Books*, 5 April 2012.

19. Jean-Paul Sartre, *Critique of Dialectical Reason, Volume One*, Verso, London 2004 [1960], p110.

20. Pat Devine, Andrew Pearmain, Michael Prior and David Purdy, *Feelbad Britain*, Lawrence and Wishart, London 2009, p32.

21. Gareth Stedman Jones, *Karl Marx*, Allen Lane, London, 2016, p492.

22. Inaccurate press coverage of the Commune boosted Marxism's profile. Engels, reflecting on 1871 in 1884, freely admitted that 'the majority of the participants in the uprising had been Blanquists ... nationalistic revolutionaries who placed their hopes on immediate political action and the authoritarian dictatorship of a few resolute individuals. Only a minority had belonged to the International, which at that time was still dominated by the spirit of Proudhon, and they could therefore not be described as social revolutionaries, let alone Marxists. That did not prevent the governments and the bourgeoisie throughout Europe from regarding this insurrection ... as a conspiracy hatched by the General Council of the International'. Quoted in Walter Benjamin, *The Arcades Project*, Harvard University Press, London 1999, p793.

23. Nikita Khrushchev, March 1963, quoted by Francis Spufford, *The Guardian*, 7 August 2010.

24. The over-priced professors A.C. Grayling and Richard Dawkins are often seen as promoting these themes. Frank Furedi and people in the network he influences are amongst other assertive enthusiasts for 'Enlightenment'. In its name, and believing that human ambitions to 'master nature' were thoroughly progressive, its members oppose green politics. As an example, see Mick Hume's claim that 'if Marx were alive today, he would surely be a ruthless critic of sustainable development, environmentalism and all the other fashionable "anti-capitalist" doctrines that justify the elite's loss of nerve and help hold back the potential for further progress within the existing system'. *New Statesman*, 14 January 2002. Furedi's own trajectory has taken him from promoting simplistic revolutionary communism as classical Marxism, to attempting to discover what Marx 'really said', free of all later encumbrances (though it is inevitable and necessary that we interpret from 'later'), only to end up arguing for positions which preceded and were criticised by Marx – in Furedi's case in recent years, the importance and value of subjectivity, counterposed to 'the social', and the absolute value of 'freedom of speech'.

# 4. Forward from liberalism?

## THE EMERGENCE OF THE LEFT

As the eighteenth century ended, strong links developed between the political push for democracy and radical approaches to economic questions. A range of figures – including the radical pamphleteer and activist Thomas Paine and the French revolutionary administrator de Condorcet – made the radically new argument that poverty was not some kind of divine punishment for humanity's sins. As Gareth Stedman Jones has pointed out, poverty became seen as 'remediable in principle, since it was man-made in practice'. The possibility began to emerge of 'a planned world in which predictable misfortunes would be addressed, so that they could no longer plunge people into chronic poverty'.[1]

Such ambitions were claimed by the pioneers of an emerging left. As industrialisation spread across Europe, socialism took shape as a radical version of democracy. This was expressed through various forms of break, independence from and continuity with liberalism. The socialist consensus was that co-operation and solidarity between working people should replace the class divisions which define capitalism.

But there were different kinds of socialist: advocates of friendship rather than enmity between workers and their bosses; enthusiasts for co-operative self-organisation by small groups of producers; Christians who opposed capitalist excesses and promoted responsible paternalism 'in the name of the Father'; and radicals who saw defeat of the capitalist ruling class as a precondition for their new system.

These various socialisms took different distances from liberalism, a tradition which inspired – and inspires still – a range of progressive activities, and which has evolved and developed over time. But liberalism, although it emerged as an ideology of emancipation from arbitrary government and hereditary privilege, is shaped by contradictory economic and social agendas.[2] Liberals promoted freedom and plurality – of ideas, opinions, pleasures and interests.[3] But their conception of society as consisting of autonomous individuals created problems: they tended towards the fragmentation of human community. Not only was liberalism disruptive of the old 'unity' of 'traditional' society in which all had their allotted places – which reactionaries wished to defend – it was also often antagonistic to the goal of unified equality for which the emerging socialist movement was working.

As David Purdy has described:

> until the mid-nineteenth century ... the European left was primarily concerned with civil freedom, political reform and national liberation. But as liberal demands were achieved without disturbing the prevailing class structure, the mantle of the left passed to socialists and anarchists, hitherto minority sects, who argued that the ideals of 1789 could not be realised within the framework of bourgeois or liberal democracy, but would require radical changes in the ownership of property, the organisation of the economy, and the distribution of life-chances. Thus, the entire political spectrum shifted to the left.[4]

Marx was part of this shift, and was critical of such liberal ideas as individual independence, the integrity of private property, free trade, limited government, tolerance, and the rhetoric of equal rights. However positive these sounded, they often provided cover for oppressive practice – through colonial rule over subject peoples, and through exploitative class relationships everywhere. Their over-riding respect for capitalist property relations meant that many liberals were content to live with a significant degree of inequality and social exclusion. They might well allow the importance of measures of social insurance or the virtues of compassion, but in the end the ideology of private property represented the bad faith of the powerful.

This argument further established the importance of 'ideology' for the emerging left. Kicking against the liberalism he himself had been part of as a young journalist, Marx's emerging thought aimed at consistently applying the principles of equality, liberty and solidarity. Liberals *said* they meant and wanted these things. But their actions told another story.

## DEMARCATIONS: LIBERALISM AND THE LEFT

Liberal theories of democracy conceive of 'freedom' as being split into two different parts – economic freedom and political freedom. Its default position is that politics is not 'free' to determine economics. Instead, the 'realities' of the economy, the market and the rights of property owners are 'givens', which politics then has to adjust itself to. Through promoting this understanding, liberal democracy's basic concept of individualism was bound up with the modern notion of ownership. As Jeff Noonan has pinpointed, liberalism's language of political rights confirmed the economic sphere of society as private, free from interference from above (the state) or below (workers and other groups made dependent for their survival on the state of market forces).[5]

This is the historical root of left-wing suspicion of liberal democracy. Liberal democracy accepts that there are 'two realms': 'politics' and law-making are managed by the state, democratic or otherwise, but rulers of 'the economy' arrogate to themselves what David Purdy describes as 'the tasks of marshalling the workforce, developing new technologies, launching new products, investing capital funds and enlarging the scale of production'.[6] They make these decisions about economic affairs on the basis of their rights as private capital owners – but without being democratically accountable about the impact of their decisions.

Democracy as constituted in capitalism fully respects these rights; by legally relegating issues of property, ownership and work to the private sector, it restricts debate over matters of power in social and public life to the narrowly defined democracy of electoral politics. As David McNally put it in his obituary of Ellen Meiksins Wood – a well-known and respected critic of democracy within capitalism – this confinement of debate 'empties democracy of its original meaning as the power of the common people, leaving workers precariously exposed to market forces'.[7]

As Chris Arthur argues, liberal democracy emancipates man 'by declaring that the real differences between men shall not affect their standing as citizens', and hence 'leaves those differences intact'. This means that relations of domination and conflict in civil society are left untouched, and it also allows 'these real social relations' to 'infect the political sphere as well': 'The modern state, in contrast with feudalism, declares wealth, education, occupation, religion, race, in short all the real distinctions, non-political distinctions'.[8]

Marxism's fundamental conception of the relationship between politics and economics, its insistence on the need to include economics in the political sphere, is at the heart of its difference from bourgeois perspectives on liberal democracy. Marxists believe that the basic mechanisms of how the economy works should be brought into the centre of democratic contestation, as the main focus of political debate.

In its development as a consistent form of socialism, communism rejected the demarcation of property rights as separate from the worlds of law and 'democratic politics', in which all were formally equal. Communists' central assumption was that economics should be entirely subject to political control. They believed that such control should be exercised in the interests of the rising class: the proletariat, or wage-labouring working class, whose numbers grew so rapidly during the nineteenth and twentieth centuries, and who would in time come to be the only class. Pursuing class struggle was therefore positive: it would lead to short-term gains for ordinary people, and was in the longer-term interests of society.

The left reaction to liberalism involved many salient criticisms. Liberalism's myths of individual autonomy could not be believed. As Edward Thompson wrote, they served only too often 'as an intellectual gloss upon the status-quo'.[9] Statements of liberal dismay over unfairness – and resulting conflicts – often resulted in little more than the application of a soothing balm while accepting current relationships of force and oppression. Most noticeably, its claims of equality and liberty did not travel well to Asia or Africa.[10] For all of liberalism's stated commitment to the rights and sensitivities of 'the individual' in the metropole, it saw the tropical lands of empire as inhabited by 'masses' and 'natives'.

Unfortunately, however, the left's reaction to this hypocrisy could sometimes lead to a rejection of the importance and significance of individuals: this became, literally, a fatal flaw. At their worst, some communist leaders, instead of rejecting the limits of liberalism by extending dignity to *all* people, treated the people in the metropoles that they themselves ran as 'masses', without individuality.

The left's response to liberalism would have been more appropriately based on understanding that it was an internally divided and incomplete project, the progressive elements of which could serve as a basis for positive forms of socialism. For, as Terry Eagleton has written, 'in its heyday, middle-class liberalism was far more of a revolutionary current than socialism has ever managed to be'. And, as he does go on to argue, 'Any socialism which fails to build on its magnificent achievements risks moral and material bankruptcy from the outset'.[11]

As Elaine Coburn has argued:

> with liberals, Marx calls for freedom and equality, both essential to democracy. Against liberals, he argues that capitalist market relationships are fundamentally incompatible with real freedom and equality.[12]

Two broad readings resulted from Marx's critique of liberalism, given its combined and unstable commitment to capitalism *and* to democracy. In one reading, Marxism can be seen as an utter rejection of liberalism, and as a politics which promotes social conflict rather than seeking consensus and understanding. But on another, it can be seen as an attempt to meet the agenda set by liberalism, going beyond it in order to achieve social equality, and thus establish the real conditions for mutual respect between people.

Demands for social and economic reform led to a pattern of separation of 'the left' from liberals within the democratic struggles against the old regimes in America and across Europe. These divisions occurred even though liberals were not normally part of any European country's ruling bloc during the nineteenth century. According to Eric Hobsbawm's interpretation:

> ... the new socialists ... made their case by pushing the arguments of classical Franco-British liberalism beyond the point where bourgeois liberals were prepared to go ... A world in which all were happy, and every individual fully and freely realised his or her potentialities, in which freedom reigned and government that was coercion had disappeared, was the ultimate aim of both liberals and socialists. What distinguishes the various members of the ideological family descended from humanism and the enlightenment, liberal, socialist, communist or anarchist, is not the gentle anarchy which is the utopia of all of them, but the methods of achieving it ... [it was over these issues that] socialism parted company with the classical liberal tradition. In the first place it broke radically with the liberal assumption

that society was a mere aggregate or combination of its individual atoms, and that its motor-force was their self-interest and competition. In doing so the socialists returned to the oldest of all human ideological traditions, the belief that man is naturally a communal being ... society was not a necessary but regrettable diminution of man's unlimited natural right to do as he liked, but the setting of his life, happiness and individuality.[13]

At the same time as distinguishing different but related ideological trends, this account captures the aims of the liberal revolution in terms of its own stated ambitions: the problem for socialists was that it did not go far enough in realising those ambitions. This was because liberalism in bourgeois society was the prisoner of its own contradictions. What differentiated Marx from liberals was his argument that capitalist market relationships are fundamentally incompatible with real freedom and equality – and with genuine democracy.

Thus socialism emerged from liberalism partly as a reaction against it, representing both break and discontinuity. But it was also, at least partly, an attempt to 'make it real': continuity and fealty. Increasing numbers of socialists started to believe that the realisation of liberal agendas might require illiberal means: this viewpoint would in due course draw some liberals first to socialism, and then towards communism, while at the same time repelling some people from communism, because of its use of coercive, illiberal approaches.

Overall, the story of Marxism was that, in its incarnations that achieved state power, its move beyond liberalism became a *rejection* of liberalism, rather than an attempt to realise it more fully. This problem was compounded after communism became a practical project of government in the hands of the Russian Bolsheviks – the dominant wing of one of the working-class parties least used to the practice of democracy, and most hardened in its culture, in reaction to the autocratic character of the regime they had been fighting against.

## MARX AGAINST DEMOCRACY?

Many opponents of socialism and communism assert that there is an essentially anti-democratic core in Marx's thinking. Against this, a common position on the left is to present undemocratic practice as resulting from the corruption of the entirely positive intentions and politics of the early founders.[14] Marx himself is presented as a democrat in every sense of the word, consistent and thoroughgoing. Distortion and error is said to have been introduced to Marxism by Stalin, or through the earlier 'wrong turning' of Bolshevism.

The reality is that some of the roots of the anti-democratic practices which marked Bolshevism in Lenin's day, and later entirely shaped Stalinism, can in fact be traced back, at least in part, to Marx and Engels: elements of arrogance and instrumentalism are present there, though in tension with other elements which *were* consistently democratic.

Such contradictory signals resulted from the character and tone of Marx and Engel's critique of the limitations of bourgeois or liberal democracy, and of the moral hypocrisy on the part of liberals that went along with this. Marx and Engels were impatient with bourgeois norms and values because the bourgeoisie espoused positive values but did not support the practical steps that would be necessary and appropriate to realise those values on a universal basis. This sometimes led to Marx and Engels displaying a certain ambivalence towards democratic practice. They did not oppose bourgeois democracy because of opposition to democracy, however: their critique was that bourgeois democracy did not deliver. As even Leszek Kolakowski, a determined critic of communism, allowed, Marx expected socialism to lead to the abolition of economic coercion 'in addition to, and not as opposed to, political coercion'.[15] But Marx and Engels had not provided their followers with a consistent and comprehensive democratic theory. They never unpacked and clarified a set of distinctions that needed to be made.

This is illustrated in *Revolution and Counter-Revolution in Germany*, a collection of newspaper articles co-produced by Marx and Engels from 1851. Their analysis before 1848 had been that, because of democracy's limited development to that date, and because the German states' kings and princes were not cushioned against the shocks of popular upheaval by parliaments, as in France or England, it was likely that a push for working-class rights would lead to a full bourgeois revolution, and the establishment of a republic. It could be seen that this view implicitly assumes that prospects for revolution would somehow be better if there were no democratic institutions in place.

During the revolutionary events of 1848, Marx's newspaper, the *Neue Rheinische Zeitung*, had urged that events should be pushed beyond the 'liberal-constitutional phase' of the revolution as quickly as possible. But such ambitions were not to be realised: events did not even go so far as to overthrow the princes and kings. The year's crises and opportunities were settled through compromises which supposedly put Germany's authoritarian monarchies under the control of parliaments in Berlin and Frankfurt. But Marx and Engels railed against these bodies, which were ineffective even in their own terms. Instead of exercising popular sovereignty and bringing the pre-revolutionary authorities under their control, the liberal representatives were more concerned to reach agreements with reactionary monarchs and to make deals with established power.

The journalism expresses scathing exasperation with bourgeois politicians, who wore out 'their short and feeble popularity … in continual bickering', and, instead of taking part in revolutionary events, 'lost all their time in idle debates upon the possibility of resisting the imperial army without overstepping the bounds of constitutional conventionalities'. The German Diet – parliament – was pilloried as 'helpless … discussing theoretical quibbles while the roof over their head was almost burning', and as suffering from the 'incurable malady' of 'parliamentary cretinism'.[16]

Engels argued that 'ineffective' bourgeois parliamentarians were in fact all too effective: whether or not it was their wish, their actions contributed to the defeat of potentially revolutionary steps:

> They allowed the insurrections of Saxony, of Rhenish Prussia, of Westphalia, to be suppressed without any other help than a posthumous, sentimental protest against the unfeeling violence of the Prussian government … they went on talking, protesting, proclaiming, pronouncing, but never had the courage or the sense to act.[17]

In his important account of key trends in the twentieth-century left, the Spanish political thinker Fernando Claudin summed up the observations of Marx and Engels after the German liberal bourgeoisie had made a pact with the absolutist monarchy:

> Marx concluded from these defeats … not that the struggle for democracy was futile, but rather that it was subversive – demonstrating in deeds the anti-democratic nature of the bourgeoisie

and the anti-bourgeois nature of democracy ... he also drew the lesson that when the revolution is faced with the need for an armed struggle, universal suffrage must be backed up by an armed strength greater than that of the bourgeoisie.[18]

Here is the Marxist criticism of bourgeois liberalism: whatever its verbal claims, it proved ineffective against reaction, even if it did not actually fuse with it. This analysis fed the later revolutionary communist argument that fighting for 'real freedom' meant rejecting the sham appearances of 'formal democracy', including parliaments, which were actually a form of class rule – a dictatorship of the bourgeoisie. However, for all their impatience with bourgeois talk of democracy, any balanced reading of Marx and Engels shows that they cannot be seen as direct precursors of the undemocratic communist regimes of the twentieth century. As Robin Blackburn states: 'Marx's writings on Jacobinism and Bonapartism were animated by deep hostility to political formations that sought to usurp social forces'.[19]

Perhaps the most troublesome of the concepts which led to communism being positioned as inherently anti-democratic was that of the 'dictatorship of the proletariat', which Marx defined as a 'necessary' outcome of class struggle.[20] The argument was that achieving socialism would require a temporary period of class domination by the proletariat: socialism would not come about overnight, or through some happy and easily achieved consensual agreement between all classes, based on what was best for all. There would have to be a period of transition from capitalism to a better world, during which period the working class would need to be in charge. State powers would need to be used in order to expropriate the rich and take their power away – and deployed to stop the tiny minority of capitalists blocking progressive change in ways which really *would* be oppressive and murderous.

But, given that this transitional period would be one shaped by and serving the needs of the vast majority of people, Marx's clear belief was that the revolution he proposed – the new socialist society – would deliver a new and higher level of freedom than that prevalent in the existing society. Marx was not arguing that working-class power would have a dictatorial character in the sense of being brutal, harsh, cruel and oppressive. Once the political dominance of the proletariat was clearly and democratically established, such processes as expropriation could take orderly, even measured forms. Furthermore, as Terry Eagleton points out, the term 'dictatorship' did not have the same associations in Marx's usage as it usually has today.[21] And, as Eric Hobsbawm argues, in Marxist terms the 'dictatorship of the bourgeoisie' could exist with or without universal suffrage: the focus was on the *class content* of government rather than its *institutional form*, and the term 'dictatorship' was not to be understood as being in opposition to a democratic state.[22] The best thing would be for the workers' party to campaign for its programme through elections, and use the power resulting from political success to dispossess what Geoff Eley describes as 'an ever-narrowing circle of exploitative capitalist interests', as part of a process of 'reorganising society's economic, social and cultural goods'.[23] In this way, the institutional forms which had characterised the emergence of liberal democracy, and which had initially established themselves as vehicles for bourgeois rule – parliaments, freely contested elections, argument and dispute through the press and in public spaces – could become key elements in the system through which the working class would reorganise society and the economy away from the class divisions and exploitation which the bourgeoisie depended on.

The insistence that class struggle was an actual phenomenon, inherent in real social arrangements, rather than being an unfortunate notion resulting from 'divisive' socialist activity, was one way in which Marx and Engels marked their differences with those they characterised as 'utopian socialists'. Many socialist intellectuals had proposals for re-ordering economic affairs, but they did not have a concept of class struggle as the motor of history, or a conception of the historic role of the working class in overcoming capitalism. As Willie Thompson puts it, 'the fateful conjunction' arrived when socialist ideas were interpreted as being 'the responsibility and the destiny of the new class of hereditary wage-workers central to the capitalist production process'.[24]

In making this 'conjunction', Marx and Engels presented their thinking as 'scientific socialism'. There was some condescension in this, but not a wholly contemptuous rejection of the 'utopians'. Marxism emerged from serious critical engagement with all the radical political currents and thinkers in Germany, France and Britain in the 1840s. As Gramsci recognised, the followers of Fourier and Saint-Simon, and of the Welsh social reformer Robert Owen, recognised that in the types of society they envisaged for the future, economic equality was 'the necessary basis for the projected reform'.[25] Moreover, their followers were responsible for a range of concrete, practical projects, from the establishment of long-term co-operative communities to the organisation of the French railways, and the building of the Panama and Suez canals – two of the ambitious and large-scale development projects proposed by Saint-Simonians that were actually realised.

For Marx, the problem with the utopian socialists was their political approach and method: as the Russian Marxist Georgi Plekhanov would later put it, 'the utopian is one who, starting from an abstract principle, seeks for a perfect social organisation'.[26] The usual scenario envisaged by utopians was that people from all classes and backgrounds would be converted to schemes for the comprehensive reorganisation of social arrangements. Some thought that this would happen simply through large numbers of people coming to recognise and support the rational arguments that socialists advanced. If enough people woke up one morning, realising the truth, the world would be made anew. Unfortunately, the argument that rational argument has the power to change things for the better was never, itself, a rational argument.

According to Gramsci, the 'utopian character' of these theoreticians and activists was the result of their belief that it was possible to introduce economic equality 'with arbitrary laws, an act of will'.[27] This scenario did not convince the 'scientific socialists'. As Vincent Geoghegan argues, what they were attacking was not a utopian anticipation of a better world, but, rather, a failure to root this anticipation in a theoretical framework that understood the essential dynamics of capitalism. Socialism had to draw its energy from the social forces that were destroying the old society and ushering in the new. 'For Marx and Engels, this meant becoming a part of the proletarian movement'.[28]

The future would emerge from the dynamics of history and struggle: not from grandiose schemes and precise instructions on the best way to arrange all aspects of life and daily routine. Rather than promoting visions or blueprints of what the ideal society would look like, or appealing to the good sense and generosity of an imaginary fair-minded elite, there was a need to *organise*.

## NOTES

1. Gareth Stedman Jones, 'A history of ending poverty', *The Guardian*, 2 July 2005.

2. Willie Thompson, *Ideologies in the Age of Extremes*, Pluto Press, London 2011, p5.

3. Francois Furet, *The Passing of an Illusion*, University of Chicago Press, London 1999, p11.

4. David Purdy, in Pat Devine, Andy Pearmain and Purdy (eds), *Feelbad Britain*, Lawrence and Wishart, London 2009, p234.

5. Jeff Noonan, *Democratic Society and Human Needs*, McGill-Queen's University Press, Montreal 2006, p45.

6. David Purdy, 'Keywords: Democracy', *Perspectives*, Democratic Left Scotland, Dundee 2007.

7. David McNally, obituary of Ellen Meiksins Wood, *The Guardian*, 10 February 2016.

8. C.J. Arthur, 'Editor's Introduction', Karl Marx and Friedrich Engels, *The German Ideology*, Lawrence and Wishart, London 1991 [1970], p10.

9. E.P. Thompson, *Writing by Candlelight*, Merlin Press, London 1980, pp8-9.

10. In Chapter One of *On Liberty* [1859] John Stuart Mill had stated that 'despotism is a legitimate mode of government in dealing with barbarians, provided the end be their improvement'.

11. Terry Eagleton, *Reason, Faith and Revolution*, Yale University Press, London 2009, p94. Some radical pre-socialists developed liberal themes through proposals that would still constitute progressive change today. By the end of the eighteenth century, Thomas Paine and Mary Wollstonecraft had, in different ways, pushed the liberal argument further than would be matched by its practice for the next century and more.

12. Elaine Coburn, 'What is socialism? What are socialist studies?', *Socialist Studies*, Canada, Fall 2009.

13. Eric Hobsbawm, *Age of Revolution*, Weidenfeld and Nicholson, London 1975, pp242-5.

14. When reform communism began in Western Europe, even its most thoughtful partisans could only ask whether 'the errors, faults, distortions [had] started with Stalin? With Lenin? In those days nobody dared say "with Marx"'. Rossana Rossanda, *The Comrade from Milan*, Verso, London 2010, p163.

15. Leszek Kolakowski, 'The Marxist Roots of Stalinism', *Is God Happy?* Penguin, London 2012 [1975], p93.

16. Friedrich Engels, 'Revolution and Counter-Revolution in Germany, XI: The Vienna Insurrection', *Marx and Engels Collected Works, Volume 11*, Lawrence and Wishart, London 2010, [1852], p58 (digital edition).

17. Friedrich Engels, 'Revolution and Counter-Revolution in Germany,

XVII: Insurrection', *Marx and Engels Collected Works, Volume 11*, Lawrence and Wishart, London 2010 [1852], pp86-7 (digital edition).

18. Fernando Claudin, *Eurocommunism and Socialism*, New Left Books/ Verso, London 1978, pp68-9.

19. Robin Blackburn, 'Fin de Siècle: socialism after the crash' in Blackburn (ed), *After the Fall*, Verso 1991, pps176 and p179.

20. March 1852, letter to Georg Weydemeyer.

21. Terry Eagleton, *Why Marx Was Right*, Yale University Press, London 2011, p204.

22. Eric Hobsbawm, *How to Change the World*, Little, Brown, London 2011, p56.

23. Geoff Eley, 'Exile to the ages', *Los Angeles Review of Books*, 28 October 2013.

24. Willie Thompson, *The Left in History*, Pluto Press, London 1997, p21.

25. Antonio Gramsci, *Prison Notebooks*, Joseph A Buttigieg (ed), Columbia University Press, New York 2011 [1930-32], Volume Three, p11.

26. Georgi Plekhanov, *Anarchism and Socialism* [1895].

27. Antonio Gramsci, 2011 [1930-32], op cit, p11.

28. Vincent Geoghegan, *Utopianism and Marxism*, Methuen and Co, London 1987, p27.

# 5. Socialism, Engels, Marxism and democracy

## THE GROWTH OF SOCIALISM

In the second half of the nineteenth century, socialism developed quickly across Western and Central Europe, as a widespread and deep-rooted movement of reaction to capitalist exploitation. It also expressed the massive shift of ordinary people into political life and social consciousness after the industrial revolution, and gave voice to their attitudes, reactions and hopes. At first strongly focused on building trade unions to defend workers' rights, it soon went much further than this, proposing a different way of organising society. One of its key aims was to transform the position of workers from being 'a multitude of desperately competing individuals' so that they would 'become a class'.[1]

What was socialism? Key principles were shared by all who took the name.[2] The social imaginary that formed its basic outlook was framed by the idea that a polity's issues and problems should be dealt with on the basis of the interests of the community as a whole. Collectivist approaches should be put in place that could implement overall conceptions of how society should be organised, so that everybody could live fairly and well. Production would be for need, not greed. Decisions about manufacture, exchange and administration would be taken democratically, with the active participation of all. People's working lives and jobs would not depend on the judgements of capitalists about how they might make a profit. Instead, social needs would be assessed, and production and services would be arranged so that all members of society who were able to work would have a range of tasks to carry out to meet those needs. Individual ambitions would be aligned with social objectives; and the costs of foregoing the gains that a small minority could achieve through selfish endeavour would be more than compensated for by the benefits that social co-operation would deliver for all.

Given the gross inequalities and injustices which ordinary people faced during the nineteenth century, socialism's immediate demands were for wealth redistribution, greater rights for workers, a range of social goods from education to health care, and a massive shift of power away from those currently in authority. In every country, thousands took up the political ambitions it espoused. As Eagleton describes it, they objected to the fact that 'the great majority of men and women in history have lived lives of suffering and degradation', and believed that this could be altered in the future.[3]

In their campaigns for change, socialists subjected class inequalities to merciless criticism. They understood that it was the uncontrolled concentration of wealth and the pressures of competition between capitalists that were causing their misery. Their aim was therefore to overturn the old system and re-organise society in the interests of working people.

Opposition to present unfairness fuelled the movement. But its engine was a vision of the future. Short-term goals were seen as marking the way to an entirely different way of living. The detail may have needed more work, but the goal could still be clearly stated: socialism would be a classless society in which human solidarity would go along with the harmonious satisfaction of all reasonable needs. The whole community, in a democratic commonwealth, would own land and resources collectively, and use them for the good of all. Factories and productive equipment would be socialised. The economy would be planned: politics would be in command of the economy, and would determine the organisation of work, instead of investment and production levels being determined by private businessmen. Work would be organised for all to carry out, within the limits of their abilities. It would be fairly shared, purposeful, and decently rewarded: even if some management or even direction were still needed, this would be co-ordinated and controlled by those whose interests it served. Justice, mutual respect between people and equality of opportunities would mark social relations, and these arrangements would be freely and more or less unanimously supported. The view also grew – unevenly and in the face of resistance and suspicion even within the movement – that these principles should extend to relationships between women and men, and between people of all races. The common good and self-realisation through education, culture and fellowship would be the defining social values, instead of accumulation and greed.

Those working for a shift to such conditions took an understanding of the French Revolution as a template for next steps. They saw the next revolution as belonging to the working class. They too were a class that had been born and grown to irresistible strength 'within an old society they were destined to take over', as Eric Hobsbawm puts it:

> just as bourgeois society had been in relation to the feudalism that preceded it and that it had overthrown, the new socialist society would be the next and higher phase of the development of human society.[4]

By the end of the nineteenth century, socialism was the strongest social movement to have emerged during the previous few hundred years; it had created enduring institutions and established new traditions and outlooks. Adherents of the socialist red flag had built up increasingly successful electoral parties, trade unions, newspapers, friendly societies, consumer co-operatives and educational and cultural bodies. Joining organisations and accepting the disciplines of shared endeavour became a widespread practice. People saw themselves as members of the movement, and were confident that they shared the same outlooks and ambitions as many thousands of others who they had never met.

## BANKS OF RAGE

As suggested in the previous chapter, the socialist parties of the 1800s could be seen as 'banks of rage'. They gathered together different potential responses to the separate concerns and problems of working people, and sought then to combine these through strategic long-term struggle. This meant that workers' anger would not be frittered away and wasted in immediate reactions, but could be organised and applied to programmes of sustained action which actually removed the sources of their oppression and exploitation.

Internationally, the movement took multiple forms. Some socialists railed against the fundamental and self-evident injustice that the rich had gained their wealth at the expense of the poor: restitution was the goal. Others limited themselves to putting in place social insurance, welfare and self-help institutions such as consumer co-operatives, in order to alleviate and offset the effects of capitalist wealth production.

Variations in programme, tone, style and organisational form reflected the specific circumstances of the left in each country. Different traditions were strong in different places, but there was much overlapping, as well as attempts at dominance. The German Social Democratic Party (SPD), founded in 1875, was the biggest political party in the world by the end of the nineteenth century, winning elections and promoting its own programme for government. In Italy, the anarchist movement was stronger than that of socialists seeking governmental power, and in France and Spain, syndicalism flourished, a movement that emphasised industrial action as a method of struggle, and workers' control as a mechanism for social administration. Syndicalists had much in common with anarchists: they repudiated participation in elections and all 'collaboration' in legislative bodies. British socialism brought together campaigns for political reform which had been initiated by the Chartist movement of the 1830s and 1840s; trade unionism around wage disputes, and demands for better health and safety; syndicalist outlooks; and the co-operative movement.[5]

As the First International was being put aside as a vehicle for the European left in the late 1870s, the prosperity of the mid-century was giving way to a period of depression. In these conditions the European labour movement became more combative. Between 1873 and 1896, strikes broke out on an unprecedented scale in one country after the other. Independent mass labour parties now organised separately from liberal parties in many countries; and this was also a time when many radical groups broke away from conspiratorial practice and won broad support through operating openly in conditions of increasing democratic freedom. Marx, Engels and their followers put forward the view that workers needed a political movement which valued trade unionism but looked forward to acquiring state power, taking maximum advantage of the new frameworks of parliaments and the rule of law.

As we saw in chapter 3, the main lesson Marx drew from the Paris Commune in 1871 was that large and legal working-class parties in each country were the necessary prerequisite for socialist revolution. In the wake of the violent crushing of the Commune, most socialists turned their attention to campaigning as pressure groups, agitating and arguing for the reform of particular abuses, and for the right of labour to advance its claims by industrial or political action; and where they operated in states with some measure of responsiveness, they argued that the state should concern itself with the demands of the masses and the social dimension of public affairs.[6]

In July 1889, a congress in Paris, marking the one-hundredth anniversary of the storming of the Bastille, formed a new 'Second International' with the aim of forming a federation of the emerging large working-class parties. The Congress brought together an impressive network of labour parties that had growing support in most European countries, as well as elsewhere. Paul Lafargue, Marx's son-in-law, made the keynote address. And as this strong and socially grounded movement developed, Marx's followers succeeded in getting its key leaders to conceive of their efforts as building on his pioneering work. This did not happen automatically. As Giovanni Arrighi describes it, Marx and his followers were only able to establish their hegemony over the nascent European labour movement 'after protracted intellectual struggles'.[7]

One key division had concerned the possibility of co-operative production as a potential system to replace capitalism. This was the view propounded in an earlier period by the Owenites in Britain and the Fourierists in France, and it was now supported by the followers of Mikhail Bakunin and Ferdinand Lassalle. But in 1891, Lassalle's followers among the German social democrats, who believed that socialism could be brought about through state-aided mutuals, were defeated at the party's congress in Erfurt.

This result consolidated 'Marxism' as the dominant outlook within the Second International. Three key positions shaped this outlook: the conviction that the present capitalist system was unfair and wasteful; the belief that history proceeded through stages; and a view that members of the working class, the labouring 'proletariat', shared fundamentally similar experiences and interests, whatever differences of nationality and identity might exist between them. Moreover, a romantic-heroic image began to be promoted of a relatively isolated and misunderstood Marx, who had been labouring away over long years at theoretical analyses, and was now posthumously being vindicated as his work became the underpinning for the programmes of large socialist organisations that were preparing for power.

## ENGELS: THE INVENTOR OF MARXISM

Engels had shared, promoted and supported Marx's ideas from 1844 until his death in 1883. In 1870 Engels had allowed himself to be bought out as the junior partner in the Manchester branch of his family's successful multinational cotton business, and on the proceeds of this deal had moved to London to devote himself to his real enthusiasms: supporting and advising his friend Karl Marx, and activity in the socialist movement.

From his Primrose Hill townhouse, Engels had worked voluntarily as corresponding secretary for the International Working Men's Association, entertaining and influencing a roster of remarkable visitors – activists, intellectuals, journalists, revolutionaries. Following Marx's death, and inspired by the increasing strength of the German socialists, Engels had committed himself even more fully to developing and promoting his old comrade's perspectives.

Though the movement faced many barriers, Engels believed there was a real possibility of a transition to socialism through proletarian governments being voted in by the enfranchised working class. It certainly looked this way in Germany, where it seemed possible to extrapolate the possibility of the socialists coming to power through mathematical calculation. The socialist vote had risen from 550,000 (9.7 per cent of the electorate) in 1884, to 1,427,000 (nearly 20 per cent) by 1890.[8]

Recognising democracy as a route to socialist victory had led Engels to reject vanguardist adventurism: 'the time of surprise attacks, of revolutions carried through by small conscious minorities at the head of the masses lacking consciousness, is past'.[9] This commitment to legal and incremental means was no rejection of the revolutionary goal, but a tactical judgement about the most effective way to advance. Through 'long and persistent labour', the workers' party could win support from the lower middle classes. In the particular circumstances of the 1890s, parties like the SDP had the most to gain through legal means. As Hobsbawm has commented, in Germany 'violent and armed confrontation was ... likely to be initiated not by insurrectionists but from the right against the socialists'.[10] If such a situation were to arise, the left would have a legal and democratically grounded basis for authorising the necessary use of violence to suppress counter-revolutionary reaction.

Whilst some radicals believed that their continuing oppression in countries that proclaimed the existence of 'democratic rights' proved that these were a fraud and a sham, many others felt that the continuing restrictions they faced proved that the ruling class feared democracy. The task, therefore, was to push harder for democratic rights. Engels lent his authority to this position and asserted the 'inevitablity' of victory. As David McLellan recounts, looking forward to socialist transformation, Engels predicted in 1891 that the SPD would come to power in 1898. 'This victory was mathematically calculable and he even had a graph to prove it'.[11]

Through his writings and activity, Engels popularised his late friend's work as a unified objective system encompassing Nature and History, and associated Marx with the then widespread enthusiasm for science. Thus, as Fredric Jameson notes, 'it was not Marx but Engels who invented Marxism'.[12] This systematisation was most evident in *Anti-Duhring*, written in 1888. Here Engels sets out general propositions about the universe and the laws governing everything in it, attempting to set out a philosophical system based on the idea that nature itself moved dialectically. The book was highly influential and was to shape the views of important socialist leaders over the next couple of decades, including Karl Kautsky and Eduard Bernstein in Germany and Georgi Plekhanov in Russia.

But Engels's systematisation could on occasion distort and obscure some of the most creative impulses in Marx's work.[13] These included an emphasis on the importance of subjective, human agency and the ways in which this could change objective conditions, alongside the simultaneous recognition that 'subjective forces' were themselves constructed and shaped by objective conditions, and acceptance that objective conditions set limits to what subjectively motivated effort could achieve. These ideas were most explicit in early texts shaped by and at the same time breaking from Left Hegelianism, but they were retained in Marx's work to the end.

Engels downplayed the importance of 'the subjective' in effecting social change, suggesting that this happened 'inevitably', 'objectively', 'necessarily'. He suggested that nature itself conformed to the philosophical principles that Marx had formulated. In fact, as Paul Thomas argues, the idea that human history and thought are 'but special fields of play for nature's general laws of motion and development ... appears to owe little, if anything at all, to Marx'.[14]

Serious problems partly resulted from inflated claims that Marxism was a way of comprehending everything. This outlook might instil confidence, but it was also a source of arrogance. The idea that those who possessed the imprimatur of Marxism were acting with the knowledge and authority of nature itself led to attempts to force progress through short cuts.

Marx's own position was quite focused and limited. As a British communist philosopher wrote nearly forty years ago, for Marx, materialism was a way of comprehending our relationships with one another in our material environment.[15] More generally, the appropriate counter to *excessive* Marxism is to understand Marx's work as itself a historical phenomenon, shaped by forms of thinking very much of their times.

## THE FORWARD MARCH OF LABOUR AND DEMOCRACY

The socialism that developed from the 1800s took many different forms. But it is important to recognise that it emerged in tandem with modern democracy. Neither was established before the other. In many ways the movement's growth directly generated the system: growing support for democratic principles in the nineteenth and twentieth centuries can be seen as one of socialism's main achievements. The movement drew on ideas about democracy to assert the need for ordinary people to be involved in political determination. At the same time, many of the mechanisms and practices of liberal democracy that were developed during its emergence were instigated as a means of containment: structures and procedures were put in place by the more astute bourgeois representatives to avoid, limit and manage socialism's content and ambition.

The ambivalences of some radical socialists towards democracy are connected to this duality in the formation of democratic institutions. But, as we have seen, socialists were also critical of liberalism's unwillingness to include the economy within their definition of democracy and sought to extend it: their first focus was therefore political struggle against liberals and conservatives who were convinced 'that democracy was incompatible with the preservation of private property, and thus demanded severe restrictions on the right to vote and the freedom of parliaments'.[16]

This struggle resulted in the slow and uneven extension of suffrage. Republican France was the first nation to abolish all property requirements for voting, instituting universal male suffrage in the revolutionary year of 1792 (though French women were not to be granted the vote for a further 153 years). As the vote was extended and political enfranchisement grew, pressure was exerted for further reform, and potential support for such reform increased among the electorate.

In Britain, campaigns for the extension of suffrage to the working class began in the 1830s, with the Chartists, but it was a long time before their aim of universal male suffrage was achieved. The 1832 Great Reform Act had granted an extension of the suffrage to the male urban middle classes, increasing the size of the electorate to one man in five. Further reform in 1867 extended the vote to skilled urban male workers. Only after 1884 did the majority of men – two out of three – have the vote. Women's campaigns for suffrage took off at the end of the nineteenth century, and they finally achieved their aim in 1918 – so long as they were over thirty. It was 1928 before all women and men over 21 had the vote. Only since 1969 has the voting age been 18.

The German Empire instituted universal male suffrage for the Reichstag from its formation in 1871. But this lower house's powers were counterbalanced by the upper house, the Reichsrat, to which access was much more carefully controlled. Democracy was further distorted by 'Anti-Socialist Laws' that were put in place from 1878 to 1890, which prohibited organisations 'that seek by means of Social democratic, Socialistic or Communistic activities to overthrow the existing political and social order'. Meetings were banned, trade unions outlawed, and newspapers closed.

The main result of the Anti-Socialist Laws was that the socialist movement grew exponentially. Support for socialists increased from 493,000 votes and twelve Reichstag seats in 1877 to almost 2 million votes and forty-four seats by 1893.[17] German socialists developed a hard, combative edge. Responding to state prosecution, they became more radical in terms of their political outlooks, and they learned the skills of underground organisation. Using creativity and subterfuge, socialists often ran as 'independents' and printed their journals and books outside Germany, to be smuggled back across the border.[18]

Creativity and political intelligence are not exclusive to the left, though. German Chancellor Bismarck decided to shift from seeking to ban the SPD to a strategy of competing with it by introducing measures of social protection in the form of insurance-based social security programmes that covered retirement pensions, healthcare and industrial accidents. This was the origin of Germany's social-market economy – and it was perhaps even more challenging to the left than the earlier repression and discrimination had been.

Such experiences sharpened awareness of the limitations and ideological deceptions of 'bourgeois democracy'. Would it really serve as the procedural basis to achieve socialism?

The repressive apparatuses of the state bureaucracy – the police and army – seemed fully under ruling-class control, however many votes the socialists secured. And, even if electoral support for working-class parties could be built up, it was not clear how a changeover to socialism might actually come about.

Some socialists preferred not to think about these difficult issues, which raised the prospect of significant social conflict. But others could clearly see that the extension of democratic principles into the economic sphere would require the expropriation of propertied interests. This would obviously be resisted by those who stood to lose their possessions, wealth, power and identity. There was therefore an unavoidable tension between an optimistic belief that extensions in democracy would have a cumulative effect, through which they would somehow deliver socialism, and the hard reality that periods of rupture, change and transition – harsh, severe and authoritarian moments – would be needed if democracy was to be extended to the point when it became socialist democracy.

In relatively rich countries such as Germany and France, most socialists believed that when democracy eventually included everybody, the social weight of working-class people would inevitably lead to the implementation of socialist programmes. Wealth redistribution and the correction of power imbalances would follow on 'naturally' from electoral victories for parties that represented ordinary people. Meanwhile, agitating for better working conditions and welfare provision would deliver benefits in the short term, build support and point the way forward.

There would need to be a definite transition at some point: a socialist society could not result simply from cumulative reforms and concessions on the part of the capitalist class. But there was no requirement in principle for this to involve armed violence. The German socialist Karl Kautsky, a leading theoretical figure within the Second International and a close associate of Engels, took the view that the potential for the revolution to take a non-violent form would be positively correlated with the extent to which the working class was properly organised, operating in line with party discipline, well-informed about the nature of historical processes and familiar with participating in democratic institutions. According to the Italian historian Massimo Salvadori, Kautsky imagined that the transition route to new social arrangements would emerge clearly in due course: social democrats 'would harvest the ripe fruit of power when the ruling-class lost subjective vigour and confidence'.[19]

The later disillusion of sections of the socialist left with democracy results from the fact that it did not deliver their goal for them in the way they had hoped. Disappointment led to two possible conclusions: settle for what could be delivered by democracy, even if it fell short of socialism; or reject democracy as an essential element of socialist politics. The bitter realisation that democratic advance had not led 'inevitably' to socialism pushed some comrades towards impatient activity. For them, 'democracy' would be, at best, a tactical means of advance towards socialism, to be used if useful, to be dropped if not. This history explains how the twin errors of 'gradualism' and 'insurrectionism' became linked. The third possible position became relatively marginalised: to continue working for real socialism, but to insist that socialism would need to be democratic, or it would not be socialism at all.

Difficulties for the left in simply advocating 'democracy' were compounded when far-sighted bourgeois politicians started to recognise the need to adapt and reposition themselves to succeed within the democratic political settlements which were clearly coming. Thus, for example, during the years of Benjamin Disraeli's leadership, British conservatives cured themselves of the fear that extending the vote to working people would inevitably lead to democracy being used to take power and wealth from the rich. In making this shift, they drew on the thinking of the great conservative intellectual Edmund Burke, described by Francis Mulhern as 'the first European thinker to pose the question of popular political representation as ... that of maintaining oligarchic class rule in the conditions of emergent democracy'.[20] They also picked up themes from liberal thinkers such as Jeremy Bentham and John Stuart Mill, who recommended representative government as the practical form of democracy in large and complex societies, and further argued that it would enhance people's capacities and achievements, and foster a positive political culture. Nevertheless, Bentham and Mill also cautioned that suffrage should be introduced step by step, rather than all at once, for the sake of social stability. Conservatives started to tone down their opposition to extending the franchise and began instead to establish themselves as – according to their critics – an effective conspiracy to get the majority of people in the country to support policies which served the interests of the minority.[21] In Germany and Italy, too, innovative and audacious conservative politicians also made 'deft defensive gambits' in response to the extension of the franchise.[22] As Gramsci puts it, after breaking the first attempts by the proletariat and the peasantry to rise up against the state, 'the strengthened Italian bourgeoisie was able to adopt the external methods of the democracy to impede the progress of the working-class movement'.[23]

Through all the debates detailed above, socialists gave little consideration to the concern that their policies might – to adopt a term favoured by those who see capitalists as wealth creators – 'kill the goose that lays the golden egg'. Marx and his followers argued that instituting socialism and then communism would increase economic productivity, ending the 'block' within capitalism which means that the main determinant of whether or not production is carried out is its potential for creating private profit. The counter argument to this is that abolishing the capitalist economic motor does not lead to an unbridled drive to productivity, capitalism having been 'finally delivered of its impediment'.[24] In fact, the productivity that seems to be both generated and simultaneously thwarted by capitalism would be lost. This argument is offered by Slavoj Zizek as a 'possible critique' of Marx, rather than as being his own position. Nevertheless, he precisely identifies the problem which would face the ruling communist parties of the twentieth century. Their 'success' in abolishing the market and suppressing the principle of profitability as the motor of economic life left them with a new problem which the capitalist system had previously, much of the time, 'successfully' solved – that of generating successive rounds of industrial production, innovation and enterprise.

## NOTES

1. Gopal Balakrishnan, 'The Abolitionist: part 2', *New Left Review*, January – February 2015.
2. The term itself was minted by Saint-Simon in the early nineteenth century.

3. Terry Eagleton, *Walter Benjamin or Towards a Revolutionary Criticism*, Verso, London 2009 [1981], p112.
4. Eric Hobsbawm, *Echoes of the Marseillaise*, Verso, London 1990, p8.
5. The Labour Party, which emerged in the first decade of the twentieth century, and organised most socialists in Britain, was not founded on any distinct programme. Instead, through the Labour Representation Committee, labourism began as a kind of identity politics, a call for a greater proportion of parliamentary candidates to be drawn from a particular demographic background. With its political thinking at first still orientated to the programmes of the Liberal Party, the committee's main position was that working-class constituencies should have working-class representatives.
6. See Willie Thompson, *The Left in History*, Pluto Press, London 1997, p25.
7. Giovanni Arrighi, in Robin Blackburn (ed), *After the Fall*, Verso, London 1991, pp132-3.
8. Massimo Salvadori, *Karl Kautsky and the Socialist Revolution 1880-1938*, New Left Books/Verso, London 1979, p29.
9. Friedrich Engels 'Introduction' to Karl Marx's *Class Struggle in France* [1895].
10. Eric Hobsbawm, *How to Change the World*, Little, Brown, London 2011, p68.
11. David McLellan, *Engels*, Fontana/Collins, London 1977, p49.
12. Fredric Jameson, *Valences of the Dialectic*, Verso, London 2009, p8.
13. This is not to suggest that Engels was a crude, inferior thinker as compared to Marx, though he himself would have insisted that this was so. Engels was usually far less fierce, sharp and polemical than Marx: his style and tone were more urbane, sophisticated and patient.
14. Paul Thomas, *Karl Marx*, Reaktion Books, London 2012, p14.
15. Maurice Cornforth, *Communism and Philosophy*, Lawrence and Wishart, London 1980, p55.
16. Goran Therborn, 'Class in the twenty-first century', *New Left Review*, November – December 2012.
17. McLellan, op cit, p49.
18. The counter-productive nature of the anti-socialist legislation was nicely mocked by Engels in his 1887 preface to a pamphlet that collected together fifteen-year-old newspaper articles, *On The Housing Question*: 'the fact that a new reprint has now become necessary I owe undoubtedly to the solicitude of the German government which, by prohibiting the work, tremendously increased its sale, as usual, and I hereby take this opportunity of expressing my respectful thanks to it'.
19. Salvadori, op cit, p67.
20. Francis Mulhern, 'Burke's Way', *New Left Review*, November – December 2016.
21. Crude anti-socialist arguments, to the effect that socialism is envy and

jealousy raised to the level of politics by those who do not wish to face up to their own failures in life, are matched by equally unfair and inaccurate anti-conservative lines to the effect that conservatism is merely the self-serving agenda of the selfish privileged. In fact, most conservatives genuinely believe that the system and policies they advocate will deliver the maximum possible benefits for all. The belief that rivalry between companies competing for business will elicit a high level of performance and benefits for consumers is coherent and evidenced: critique had best be on this basis.

22. John Dunn, *Setting the People Free*, Atlantic Books, London 2005, p153.

23. Antonio Gramsci, *Selections from Political Writings 1912-26*, Lawrence and Wishart, London 1978, p 348.

24. Slavoj Zizek, *The Parallax View*, MIT Press, Cambridge MA 2006, p266. One of the things many readers find infuriating about Zizek is that it is often hard to tell whether he is promoting a view sincerely, presenting it 'ironically', or advancing it as a focus for systematic critique. Urging indulgence, Adam Kotsko argued in the *Los Angeles Review of Books*, 2 September 2012, that Zizek's style 'fits with his goals and with the kinds of phenomena he is trying to get at ... [his] reversals are part of a strategy to keep the thought in motion. Instead of proposing a solution or finding a resting-place, Zizek relentlessly seeks out further conflicts and contradictions ... the goal is not to arrive at a settled view, but to achieve greater clarity about what is really at issue, about what is really at stake in a given debate'. Whether or not Zizek's 'reversals' and inconsistencies are some kind of Socratic philosophical method, or whether they are wilfully disorientating, mischievous and provocative – or whether they express simple incoherence – it cannot be doubted that they are a factor in the stimulating character of his work, and its commercial success.

# 6. Inescapable debates

## REFORM OR REVOLUTION: DEBATES IN SOCIAL-DEMOCRACY BEFORE 1917

As Marxist concepts became widespread within the European labour movement, a range of debates opened up. One major conundrum was the question of how the move from capitalism to a socialist society would actually take place. Would there be a sudden break, a short and necessarily violent moment of dramatic radical change – a 'revolution'? Or would there be a transformative process in which socialists achieved gains bit by bit, and current social relations were somehow changed over time into something entirely different, almost without anyone noticing?

Though these conflicting approaches were sometimes obscured by the comradely culture of the Second International, some positions within these debates delineated the ground on which twentieth-century communism would later stand. But in the late 1890s, the concept of 'social-democracy' was used to denote the whole socialist movement: the term embraced a number of different positions. There were gradualists who believed that reform would occur incrementally, and that capitalism would inevitably break down over time. Then there were the revisionists, who believed that efforts should be focused on achievable gains given that the imminent demise of capitalism seemed unlikely. Finally there were those who believed that main task of social-democrats was to prepare for a revolutionary break. There were also positions that combined these different emphases in differently nuanced ways.

Perspectives of 'gradual transition' tended to take hold amongst socialist leaders in the richer countries. Their long-term aim was radical, of course. But in the 'here and now', gains could be made by dealing 'realistically' with those in power. A joke developed, shared knowingly between the well-to-do, and bitterly by working people, that the leading social-democrat politicians had become so confident in the inevitability of the coming transition to socialism that they increasingly preferred to await it in the company of the very rich.

The notion that capitalism would inevitably break down, and that socialism would necessarily result, left open the question of how it would actually be achieved. Karl Kautsky remained committed to the idea of a radical break with capitalism, but believed that certain conditions needed to be in place before this would be possible. As we shall see below, he was to become a critic of the Bolshevik revolution on the grounds that it could not be democratic, given that the material conditions for a socialist revolution were not in place. It was, however, difficult – then as now – to delineate the conditions in which a break might take place, or the right conditions in which to make a revolutionary intervention.

This difficulty created a 'breakdown controversy' within German social-democracy. Some leaders hoped that the growth of working-class consciousness would develop as capitalism unfolded, and that through these processes capitalism would precipitate its own downfall: as capitalism's potential for expansion and viability was exhausted, more and more people would come to realise the necessity of a move from the current system to socialism. But the resulting political practice, which tended to focus on reform, saw socialist parties increasingly accommodating to the systems in which they operated.

Whilst Kautsky was waiting for the inevitable but mysterious moment of transition, a younger generation were observing that actual developments appeared to contradict some of the political predictions set out by Marx and Engels: the development of capitalism thus far did not appear to be creating the conditions for the growth of a revolutionary consciousness within the working class. So as not to appear heretical, they stressed that this was not a problem of 'the founders' having got some things wrong: it was a matter of the world having moved on. Engels's literary executor Eduard Bernstein was central to this 'revisionist' tendency. As Vincent Geoghegan comments, his views were 'pithily expressed' in a jotting found in his papers after his death: 'peasants do not sink; the middle-class does not disappear; crises do not grow ever larger; misery and serfdom do not increase'.[1] Bernstein judged that the world was not rapidly heading towards revolution after all. But this, he insisted, was not a rejection of socialism. He still promoted reforms to improve the conditions of workers: their rights to join trade unions, to have a shorter working week, and to enjoy state-sponsored health insurance. For Bernstein these reforms proved that real gains came from operating constructively within the system.

Rosa Luxemburg, one of Bernstein's major critics, summarised his position as being that the movement should 'direct its daily activity toward ... the betterment of the working class within the existing order': 'It must not expect to institute socialism as a result of a political and social crisis, but should build socialism by means of the progressive extension of social control and the gradual application of the principle of co-operation'.[2]

The third social-democratic trend, to which Luxemburg belonged, asserted revolutionary politics, aggressively opposing Bernstein's 'revisionism'. In the resulting debates, 'what Marx said' and 'what Marx meant' became crucially important matters, establishing a practice of quoting and counter-quoting authorities which has marked much left-wing argument ever since. In these debates, leaders of the revolutionary trend, such as Lenin and Luxemburg, were by no means simple defenders of a pre-established orthodoxy. Like the revisionists, they recognised that times had changed: it was 'a duty' to understand and respond to new trends. But the revolutionaries drew quite different conclusions from their analysis. They agreed with the revisionists that the commitment of the Second International leaders to revolution had become rhetorical, symbolic, decorative. But whereas the revisionists' conclusion was to drop the symbolism, the revolutionary approach was to make the commitment to revolution central again, and relevant to the times. Make it real.

Another way of understanding these issues is to seek to distinguish between oppression and exploitation.[3] The earliest stages of industrialisation involved the harsh oppression of working-class people: force, coercion, difficult living conditions. But, over time, employers found that exploitative relationships could be established perhaps even more effectively through providing benefits and rights. The fact that the ruling class would settle for, and even benefit from, exploitation without oppression allowed socialists to put forward real, desirable and achievable goals within the limits of the existing economy. But this left the dilemma of how to bring about systematic change. For some this question gradually became less important. Others continued to argue about how to bring it about and what conditions would make it feasible.

From the 1890s onwards, the context for these debates included trends towards improved living standards in the richer European countries, alongside ongoing inequality. There was also relative international stability, and a social climate of expansive optimism. In Germany, the world's largest social-democratic party focused on building parliamentary influence, alongside trade union campaigns for improved wages and working conditions. The working class appeared to be increasingly integrated into society rather than alienated from it.

Even so, during the period before the 1917 Russian revolution, the main parties of the Second International kept up their revolutionary talk. This matched the actual views of key activists in the East European parties, which were often illegal. Many of these comrades were living in exile, and developed a sense of solidarity based on shared political goals that superseded differences of nationality and language. Leaders from this milieu opposed the new 'revisionism', which, they argued, gave too much credence to the claims that capitalism would improve the workers' lot. Luxemburg's view was that recent advances resulted from a temporary economic situation that would not be maintained indefinitely. Bernstein was therefore mistaken in wanting to preserve positive elements of the capitalist system. The changes that socialists wanted could not come other than through thorough-going transformation.

'Red Rosa' insisted that revisionism and reformism would result in the abandonment of any commitment to real socialism. For her, socialism was a response to and consequence of the growing contradictions of the capitalist economy: the task of the working class was to overcome these contradictions through a social transformation. When revisionists denied these contradictions, and rejected the need for transformation, 'the labour movement finds itself reduced to a simple co-operative and reformist movement'.[4] In her key works, Luxemburg posed a choice between reform 'or' revolution. These were presented as different in nature, not merely in degree or speed. Reform was not a gradual variant of revolution. Revolution was not accelerated reform.

This counterposition would have surprised Marx. As Terry Eagleton has stated:

> most revolutionaries are also champions of reform. Not any old reform, and not reformism as a panacea ... where [revolutionaries]

differ from reformists proper is not, say, in refusing to fight against hospital closures because they distract attention from the all-important Revolution. It is rather that they view such reforms in a longer, more radical perspective. Reform is vital; but sooner or later you will hit a point where the system refuses to give way … or, in less politely technical language, a dominant class … controls the material resources and is markedly reluctant to hand them over.[5]

In some cases, demands for even modest reforms could lead to revolutionary possibilities. In other circumstances, reforms could be offered as a way of avoiding revolution. Context and balance of power were the key variables here, rather than questions of principle. Nevertheless, the challenge of relating the two forms of political movement was a real one. These were issues which had hardly been focused, let alone resolved, by Marx.

During these arguments, the concept of 'the dictatorship of the proletariat' was reviewed. As described in chapter 4, this term has had varying interpretations, with some arguing that the intention behind the phrase is to counterpose the bourgeois dictatorship that exists under capitalism with its opposite in socialism. On this understanding, the word 'dictatorship' could simply be replaced by the word 'control'. However, there is no doubt that the Bolsheviks were to later to give a thoroughly authoritarian meaning to this term. Bernstein issued warnings about the logic of his revolutionary opponents which must now be recognised as prescient. He argued that a 'truly miraculous belief in the creative power of force' would end in violence to people.[6]

Kautsky's position was that after the political rise of a proletariat, through majority support, the question of violence would be decided by the reaction of the ruling class. He stated that 'we are neither supporters of legality at any price, nor [extra-legal] revolutionaries at any price'.[7] Being 'for' or 'against' violence was not a matter of principle. The issue was always situational and tactical: distinctions had to be made between the *political content* of different forms of violence, in different contexts. From the point of view of revolutionaries, effective violence to overthrow the old rulers through revolution was justifiable. The issue of legality was closely connected: popularly supported revolutionary violence to overthrow an unjust system of rule could not be regarded as 'illegal', since existing laws reflected the self-serving law of established rulers, whose efforts to restore their power would in any case include counter-revolutionary violence. Furthermore, a successful revolution would open the path to transformative social change that might itself involve some violence, as social relations were changed through programmes steered by the revolutionary power. Such progressive violence could, in principle, take place under democratic control, and the moments of force and repression which they would involve could be carried out in legitimate ways, avoiding excessive measures and cruelty.

## ADVANCE THROUGH A SERIES OF STAGES: THE RUSSIAN DEBATES

One position that crystallised through these debates was that defeating bourgeois class power would only become possible when the economic conditions for socialism had been fully realised under capitalism. This was a particularly important issue in Russia, where the working class was demographically weak. As the Menshevik leader Julius Martov commented in 1904, 'the riddle' that society had posed to Russian social-democracy was the 'reconciliation of revolutionary-democratic with socialist tasks'.[8] After the failed 'bourgeois democratic' revolution of 1905, the question of how to solve this riddle became a major issue. Debates around the class nature of the coming revolution shaped splits and shifting alignments between the Menshevik and Bolshevik wings of the Russian Social-Democratic and Labour Party (RSDLP) from 1903 onwards.[9]

For Mensheviks and many other socialists at this time, it was only after completing the 'first stage' of developing a capitalist economy and bourgeois democracy that it would be sensible to consider the 'second stage', the socialist horizon. In the 1890s, 'Legal Marxists' had set liberal democracy as the key goal for Russia, and had seen socialist agitation as a way of bringing this about. The Menshevik position was distinct from this: they were clear that a new socialist order was their aim, but they regarded democratic freedoms as important and valuable in themselves. The Bolshevik leader Lenin, by contrast, believed that the use of 'democratic principles should be exclusively subordinated to the interests of our party'.[10]

The situation could not be crudely characterised as a division between Mensheviks waiting for the bourgeois revolution and

Bolsheviks proposing an immediate workers' revolution. For many years, both tendencies in Russian social-democracy shared the view that socialism would not be on the agenda until capitalism had exhausted its capacity to develop the means of production. They welcomed the development of capitalism in their country, and sought to promote the position of the working class within the new system.

The Mensheviks aimed to build a strong workers' movement within the framework of a classic bourgeois revolution, which would and should be led by the liberal bourgeoisie. This position was expressed forcibly by Plekhanov, a founding father of Russian Marxism who became a sharp critic of Bolshevism, but nevertheless continued to be honoured by Lenin after his death in 1918. From 1905, Plekhanov insisted on the need for an exclusively bourgeois Russian revolution, in which the working-class movement should accept the liberal bourgeoisie as its senior ally.

Though they saw themselves as revolutionaries rather than reformists, the logic of the Menshevik position was to urge restraint on the part of workers, wherever their actions might be seen as a threat the liberal bourgeoisie's efforts to develop the economy. This limit was justified on the grounds that any attempt on the part of the working class to overstep it would be wholly counter-productive, because it would drive the bourgeoisie towards reactionary politics, and thus spoil the chances of the revolution.

The radical left has often portrayed Menshevik arguments as cautious and defensive. But they were put forward as the best way to win class struggles. At the beginning of the twentieth century, political alliances between liberals and socialists were in their early days. But the Russian social-democrats were well aware of instances where such approaches had already proved effective, such as in Sweden. In 1905 the Swedish Workers' Party had allied with progressive liberals to head off efforts by the ruling conservatives to use military force to prevent the secession of Norway, where people had voted overwhelmingly for independence in a referendum. And in 1907, Swedish liberals and socialists had worked together for a massive extension of the right to vote, and for a properly parliamentary form of government. The threat of a workers' general strike had proved an important element in this successful campaign, which pushed a reluctant conservative government to concede adult male suffrage.

Whether or not particular political strategies will be effective depends on national circumstances and the wider international context at any one time. Although his views fluctuated, Lenin increasingly identified the limitations of the 'two stage' approach in the Russian context. He felt that the defeat of 1905 had proved the danger of being overly cautious. He began to think that a proletarian attempt to take state power should be made if and when the opportunity presented itself. Waiting until all the preconditions were in place would only and always leave class power in the hands of the bourgeoisie. Lenin's view was that the bourgeoisie had proved unreliable allies for the workers' movement: the alliance which workers needed was with the peasants. The resulting revolution would be initially liberal-bourgeois in character, he agreed, and it would lead to the development of modern capitalism. But the weakness of the Russian bourgeoisie, and the fact that they had not yet managed to overthrow autocracy, meant that the revolution would now need to be led by the growing working class. Lenin argued that if the proletariat and peasantry were ever going to benefit from the success of a bourgeois revolution in Russia, they would have to take responsibility for making it themselves. This could be seen as a reasonable position, given the continuing failure of the Russian middle class to overthrow the Tsar.

In the early 1900s only a few socialists promoted another, entirely heterodox, ambition. Given that, as the Bolsheviks argued, the coming revolution needed to be led by the working class, why should the revolution not be a socialist one from the beginning? This position was argued by Leon Trotsky from 1905. Trotsky, a leader of the short-lived St Petersburg Soviet in 1905, had sided with the Mensheviks in 1903 but had later tried to operate outside the party factions. He accepted that a purely workers' revolution had no chance of succeeding in Russia alone, given the country's low level of social and economic development. But he believed Russia could prove to be a 'weak link' in a chain of international relationships: a good place to start a wider, European revolutionary wave. By linking up with simultaneous 'events in the west', the Russian working class could open up 'permanent revolution', which would see socialists complete the tasks of a bourgeois revolution through aiming from the start for socialism. This was a further shift away from the old models of revolution: the bourgeoisie, and ideas about allying with them to make a democratic revolution, were being edged out of the picture. As Ernesto Laclau put it, Trotsky's arguments loosened the understandings which socialists had developed about the 'connections between revolution, democratic tasks and agents'.[11]

These differing views shaped intense and detailed polemics. But they had little impact on the wider population: social-democratic publications were clandestine, and read only by a few.

## THE PROFESSIONALS: BOLSHEVIK APPROACHES

From the early 1900s, Lenin insisted on defining political differences in strict organisational terms. For him – and this was the cause of the 1903 split – it was more important for a small number to organise on the basis of a jointly held clear position, rather than to have relatively large numbers of people share space together in the same party whilst fudging disagreements over theory and policies. This was at odds with the cultural norms of the wider International, which held that 'unity is strength'.[12] The German movement, whose culture dominated the International, had found that growth and electoral success had followed mergers between groupings with different ideological positions. Debates over alternate policies were seen as conversations amongst friends.[13] In most countries, radically opposed positions were held within the same party, without anyone arguing for organisational separation through splits, expulsions or purges. There was strong moral pressure for unity at all costs and, until the Bolsheviks took power in 1917, very few of their comrades across the Second International understood or sympathised with their determined and constant factionalising.

Nevertheless, Lenin's sincere concern was to work effectively for democratic rights and for socialism in the autocratic context of Russia. His assertion that 'professional revolutionaries' needed to introduce political theory and strategic approaches into the workers' movement was part of this approach. Workers' interests would not be served simply through efforts to achieve the demands that arose 'spontaneously' from day-to-day struggles, such as wage demands or calls to deal with a particular instance of workplace oppression.

Lenin's concern for defining the correct positions, and the need for a small group to adopt these positions and lead the movement, has been characterised as 'vanguardism'. It built into the communist tradition a certain authoritarianism, elitism and cult of 'correctness'.

It was a version of political theory that asserted that those who had rational understanding were best placed to direct other people. But this did not mean that the Bolsheviks were 'purist'. They developed and changed their positions as the situation changed, and learned how to adapt to different situations: their politics was in no way crude, dogmatic, or simplistically confrontational. Bolshevism's flexible adherents were well used to tactical manoeuvres and alliances.

The broader context for Bolshevik culture in the early twentieth century was an absence of democracy and tolerance in the wider society within which they existed: the Bolsheviks took into themselves and reflected some of the characteristics of their autocratic opponent. It is sometimes possible to use the rhetoric of the oppressors against them: to claim more strongly the democracy that the government claims to promote. But such a tactic was not available in Tsarist Russia. There was no democratic content that the revolutionary opposition could take from the ruling class.

Furthermore, the Bolsheviks had to operate in conditions of deep clandestinity. They had never experienced the freedom to contest open elections, and this may have made them more readily accepting of the view that the state was simply an apparatus for the exercise of ruling-class power. They were vehement that revolutionary politics neither depended on, nor needed to be shaped by, bourgeois democratic norms. As Vasily Grossman later suggested, the Bolsheviks developed a tradition in Russian revolutionary politics marked by 'sectarian single-mindedness, [a] readiness to suppress today's living freedom for the sake of a hypothetical freedom, to transgress ordinary, everyday morality in the name of the future'.[14] Russian revolutionaries also used an abstract concept of 'the people': a vision of who they were working for which did not necessarily match the people as they actually were. Lenin's 'professional revolutionaries' combined this with a Marxist conception of the working class as a unified subject, and with an ambitious vision of their party as the agent of that class. Bolshevism's approach to demo-cratic matters must be explained in terms of the development of the movement from such roots: it was not caused by 'Asiatic characteristics' – that racist trope; nor could it be accounted for by the only slightly less essentialising idea that Russian national culture is somehow 'primitive', 'masochistic', and 'wants' a despot.

As the French writer Jean-Paul Sartre would later note, 'revolution, whatever it may be, does not work miracles; it inherits all the wretchedness produced by the former regime'.[15] Thus defensive, secretive and conspiratorial practices became normal in political groups that were hounded and infiltrated by the Russian imperial secret police. Being forced to operate deep underground generated a Bolshevik temperament which was exceptionally combative, intransigent and serious. Ruthless habits became ingrained: the illegal Bolsheviks prioritised discipline and unity in action. Heroic self-conception formed in response to severe odds. A deeply-held conviction of the importance of their activities maintained resilience, and helped sustain commitment in adversity. Patience, said Lenin, was a *revolutionary* virtue.

Lenin did not start off with the intention of abandoning the models that had developed in countries that enjoyed more freedom and political rights. Until 1914, he praised the west European mass party strategy, stating that he would have followed that approach in Russia, had circumstances allowed. But events at the outbreak of the first world war, when the majority of social-democratic parties – in stark contrast to the Bolsheviks – after years of proclaiming international working-class unity decided to back the war efforts of their national governments, created the conditions for a break. As Eric Hobsbawm writes:

> a range of international events [had] recurrently suggested to Lenin the need for a more general promotion of Bolshevik approaches. 1914 and the collapse of Second International socialism, and the experience of the anti-war network known as the 'Zimmerwald left', showed to Lenin and his followers that proletarian internationalism needed to be embodied in a particular political form, i.e. the vanguard party.[16]

These differences were consolidated after the Russian revolution occurred (see next chapter). Communism came to mark break and discontinuity from the Second International. From 1917 onwards, the ways in which Bolshevism had taken shape under Tsarism – an oppressive dictatorship in which the state stood in opposition to 'the people' – would in turn shape international communist culture. And this Bolshevik influence was to lead to communists in the mainly or partly-democratic countries presenting themselves at key moments as being against 'bourgeois democracy.'

## ON MENSHEVISM

Up until 1917, Mensheviks had emphasised the importance and intrinsic value of democratic tactics, and the need for basic preconditions – economic, social and political – to be in place before a socialist transition could occur. They warned that premature or isolated seizure of power would lead only to defeat, discrediting social-democracy. You could set off and make a revolution in a hurry if you wanted to: you might even get there quickly. But you would most likely find that when you got there, you had forgotten to pack some of the things that you needed.

During the tumultuous events of 1917, the Mensheviks remained committed to the 'stages theory'. They believed that social-democracy's task was to create an independent, politically conscious working class, which was capable of participating in running the affairs of the Russian state. The organised proletariat should help to bring about the bourgeois revolution, but should not then attempt to establish socialism before capitalism had run its course. These theoretical perspectives reinforced some highly practical considerations. As crises mounted, Mensheviks were concerned to hold the state and economy together in the hope of preventing a calamitous collapse and averting destructive civil war.

Whilst the Bolsheviks became ever more coherent and influential, the Mensheviks were thrown into disarray when the revolution happened at a time when, according to their analyses, it should not have done so. As the Menshevik Stepan Ivanovich would reflect, 'the problem with revolutions is that they always occur at inopportune moments'.[17] The subsequent unfolding of the various crises of 1917 constantly wrong-footed them, leading to a series of splits and their gradual disintegration. As Isaac Deutscher pointed out, in contrast to this:

> the story of Bolshevism [in 1917] is ... one of continuous integration and unification ... radicals who had been at loggerheads with Lenin for nearly a decade were returning to the fold ... Lunacharsky ... Manuilsky ... Trotsky and a large galaxy of brilliant revolutionaries, former Mensheviks most of them, [entered] the Bolshevik party.[18]

A recurrent feature of revolutions came into play: the logic of the events for which the Menshevik leadership, with others, had been working over the years, was rolling on further than they had wanted, and was out of their control.

As Lenin and his comrades began to establish a government based on socialist aims, the Mensheviks divided even further.[19] Some stuck with their insistence that the government had to be a liberal one: either the Bolsheviks would become such a government or they would be replaced. Whilst holding these perspectives, Mensheviks tried to work within the structures of soviet power. Their leader Martov sought to stand close to the Bolsheviks to avoid one-party rule; to avoid losing working-class support; and to relate to the sizeable group of Bolsheviks uneasy about ruling by themselves. But a Menshevik right wing, led by Pavel Axelrod, denounced the Bolsheviks as having destroyed democracy.

Over the coming years, Menshevik positions were amplified by Kautsky, who attacked the abuses of party dictatorship, especially after Stalin consolidated his power over the party. As Robin Blackburn argues:

> Kautsky was on firm ground in arguing that Marx had insisted on the primacy of the struggle for democracy, and had outlined his notion of a 'dictatorship of the proletariat' in terms that were irreconcilable with a narrow party dictatorship ... his critique of Bolshevik strategy was centred upon its ominous implications for the cultural and political development of the toilers. He warned that conspiratorial, secretive and hierarchical organisation 'may be rendered necessary for an oppressed class in the absence of democracy, but it would not promote the self-government and independence of the masses. Rather it would further the Messiah-consciousness of leaders, and their dictatorial habits'.[20]

Kautsky would later judge that, however much the Bolsheviks had inspired 'great enthusiasm' for revolution, the reality was that

> their dictatorship ... is in contradiction to the Marxist teaching that no people can overcome the obstacle offered by the successive phases for their development by a jump, or legal enactment.[21]

Emphasising the need for democracy and socialism to work together, Kautsky had continually promoted the classical Marxist position that 'social production without democracy could become a most oppressive bond'.[22] Rather than answer such criticisms, however, the Bolsheviks simply asserted that the Menshevik position amounted to systematised cowardice: they just did not have the nerve to act when the time came for revolutionary action.

As they proceeded to the early 1920s, the Bolsheviks faced two surprises. Firstly, their effort to hold on to power succeeded, even though Menshevik perspectives that this would prove impossible corresponded to classical Marxism. Secondly, the revolution did not spread to other places, apart from in the form of a short-lived soviet republic in Hungary in 1919, and brief risings by Czechs and Germans which quickly went down to defeat.

Over the coming decades, in different ways and at different moments, the Menshevik critique kept coming back, as the recurrent return of a repressed but valid argument.

## NOTES

1. Vincent Geoghegan, *Utopianism and Marxism*, Methuen and Co, London 1987, p40.
2. Rosa Luxemburg, *Reform or Revolution*, Pathfinder Press, Atlanta GA 2011 [1900], p18.
3. Jean-Paul Sartre later commented: 'Oppression leads to the extermination of the oppressed if they should revolt, while exploitation demands their (at least partial) co-operation as a workforce'. *Critique of Dialectical Reason, Volume One*, Verso, London 2004 [1960], p781.
4. Luxemburg, op cit.
5. Terry Eagleton, *Why Marx Was Right*, Yale University Press, London 2011, p190.
6. Eduard Bernstein, *Preconditions of Socialism*, [1889].
7. Karl Kautsky, *The Road to Power*, [1909], Chapter 5.
8. Julius Martov, quoted in Israel Getzler, *Martov*, Cambridge University Press, Cambridge 1967, p219.
9. In classical Marxism a distinction was made between a bourgeois revolution (such as the French Revolution), which marked the defeat by the rising capitalist class of the old feudal classes, and instituted a period of liberal (to a greater or lesser extent) rule based on capitalist property relations, and a socialist revolution, in which the working class would take power and overthrow capitalism. The split of the Russian Social-Democratic and Labour Party into Bolsheviks (in Russian 'the majority') and Mensheviks ('the minority') took place in 1903, over differences about party discipline and the size of the party. Subsequently many in the

party changed sides, including Trotsky (initially Menshevik) and Plekhanov (initially Bolshevik), and divisions within the party were for some time quite fluid.

10. This formulation was initially used at the 1903 RSDLP Congress by V.E. Mandelberg, whose party name was Posadovsky.

11. Ernesto Laclau, *On Populist Reason*, Verso, London 2005, p126.

12. Second International leaders failed to understand the significance of the splits in Russian social-democracy. In the summer of 1911, for example, Kautsky 'had visits from Bolsheviks, Mensheviks, Otzovists and liquidators. They are all dear people and when talking to them one does not notice great differences of opinion'. Letter to Plekhanov, quoted in Getzler, op cit, p103.

13. Writing in the 1950s, Frank Tanner recalled that the many different groupings of British socialists in the first decade of the twentieth century were 'a constant source of astonishment to foreign comrades, accustomed as they were to a single mass party covering all trends'. *British Socialism in the Early 1900s*, Socialist History Society, London 2014, p6. Another feature of the British labour movement up to the first world war was a relatively strong syndicalist tradition, with trade unions being regarded as a mainstay of the movement, and as more important than political groups.

14. Vasily Grossman, *Everything Flows*, Vintage, London 2011 [1964], p181.

15. Jean-Paul Sartre, *The Spectre of Stalin*, Hamish Hamilton, London 1969 [1956], p51.

16. Eric Hobsbawm, *On History*, Weidenfeld and Nicolson, London 1997, p323.

17. Stepan Ivanovich, unpublished aphorisms [1938], quoted in Andre Liebich, *From the Other Shore*, Harvard University Press, Cambridge MT 1997, p47.

18. Isaac Deutscher, 'The Mensheviks', *The Listener*, 4 February 1965.

19. For a careful discussion of shifts and splits within Menshevism during 1917, see Francis King, 'Introduction' to Fedor Il'ich Dan, *Two Years of Wandering*, Lawrence and Wishart, London 2016, pp8-14 and 22-5.

20. Robin Blackburn, in Blackburn (ed), *After the Fall*, Verso, London 1991, pps176, 179.

21. Karl Kautsky, *The Dictatorship of the Proletariat*, [1931].

22. Karl Kautsky, 'The Prospects of the Russian Revolution', *Neue Zeit*, 6 April 1917.

# 7. 1917

## THE FIRST GOVERNMENT FORMED BY SOCIALISTS, ANYWHERE IN THE WORLD

In February 1917, evidence that the Tsar was losing his authority in Russia led his generals to advise that he stood down. A provisional government was then formed of politicians committed to continuing to pursue the war effort. Its provisionality was based on a declared intention to hold universal elections to a Constituent Assembly, a proto-parliament that would draw representatives from across the whole country.

Some Bolsheviks immediately saw the possibility of pushing for power. There were mass movements across the major cities of striking workers and mutinous soldiers and sailors, and a widespread popular rejection of Russia's disastrous involvement in the first world war. Bolsheviks encouraged the feeling that the provisional government was too weak and incompetent to maintain support: it was out of touch with the mood of the people and was not a sufficient break with the established powers.

In April 1917, Lenin returned from exile, and issued 'theses' which developed the Bolshevik programme in ways which converged with the view that Trotsky had developed after 1905: even though the proletariat was a minority in what remained a semi-feudal and industrially underdeveloped country, it did not need to wait for there to be a long period of industrialisation under bourgeois rule before taking power.

Whilst some leading young activists in St Petersburg, such as Vyacheslav Molotov, also advocated confrontation against the provisional government, Lenin's arguments surprised a large majority of his own colleagues.[1] As Slavoj Zizek describes it, at first no prominent Bolshevik leader supported the call for revolution: 'Far from being an opportunist flattering and exploiting the prevailing mood in the party,

Lenin's views were highly idiosyncratic'.[2] Experienced colleagues such as Lev Kamenev and – initially – Joseph Stalin, just returned to the turbulence of St Petersburg from Siberian exile, felt only consternation and trepidation as their respected leader pushed for power.

There was a sudden reprise of debates long familiar to Russian social-democrats as to whether the country was ready for a 'proletarian revolution'. Different positions which had once only shaped obscure polemics were now choices in national politics. Mensheviks argued that the bourgeois revolution of February 1917, which had brought the provisional government to power, ought to be allowed to stand, with revolutionaries waiting for the 'conditions' for socialism to mature.

But increasing numbers united around Lenin's new position that the weakness of the provisional government, together with the growing dissatisfaction of the broad mass of the population, offered the Bolsheviks a unique chance to 'jump over' step one, democratic bourgeois revolution, and of 'condensing the two necessary stages (democratic bourgeois revolution and proletarian revolution) into one'.[3]

Trotsky, who had pushed for the compression of 'stages' long before this had seemed appropriate to anyone else, now joined the Bolsheviks along with his network of followers. He was quickly promoted to top roles, and this generated unspoken resentment amongst some long-standing Bolshevik cadre.

Soviets (councils) of workers, soldiers and peasants, which had first appeared in the 1905 revolution, were springing up everywhere. These were a form of direct democracy in which people came together to self-manage local districts or factories; and they now became the beating heart of a remarkable and widespread social movement that sought new and popular forms of self-government. As the revolutionary situation developed, and more and more Bolsheviks were being elected to these councils, the Bolsheviks declared that the soviets were the true representatives of the people. They described the situation in Russia as being one of 'dual power': on the one hand, there was the provisional government which had taken over from the Tsar, and on the other, there were the soviets, which were now actually running things at the level of the factory, city, town, and neighbourhood.

In July 1917 a demonstration against the provisional government was fired on by government troops; one of the demonstrators' slogans was 'All power to the Soviets'. In the following repression Lenin went underground. His instinct now was to support almost anyone who defied authority, whether or not their actions or aims corresponded to his previously worked-out 'correct lines'. Correction could come later. The point now was to encourage revolution. In St Petersburg and other cities, support flowed to the Bolsheviks – the only political force in tune with the mood of workers and soldiers. By the autumn of 1917, popular radicalisation was so deep and widespread that, as Hobsbawm notes, it simply swept the provisional government aside; 'by the time of the October revolution, power didn't so much have to be seized as picked up from where it had been dropped'.[4]

The Bolshevik leadership was still by no means united over whether to take this opportunity. As late as 18 October, Grigori Zinoviev and Kamenev were giving away Bolshevik plans in Maxim Gorky's newspaper, which was linked to a group of dissident ex-Bolsheviks, and expressed their opinion that it was doomed.

A Second Congress of Soviets had been organised for the 25 October and delegates were arriving from all over the country. The first Congress, which had met in June, had voted to support the Provisional government, but events had progressed very rapidly since then: the Bolsheviks could expect to carry all business, through the combined strength of their own delegates and the support of left-wing Socialist-Revolutionaries.

As the date of the Congress drew near, Bolsheviks working to Lenin's agenda activated the Military-Revolutionary Committee of the St Petersburg Soviet. This was made up of soldiers and officers who had declared support for the anti-war and socialist cause when there had been a right-wing coup attempt a few weeks previously: the Bolsheviks had seized this chance to create an armed workers' militia. At the time, this move had enjoyed the cautious consent of the provisional government, but now the armed 'reds' were ready to overthrow the government.

After a couple of days of more or less open preparations, co-ordinated by Trotsky and presented as 'precautions' against any further right-wing coup attempt, the Military-Revolutionary Committee moved to take control of key locations around the city; their actions included a visit to the Winter Palace to arrest the ministers meeting there. Lenin now declared the end of the provisional government.

The main business of the Congress of Soviets then became to approve this action, and confirm the establishment of soviet power, which it duly did. The October 1917 revolution in Russia had established the first ever government anywhere in the world formed wholly by socialists.

## LENIN'S OPEN POLITICS

In St Petersburg, the support for change was so overwhelming, and the preparedness of the government to hold onto power so weak, that the soviets' takeover of power involved hardly any violence. Moscow saw just a few days of fighting. The liberal and moderate socialist politicians who had taken power from the Tsar only a few months earlier were now themselves easily overthrown.

The course of the revolution has frequently been described – by those praising it and by its implacable opponents – as if it followed entirely and in detail the previously planned actions of its leaders. There are still those who believe, as Moshe Lewin puts it, that the route of the revolution was set out in 1902 with the publication of Lenin's *What Is To Be Done?*, and that thereafter events unfolded 'as if they had been genetically programmed'. 'The sequence Leninism – Bolshevism – Communism is constructed as a fatality'.[5]

But this is not how things happened. As Hobsbawm has it, Lenin 'was the very opposite of the Blanquist or the man who tried to make revolution by an act of will or a coup or putsch'.[6] His career was shaped by chance and contingency, and by uncertain and even clumsy responses to events. He had shared for a very long time his party's belief that Russia must pass through a liberal stage before there was any possibility of a proletarian revolution. It was the rapid unfolding of events that changed his view.

Lenin did not anticipate that the revolutionary moment would come until it was almost upon him. As late as January 1917 he had told a meeting of Swiss socialist youths that 'we, the older generation, perhaps will not live to see the decisive battles of the approaching revolution'.[7]

But the unexpected opportunity was to come within months of that speech. By the time he returned to Russia in April, the new government was weak, unstable and facing impossible choices: the country was suffering greatly because of the war, which it was losing heavily, and there were widespread rebellious movements of peasant-soldiers and factory workers. Lenin's genius was to realise that he was at one of those rare moments in history when a short period of determined activity might create a bridge to an entirely new era, and that he might be able to directly influence events.

Lenin ridiculed those who wanted guarantees about what would happen next, insisting that 'no sequence can be established for revolutions'. He was never completely confident of success, but built credibility through acting even when he was not sure what to do, and subsequently quickly understanding the new opportunities which had been generated. As Jeremy Gilbert puts it, his decision to push the revolutionary possibility to its logical conclusion 'was the product of a willingness to accept that he could not control events and that no theoretical dogma could predict them'.[8] The aim was therefore to ensure that the party was prepared for all contingencies, and could adjust its strategies and tactics to circumstances as they arose.

Lenin's intuitive style and open politics have been obscured by what came later: the big editions of collected works, hagiography, and the cult centred on his mausoleum and image. (The institution of hero worship around Lenin's corpse and memory was opposed both by his widow and by his closest political colleagues.) As Lukacs correctly comments, the 'true singularity' of Lenin had 'nothing, absolutely nothing to do with the bureaucratic ideal of a Stalinist monument of infallibility'.[9]

Very negative consequences flowed from the belief that Lenin's trajectory was as neatly joined up as was suggested by the footnotes to his works issued by the Soviet Union's official Progress Publishers, which seemed to imply that he had correctly identified in advance each step along the road to the revolution. This interpretation promoted a logocentric error – the belief that setting things out in advance is going to determine what happens – and has led to a great deal of wasted time and effort on the left. Though (some) words (sometimes) make things happen, and 'correct theory' can be important for working out political perspectives, the notion that theory can act as a failsafe guide that can deliver success to unknown forces in future struggles has fed an enduring overestimation by revolutionaries of the effectiveness of the written word. Much left scribbling has been, at best, a consoling activity for those experiencing defeat and marginalisation. Working out in fine detail what one's position would be on a 563rd step, assuming that 562 steps had already been taken, and indulging in sharp disagreements with others about the pros and cons of this 563rd step, provides a most satisfactory distraction from actually attempting to take steps 1, 2 and 3.

## THE EARLY DAYS OF A BETTER NATION? THE CONSTITUENT ASSEMBLY

1917 has been described as 'an event' after which 'everything changed'; 'a rift in the fabric' of history, creating openings for 'the truly New'; and as a foundational moment that was from then on 'actual' and 'present' in all aspects of twentieth-century life.[10] This way of thinking about the 'ten days that shook the world' is a retrospective construct.[11] This not to deny that the October revolution *was* historically momentous; but the urge to turn it into a fetish object, or to read history backwards into these events, should be resisted. Such ideas all too easily connect to the notion that, in the Bolshevik party, Lenin had somehow constructed a mechanism to solve once and for all that most difficult question for socialists: how to move from today to tomorrow, from capitalism to socialism, from oppression to freedom, from exploitation to equality.

In fact, 1917's revolution was turbulent and confused. Established structures of governance were collapsing. There was no functioning state, and no system for taxation or public spending. Debates were shaped by immediate contingencies. Difficult choices clustered around a range of issues. One of the most crucial of these was the issue of democracy, and specifically the matter of what institutional base should be developed to provide legitimacy and stability for the new government, and provide new mechanisms to mediate between the government and the people.

There was a major conundrum for the newly proclaimed government of the Soviets: what to do about the Constituent Assembly, for which, just before its demise, the provisional government had finally set elections? Though it was not their top priority, the Bolsheviks had themselves added their voice to calls for the Constituent Assembly to be convened – this was a longstanding demand of a broad spectrum of left-wingers and democrats, who saw such an Assembly as offering the means for Russia to move decisively on from its long history of autocracy and political oppression.

On 26 October, Lenin told delegates to the Congress of Soviets that the new government would indeed convene the Constituent

Assembly. His Council of Peoples' Commissars was assuming national governmental power only on a temporary basis, until the Constituent Assembly could meet.

From the beginning of November 1917, radical socialists in St Petersburg and Moscow therefore campaigned enthusiastically for elections to the new body: every worker they knew was urged to cast their vote. Buoyed by their strength in the urban soviets, Bolshevik activists were particularly keen on getting their vote out. Popular endorsement through Russia's first democratic election ever would add momentum to the great causes of settling the war and beginning to run the country in the interests of ordinary people.

But there was unease amongst some members of the Bolshevik leadership. Now that the Congress of Soviets had confirmed the overthrow of the provisional government, and proclaimed all power to the soviets, some felt that a Constituent Assembly had become irrelevant. There had been months of 'dual power' or 'double sovereignty' following the first revolution in February, during which period opposing sides had proposed different foundations for political legitimacy. Going ahead with the Constituent Assembly risked continuing the unstable situation in which there were alternative sources of governmental power. For Trotsky, writing fourteen years later with an eye to justifying Bolshevik actions:

> in the course of the events of the revolution, this chief democratic slogan, which had for a decade and a half tinged with its colour the heroic struggle of the masses, had grown pale and faded out, had somehow been ground between millstones, had become an empty shell, a form naked of content, a tradition and not a prospect.[12]

In forming a government legitimised by the support of the Soviet Congress, while at the same time confirming the pre-existing commitment of the provisional government to hold Constituent Assembly elections, Lenin had highlighted a contradiction; perhaps he had failed to recognise 'the constitutional implications of the revolutionary dynamic'. As Marcel Liebman argues, the very notion of entrusting all power to the soviets – 'which were popular institutions that did not provide for the representing of all classes' – had effectively ruled out any notion of making a Constituent Assembly, elected by the population as a whole, the sovereign organ of state power in Russia.[13]

As they came to realise that there was indeed a problem in setting up two different sources of legitimacy, the Bolsheviks identified a way they thought they could sort it out. The Constituent Assembly *would* be convened, but simply in order to grant its seal of approval to soviet power. Having endorsed and legitimised the 'real' government, it could dissolve itself and step aside.

Good plan. One problem: it soon became clear that the Assembly would *not* have a majority in favour of soviet rule, much less in favour of the Bolsheviks exercising power through the Council of People's Commissars. The first electoral returns reflected the logic of recent events: Lenin's party won in St Petersburg, Moscow and other major cities. But when the rest of the 45 million votes began to come in from rural areas and the provinces, the trend changed. The mood changed too.

The elections confirmed that the Bolsheviks' assumption of power in October 1917 rested on workers and soldiers in the industrial areas. Their support did not extend across the country as a whole, in which eighty per cent of the population were peasants. As Trotsky ruefully later reflected, although the revolution had taken place with popular enthusiasm in the big cities, there was a risk that 'the petty bourgeoisie' might still win in the Constituent Assembly election. As he noted, 'they actually did win as it turned out – a majority'.[14] Of the 707 deputies elected, the biggest groups were the 370 Socialist-Revolutionaries, who opposed Bolshevik rule, with a further forty Left Socialist-Revolutionaries (who had worked closely with Bolsheviks in the soviets); and 175 Bolsheviks, elected with about twenty-four per cent of the vote.

The resulting 'dilemma' was the main item on the agenda of the Bolshevik Central Committee meeting on 29 November, the day after the newly elected Constituent Assembly had first been due to convene. Discussion was confused and bitter. Those pointing out the irony that the party had entered into the election campaign with zeal did not generate any smiles.

Arguments were exchanged, recriminations begun. Key figures made their proposals. But the strategist who had steered the party into government, through his inspiring mixture of cool analysis and risk-taking, sat through the meeting thinking, frowning, screwing one eye up, but offering no opinion: Lenin stayed silent throughout. What was to be done? No decision was reached.

Over the coming weeks, technical reasons were offered for the delay in convening the Constituent Assembly. A campaign began to downplay the body's importance, confusing even further the already confused issues about its place in the wider processes of revolution.

The Menshevik leader Martov argued that the Constituent Assembly should provide the basis for the legitimate national government, and that socialists should put their effort into influencing the Assembly from the soviets: these, as class-based organisations, should exist alongside, but not displace, the democratically elected Assembly.[15] This position expressed Martov's desire to consolidate the freedom from Tsarist repression which was one of the main 'gains of the revolution'. His Menshevik followers saw grave risks to this freedom from the Bolsheviks' 'adventurist' policies, which they believed would only play into the hands of the counter-revolutionaries.

Lenin, in contrast, issued theses at the end of December 1917 presenting the choice between basing power on the Constituent Assembly or on the Congress of Soviets as one based on class confrontation. His position was that the soviets represented revolutionary proletarian democracy, while the Constituent Assembly was an institution of the old kind of parliamentary democracy – a liberal and bourgeois institution – whose legitimacy could no longer hold now that the proletarian revolution had progressed so much further.

A further argument was that context made it impossible to observe normal democratic procedures, or to respect the election results: in an extraordinary situation of war, social collapse and anxious awareness that the revolutionary government was about to come under attack, Lenin stated that:

> every attempt to consider the question of the Constituent Assembly from a formal, legal point of view, within the framework of ordinary bourgeois democracy and disregarding the class struggle and civil war, would be a betrayal of the proletariat's cause, and the adoption of the bourgeois standpoint.[16]

Lenin's followers insisted that the key question was the survival of the revolution: not what kind of Russian revolution there should be, but whether there would be a Russian revolution at all. Events had overtaken the Constituent Assembly: most of the politicians elected to it now represented social forces that were already spent, and programmes which rapid developments had rendered irrelevant. People had voted for programmes which no longer mattered.

Such convoluted justifications for the Assembly's dissolution continued to be advanced by Trotsky over the next few years. He dismissed the idea that government should be based on popular support as indicated in elections as an expression of Menshevism and reformism in the international movement:

> Karl Kautsky refuses to grant a birth certificate to the Russian Revolution for the reason that its birth has not been duly registered at the political office of bourgeois democracy.[17]

Eventually the date of 5 January 1918 was fixed for the convening of the Assembly. In the days beforehand, the Soviet Central Executive Committee declared Russia 'a Republic of Soviets of Workers' Soldiers and Peasants' Deputies', and determined that 'all power, centrally and locally, is vested in these Soviets'. Lenin argued that such a republic of soviets represented 'a higher form of democracy' than any bourgeois republic with a parliament or Constituent Assembly. The Assembly now being convened in St Petersburg was to be invited to endorse this declaration. When the Assembly finally came together, proceedings were chaotic; they were disrupted by pre-emptive manoeuvres, tactical votes and walk-outs: and they ended in the Assembly's dispersal by the Bolsheviks.

Over the following months, restrictions began to be applied against non-Bolsheviks in the debates within the soviet structures. Many accepted this 'centralisation' as necessary as the civil war against the Bolshevik government took off. Even so, significant dissent could still be expressed. A faction led by Nikolai Bukharin opposed the Brest-Litovsk treaty, in which the Bolsheviks and German imperialists agreed the end to Russia's involvement in the first world war, on the basis of very harsh terms for the Russians, including a significant loss of territory. Independently-minded Bolsheviks such as the economist Yevgeni Preobrazhensky had full scope to express their views. Even at the beginning of the 1920s, and in spite of growing repression, inconsistencies in government policy meant that there was some 'socialist democracy'. Policy debates took place in the trade unions. In 1920-21, some Menshevik opposition was still tolerated in some soviets, and could still present its own political platform at trade union congresses, even though its members were subject to repressive measures. And there was still a plurality of views within the Bolshevik party.

Through these years, Kamenev in particular made attempts to bring other parties back into coalition. But, although there was no Bolshevik 'grand plan' to establish a political monopoly, their responses to events as they arose meant that single party rule eventually emerged. They were facing continued disputation of their governmental legitimacy, a return by some of their opponents to the old anti-Tsarist tactic of assassination, and intervention by imperialist powers seeking to overthrow their government, as well as the beginnings of civil war by those opposed to the revolution. In June 1918, a Bolshevik press officer was shot dead. In August, a leading St Petersburg party member was killed by a young military cadet. Eleven days later, there was an attempt on Lenin's life as he came away from giving a speech at a factory: he was shot and badly wounded.[18]

The response was the launch of a 'Red Terror' campaign against those opposed to the revolution. This was implemented by the Cheka – the 'Extraordinary Commission for Combating Counter-Revolution and Sabotage', which Lenin had set up at the end of 1917. The Cheka chief Felix Dzerzhinski was a cool-headed leader, and his commission's approach at this point was systematic rather than furious. But the basis for future problems was laid by the way the Cheka operated outside the rule of law.[19]

In more orderly times, and with different political choices, it would have been possible to allow the Cheka a range of extraordinary powers within a legal framework, as is the case with 'special' forces in many democratic countries. But the times were unstable. State authority had disintegrated and enemies of the revolution were organising. The pressures which the Bolsheviks faced, their impatience, and their disdain for and ignorance of democratic norms, led them to set an ominous precedent: they created a powerful and repressive body that was able to act on direct instruction by, and according to the immediate wishes of, the inner ruling bodies of the state, without any respect for legal frameworks or procedural norms, or any oversight by a wider and more representative authority.[20] The Cheka became a *substitute* for statutory organisations and functions. It was one of the few coherent, hierarchical and nationally-organised forces to hand as the civil war began. Alongside the Bolsheviks, who were renamed as the Communist Party early in 1918, and the Red Army, it became one of the key institutions of the new revolutionary order.

The Romanov Tsar, his wife and children were not affected by the 'Red Terror': by the time it got underway in autumn 1918, they had already been killed. The royal family had at first been put into Siberian quarantine by the provisional government, but in the early part of the civil war the Bolsheviks had moved them to Yekaterinburg in the Urals, for fear that monarchists might try to liberate them. And as anti-Bolshevik forces started to advance towards Yekaterinburg in July 1918, Lenin and Yakov Sverdlov, who was the leader of the Congress of Soviets, gave the order for an act of 'cruel necessity', so as to ensure that neither Nicholas II nor any members of his family could become a focus to rally counter-revolution. This meant giving up on a plan to put the Tsar on trial for his regime's crimes: Trotsky was to have presented the case for the prosecution.

After the very intense initial period of repressive activity, there followed a period of some relaxation in which a degree of democratic opposition was possible again: this could be seen as evidence against those who claim that Leninism led automatically, cumulatively and in a straight line to Stalinism.

One area in which democratic practice was certainly reflected was in the field of culture, where writers, artists, composers and intellectuals had scope to shape a vibrant period of experimentation and variety. In its early days the Soviet state did not adopt an official line on what kind of culture was deemed to be socialist and therefore exclusively promoted.

## WHY THE BOLSHEVIKS CLOSED DOWN DEMOCRATIC SPACE

For some, including many committed Marxists, the issue of the dissolution of the Constituent Assembly is critical. As we have seen, this happened as the soviet regime became increasingly embattled and isolated. In the judgement of the British democratic communist and historian Monty Johnstone:

> Under such conditions Lenin and the Bolsheviks judged that to keep
> in power introducing widespread socialist measures they had to apply

coercive measures against other soviet parties, which were effectively banned after 1921-2. Voices were raised against such measures at the time – not only by Mensheviks like Martov, who continued to believe that authority needed to be based on general representative institutions, but also by a number of members of the Bolshevik leadership predicting undesirable consequences. In trying to establish socialism in a backward country with only minority support there began already under Lenin to be enforced restrictions on democracy which were later to expand into Stalinism.[21]

Isaac Deutscher, thinking himself into the problems of the Bolshevik leadership, reflected:

> they had always tacitly assumed that the majority of the working class, having backed them in the revolution, would go on to support them unswervingly until they had carried out the full programme of socialism. Naive as the assumption was, it sprang from the notion that socialism was the proletarian idea *par excellence* and that the proletariat, having once adhered to it, would not abandon it.[22]

But as many workers, in actuality, started to move away from active participation in and support for the Bolsheviks, a conflict arose. As Deutscher writes, if the working classes were to be allowed to speak and vote freely, they would destroy the proletarian dictatorship. But if the dictatorship were to openly abolish proletarian democracy it would deprive itself of historical legitimacy. This situation led to the Bolsheviks implementing a policy 'with which the working class, in its own interests, ought and eventually must identify itself, but with which it did not as yet identify itself'. The dictatorship would for a period, therefore, need to 'represent *the idea* of the class, not the class itself'.[23]

Democracy *should* have been centrally important to the communist project. It had emerged from socialism, a movement which had been the main expression of the democratic impulse during nineteenth-century industrialisation. From this it might have been assumed that communism – as socialism in serious form – would have been all the more serious about democracy, seeking to deepen it rather than reject it. But this did not happen.

As the Bolsheviks consolidated their rule, the lack of democracy became a major factor in their economic difficulties; and their economic policies themselves further increased the democratic deficit (this is discussed in more detail in chapter 15). Marx himself, though the practicalities of the transition to socialism had not been at the forefront of his writing, had envisaged that a programme to free humanity from exploitation would mean that social development would come about through social individuals working as freely associated producers. Leaving behind class division, and organising life without the distortions and oppressions necessarily generated by economic inequalities, would lead to democratic principles being extended more widely than capitalist bourgeois society had allowed.

But where there is not broad involvement in and ownership of social decisions, the likelihood is that a sectional clique or group will form to determine economic and other matters. This is of course what happened in the Soviet Union, and it established an undemocratic model which was then exported to other countries where communists achieved power. One justification for the soviet system was that what really mattered was economic development: through their focus on industrial growth, which would really improve peoples' lives, communists were committed to acting and delivering in the real interests of millions and millions of ordinary working people. The capitalist world's critique that communism did not make use of the multi-party system for selecting alternating elites was therefore regarded as hypocritical, reflective of a narrow conception of democracy, and driven by the aim of disrupting and disorganising the effort to build socialism. But in the Soviet Union and elsewhere, the absence of democracy turned out itself to be a block on the grand economic developments that its ruling communists sought.

## NOTES

1. St Petersburg was given the more Russian-sounding name of Petrograd in 1914 in the context of war against Germany. Bolsheviks refused to recognise the 'chauvinistic' change, and also did not use 'St', simply referring to themselves as operating in 'Petersburg'. The city was renamed Leningrad after Lenin's death in 1924.

2.  Slavoj Zizek, *Living in the End Times*, Verso, London 2010, p86.

3.  Slavoj Zizek, 'Georg Lukacs as the Philosopher of Leninism', in *The Universal Exception*, Continuum, London 2006, p105.

4.  Eric Hobsbawm, *On History*, Weidenfeld and Nicolson, London 1997, p323.

5.  Moshe Lewin, *The Soviet Century*, Verso, London 2005, p272.

6.  Eric Hobsbawm, *Echoes of the Marseillaise*, Verso, London 1990, p63.

7.  Vladimir Lenin, 'Lecture on the 1905 Revolution' [January 1917].

8.  Jeremy Gilbert, in Paul Bowman and Richard Stamp, eds, *The Truth of Zizek*, Continuum, London 2007, p74.

9.  Georg Lukacs, 'Postscript' [1967] to *Lenin: A Study on the Unity of His Thought*, Verso, London 2009 [1924].

10. Alain Badiou's idealist concept of 'the event' was formulated in the 1980s, drawing on Maoist voluntarism. Georg Lukacs promoted the concept of the 'actuality of the revolution' as a presence shaping society in *Lenin: A Study on the Unity of His Thought,* op cit.

11. John Reed's 1919 book *Ten Days That Shook the World* is the American's eyewitness account of the revolution in St Petersburg, conveying its excitement and high hopes.

12. Leon Trotsky, *History of the Russian Revolution* [1931], Volume Three, Chapter III.

13. Marcel Liebman, 'Was Lenin a Stalinist?' in Tariq Ali (ed), *The Stalinist Legacy*, Penguin Books, Harmondsworth 1984, p135.

14. Trotsky, *History of the Russian Revolution*, op cit.

15. Francis King, 'Introduction' to Fedor Il'ich Dan, *Two Years of Wandering*, Lawrence and Wishart, London 2016, p25.

16. Vladimir Lenin, *Theses on the Constituent Assembly* [December 1917].

17. Leon Trotsky, 'Preface to the reissue of this work' in 'Results and Prospects', *The Permanent Revolution and Results and Prospects*, Red Letter Press, Seattle WA, 2010 [1919].

18. The Bolsheviks – rightly – suspected British agents of involvement. See Chapters 14 and 15 of Robert Service, *Spies and Commissars*, Macmillan, London 2011.

19. The inherent dangers of governments taking 'extraordinary' steps are illustrated by the fact that the Cheka, once established in December 1917, was never disbanded. For Victor Serge, the creation of the Cheka was one of the Bolshevik's 'gravest and most impermissible errors' – alongside the 1918 introduction of the death penalty on the basis of secret procedure. Discussed in Paul Gordon, *Vagabond Witness*, Zero Books, London 2013, p5.

20. Serge's view is that, in this, 'the Central Committee probably followed the line of least resistance; it also followed psychological impulses which are comprehensible to any student of Russian history, but which have nothing in common with socialist principles'. *Memoirs of a*

*Revolutionary*, New York Review Books, New York NY 2012 [1940s], pp442-3.

21. Monty Johnstone, 'The Historical Significance of the Russian Revolution', *Socialist History*, 22, 2002.

22. Issac Deutscher, *The Prophet Armed: Trotsky 1879-1921* [1954], Chapter XIV, Oxford University Press, Oxford 1970.

23. Ibid. The italics are Makin-Waite's.

# 8. Regime change, everywhere

## THE ACHIEVEMENT OF THE ZIMMERWALDISTS

As the Russian revolutionaries took power, they encouraged others to follow their approach. They urged that other socialists should make October 1917 just the first instance of a wave of change which would be both stimulated by and become the condition for their own lasting success. This appeal was based on rejection of the 'reformist' approach of the Second International, whose leaders had failed to oppose the first world war, and which, after stumbling along for a couple more years, finally dissolved in 1916.

For years up until 1914, conference after conference of the Second International had confirmed lofty abstract principles: socialist parties were committed to solidarity with each other, and bonds of international friendship joined the workers of all countries as brothers. At times of inter-imperialist intrigue, socialist leaders asserted that their supporters enjoyed comradely ties which meant more than borders: they would always act in loyalty to each other, rather than to their own nation's 'ruling class'. The bourgeoisie's war-mongering was denounced as self-serving: it was against the interests of the ordinary working people, whose needs could never be served by nationalist militarism and conflict.

Such outlooks were not mere sentimental 'fraternity'. They reflected practical lessons drawn from 1871 and other radical episodes, which had shown that if revolutionaries took power in one particular city, region or nation, but that reactionary forces could be assembled nearby or in a rival country, then all progressive achievements would soon be challenged by hostile armies. Socialists recognised that their prospects for success in any particular country would depend on co-ordinated and effective acts of solidarity on an international basis.

But when the test came, most left-wingers had been somehow taken in by August 1914's stirring calls to rally round the flag, the initial sense of jolly adventure and the carnival atmosphere attending recruitment. This was the case in countries on both sides of the conflict. Some internationally known socialist leaders, for example Clara Zetkin of the German SPD, continued to campaign for the principled position their fellow socialists had been making for years: *now*, more than ever, was the moment to insist on peace. But such figures were isolated. For most of their former comrades, anti-imperialism had crumbled as soon as their own country was threatened with war. Most German social-democrats now supported the war effort, as did their counterparts in all the warring countries. The Kaiser – expressing his confidence in the victory of nation over class – declared that he no longer saw any political parties, 'but only Germans'. The parliamentarians of the SPD duly voted for the war, and approved big budgets of war credits. Most other socialist 'internationalists' followed suit, lining up behind 'their' national leaders – and even helped to fan the patriotic fury.

In Russia, unusually, the Tsar Nicholas's decision to go to war had not had such a unifying effect on the country. His declaration of war had partly been made in the hope of undermining the Russian Duma, the semi-democratic assembly which he had been forced to accept after 1905, and which he had long aimed to downgrade or, better, abolish. The Tsar believed that war would allow the rekindling of the mystical union between himself and the Russian people.[1] But many Russians were resistant to such a union. (This failure to win support for the war was further evidence of the Tsarist regime's lack of popular legitimacy – which its conduct of the war did little to enhance.)

When the war began, Lenin, who was living in exile in Zurich, found the SPD's 'capitulation' difficult to believe. He assumed that the edition of the German socialist newspaper *Vorwarts* that reported its unity with the government was ruling-class propaganda: there had been plenty of earlier examples of such false news as the imperial powers prepared for war. When he received confirmation that that the German party was indeed supporting the war effort, he suffered a brief nervous crisis. As Savas Michael-Matsas has commented, Lenin was 'never the unemotional icon of steel portrayed by Stalinists' – and he may even have considered abandoning politics.[2] His further response, however, once he had recovered his wits, was to identify the war as the definitive political opportunity. Its outbreak proved that the long-awaited general crisis of capitalism had now – explosively

– commenced. It was the culmination of trends over the previous decades: monopoly concentration and imperialist expansion. The room for cartel arrangements and diplomatic manoeuvre having been exhausted, the spoils were now being forcibly divided.

Lenin further interpreted acceptance by the working class of the bourgeois states' military compulsions as resulting from the malign influence of their treacherous leaders, who had been, effectively, bribed and corrupted through the bestowal upon them of a small part of the super-profits of imperialism. This had led them to act towards their class brothers in other countries as the bosses did towards them in their own country. He predicted that once the realities of the conflict began to be felt, then the working men in the trenches and factories would change their attitudes. The initial intoxication, the 'holiday mood' that had marked August 1914, would fall away as they reacted against the stupid and wasteful horror of the establishment's war. They would want to find ways to end it – and they would support movements to overthrow the old rulers and leaders who had directed them into the trenches of blood and division. International socialist revolution was no longer a distant prospect, but had now moved to the top of the agenda. The task which followed from this analysis was to re-establish as rapidly as possible an international organisation with real Marxist perspectives.

This was a challenging agenda: the Second International was in ruins, and any internationalists who might network with Lenin and his co-thinkers were beleaguered and marginalised, each facing the censorship and repression of their own belligerent government.

Nevertheless, these internationalists restarted their political campaigning, and their subsequent efforts effectively mark the foundation of the twentieth-century communist movement. Those forming the new movement rejected all 'illusions' in 'bourgeois democracy', and judged those who promoted it as the vehicle for socialist progress as fools or self-serving hypocrites. The establishment's 'democratic' politicians had willingly joined in the propulsion of young men into the horrors and massacres of war. The elites who trumpeted democratic values had presided over grossly polarised class societies. They had ruled empires in which massive numbers of people were oppressed, cast as less than human by racist ideology. With worker now pitted against worker in a war over which state would acquire the spoils of imperialism's now disintegrating empires, many radical leftists concluded once and for all that any talk of 'representative democracy' was a con-trick. This attitude fed into the founding spirit of revolutionary communism, saddling the movement with a profoundly mistaken and disabling outlook.

Small minorities of socialists in each warring nation now broke with their 'chauvinist' leaderships and networked together in a new cross-border radical left. For these uncompromising activists, the call for brave opposition to the war was a way of making sense in the madness of the conflict, and redeeming 'true' socialist values from the demoralisation caused by their 'renegade' erstwhile leaders.

For a long time the 'internationalists' seemed entirely isolated. Their occasional gatherings, such as that held in the obscure Swiss village of Zimmerwald in September 1915, were clandestine moments, making little apparent impact. Their best-known comrades, including Rosa Luxemburg in Germany, spent large periods of the war 'on leave' from history, imprisoned as long as it continued. (Zetkin was also arrested several times but released on grounds of illness.)

As the fighting continued, some socialists who had initially supported their country's declaration of war changed their positions. Bernstein, for example, had voted for war credits in 1914, seeing the hand of autocratic Russia behind efforts to create a Greater Serbia, and believing that war with Russia was inevitable and even progressive. But by early 1916 he had aligned himself with Kautsky in condemning the war as imperialist. In 1917 Kautsky and Bernstein helped set up a new party of socialists who rejected the SDP's support for the war, the USPD (Independent Socialist Party of Germany).

Lenin and a few co-thinkers opposed the war in a particular way: even amongst the 'Zimmerwaldists', already seen as a group of ultra-radical peace-mongers, they developed a left. Their minority stance – 'revolutionary defeatism' – advocated that those opposed to war in each country should work for the defeat of 'their own' state, taking the crisis and pressures their ruling classes faced as a chance to fight them harder. On this basis, they rejected the argument that all political forces should combine to pursue the war effort 'in the national interest'. Some socialists had been stung by accusations of defeatism, to the extent that they had been brought back into the national fold. But Lenin not only accepted the 'accusation', but proclaimed the notion of *revolutionary* defeatism: now, at a time when the ruling class of his own nation was reeling from the blows of war, now was precisely the time to redouble efforts to overthrow it. If socialists were not prepared to push for revolutionary change at a moment when it was more likely that they would succeed, and when they would be acting in the interest of the masses of ordinary people from whose ranks were drawn the hundreds of thousands of young soldiers being needlessly blown limb from limb in the killing fields of the war, what kind of socialists were they?[3]

Support for the war effort was so strong in most nations that Lenin and the left Zimmerwaldists knew that their stance would – initially – attract hostility and confirm their marginalisation. But 'revolutionary defeatism' was a positive agenda. The optimistic vision was that working-class governments would take over in all the belligerent countries. The war was not being fought on behalf of ordinary people, and their representatives would therefore conclude a series of peace agreements, with justice. The slaughter would end. Wives and husbands would be reunited. Mothers would welcome home their sons. The old ruling classes who had sent 'their' young men to fight each other in the blood and shit and mud of the trenches would be discredited, defeated. They would leave the stage of history. A new epoch would begin, in which working people would run their economies and societies in the interests of the vast majority.

To achieve this positive goal, Lenin's guiding concern was that people working with him should be able to resist the lure of the belligerent nationalism being promoted by their bourgeois governments, including through the associated nuances of 'social patriotism' – which quibbled with 'excessive' jingoism but still went along with the war effort. Socialists needed to stay focused on the fact that their enemy was their own ruling class, even when the expected response to the emergency of war was for the whole country to pull together. Lenin's repeated line was that this was 'their' war – the war of the ruling class – not 'ours': his summary analysis was that 'one slave owner, Germany, is fighting another slave owner, England, for a fairer distribution of the slaves'. This fed into a clear message to soldiers: they had much more in common with the men they were fighting *against* than with the men they were fighting *for*.

The validity of Lenin's approach was, for his followers, to be rapidly confirmed by events. Not much more than two years after the Zimmerwald conference, the internationalists from his own country succeeded in taking state power, precisely by exploiting the mass discontent of the population that had been greatly increased by the Tsar's conduct of the war. As Willie Thompson comments, 'the pathetic revolutionary fantasists of Zimmerwald … seized power … by a process corresponding precisely to Lenin's forecasts of how war was likely to turn into revolution'.[4]

Subsequent claims that the direct lineage of the Russian revolution could be traced back to the resolutions hammered out in the Alpine conclave were a retrospective construct. Nevertheless, the narrative was quickly established that the achievement of the left-wing Zimmerwaldists had been to restore the morality and meaning of the old International's abstract commitment to fraternal solidarity, and to give it concrete organisational form. And once Lenin's party was in power in Russia, one of its priorities was to realise, resource and build the new International which the Zimmerwald left saw had been needed since August 1914.

## COMRADES COME RALLY: ESTABLISHING THE COMMUNIST MOVEMENT

Within a few months of October 1917, the Bolshevik government had effectively broken the power and destroyed the social position of the old nobility, by means of the legal recognition it gave to the land seizures that waves of peasants had been carrying out; it had negotiated an end to Russia's involvement in the first world war – a moment in which 'class' took its revenge on 'nation'; and it had geared up to successfully defend their fledgling revolutionary state in the new conflicts forced on them by foreign 'interventionists' and domestic counter-revolutionaries.

Now renaming itself the Communist Party, Lenin's organisation put energy and resources into strengthening some of the groups, factions and fragile tendencies in each nation's socialist movement which had opposed the war. In this 'wildly fermented time', they were encouraged to break with other socialists and set up independent, revolutionary communist parties themselves.[5] These would operate collectively, and in disciplined co-ordination, as sections of a new and integrated organisation that would be effective across all borders. Thus was the Third International – the Communist International (Comintern) – inaugurated. Working-class people would act on the basis of horizontal solidarities of class, rather than the vertical solidarities through which they were asked to act in line with 'the national interest' as defined by the ruling class of each country.

Twentieth-century communism was thus established as a particular – resolute – form of socialism. The new International reinstated the old communist name from the 1840s to emphasise its undiluted opposition to the bourgeoisie, and to distinguish its parties from the social-democrats who had led the Second International to ignominy.[6] From this point on, as far as Lenin's followers were concerned, 'social-democracy' would denote those organisations which called themselves socialist but were merely reformists, content to operate within the limits determined by right-wing capitalist politicians.

The Comintern was established, with significant funds, in early 1919, and conceived of as a single centralised party – a form of world politics.[7] Its global approach would necessarily be expressed in struggle organised through national sections. These, though, were seen as integral and subordinate parts of the overall International: the communist Third International was not the result of a federation or aggregation of national parties. It was not a movement shaped by the liberal approach of recognised nation relating to recognised nation, with respect for established powers and treaties. It carried, rather, a world-wide commitment to regime change, everywhere.

The Comintern extended Bolshevik attitudes to democracy to the international movement, wiring them into the culture of this major new political formation. A number of key perspectives were made central to the whole movement: it was necessary to establish factory councils as power bases for the industrial working class; socialism could not be reached other than through a process of civil war; revolution meant the dissolution of the existing capitalist state; new mechanisms of socialist democracy needed to be created to take power; as in Russia, only 'soviets' would prove suitable for proletarian rule, and there was no possibility of a parliamentary route to socialism.

The revolutionary communists now argued that parliament and democracy were, in their essential nature, 'bourgeois institutions'. As Kautsky argued, this position was at odds with classical Marxism.[8] It was, rather, a projection of the 'lessons' and justifications the Bolsheviks had fashioned as the Constituent Assembly was closed down. For Trotsky, revolutionary politics were not a way of building on and then going beyond the positives in liberal democracy, albeit in a higher and more developed form. They were a different approach to progressive change altogether. Why should the birth of proletarian revolution have to be 'duly registered at the political office of bourgeois democracy'?[9] After all, the social classes which now set this requirement for workers' parties had not achieved their own positions of dominance by relying on 'democracy'.

As Massimo Salvadori recounts, Kautsky rejected the view that councils or soviets were the necessary form of revolutionary government. The counterposition of councils to parliament 'masked the design of a dictatorship by a minority, disguised in the formula of a democracy distinct from parliamentary sovereignty, branded as bourgeois'. In fact, 'it was impossible to adduce any evidence that a national assembly must be against socialism by nature, while a council of soldiers must necessarily be in favour of it'.[10]

Meanwhile, new communist papers such as the Hungarian *Red News* declared:

> To hell with bourgeois democracy! To hell with the parliamentary republic and politics that discourage the masses from acting! To arms, proletariat![11]

As the Comintern established itself, Lenin refined such slogans to make clear that representative democracy could – and in fact should – be used, tactically, wherever it could serve revolutionary interests. The rejection of parliamentarianism as a political form did not mean rejecting participation in elections as a tactic. He attempted to explain the issue to sceptical ultra-leftists through taking Britain as an example: his view was that, where the rules still allowed communists to stand as Labour candidates, revolutionaries should 'support' the Labour Party – but only in the sense that a rope 'supports' a hanging man.[12] This phrase had the advantage of being vivid and memorable. It had the disadvantage of still resonating in the memory of Labour activists a few years later, when communists shifted to a different position and wanted to work in genuine partnership with them: unsurprisingly, they struggled to win back trust.

## NEW FORMATIONS

The Second Comintern Congress in August 1920 set out twenty-one terms and conditions of affiliation that had to be accepted before any party could join the new International. These convey uncompromising disciplines – but they also confirmed the sense of determination and ambition of those signing up. The conditions were drawn up precisely to exclude those who could have corrupted and blunted the clear intentions of the new International.

Where did the parties come from that now joined the Comintern? In a handful of cases, the Bolsheviks directly established parties to operate in particular countries. Thus the Hungarian Party was formed in November 1918 on Russian soil, from among radical socialists who had been captured by Tsarist forces before the revolution, and had become prisoners of war.

In what was a fairly rare trajectory, the organisation which became the Communist Party of the Netherlands had been already established well before the Russian Revolution: a Marxist group opposed to 'reformism' had split from the Dutch Social-Democratic Workers' Party in 1909.

In most countries, communist parties formed through left-wing sections splitting off from established socialist parties in a period of three or four years after 1917. All these splits were rooted in domestic political impulses and differences that went back many years, but were now highlighted and exacerbated by the events of October 1917. It was usually a substantial minority of the old socialist parties that left to form the CP, as in Italy. In a few cases, a majority of socialists turned communist, casting off the socialist name which the smaller rump then held onto: this happened in France, Czechoslovakia and Norway.

In a few other countries, the example of the Russian Revolution spurred existing small groups and parties of left-wingers who were not part of the main socialist party into 'unity conferences', such as those which established the Communist Party of Great Britain in 1920.

The most promising organisation established through the Comintern's early work was the German Communist Party. It formed in late 1920 through a complex process, in which the Spartacists (who had broken from the SPD in 1915 and led a failed uprising in January 1919) fused with the majority of the Independent Social-Democratic Party that had formed in 1917, together with some other small groups. The united German communists were by far the strongest party outside of Soviet Russia until they were virtually destroyed by the Nazis.

Whichever route was taken to establishing an independent communist party, the result was to lock all but the tiniest fragments of the far left in nearly every country into behaviours, styles and approaches which drew on the particular circumstances and history of Russian Bolshevism – circumstances and history wholly removed from their own. The style, policies, and prospects of European radicals were now hitched to the fortunes of the Soviet project: twentieth-century communism came into being as that wing of the wider socialist movement which saw the 1917 Russian revolution as inaugurating the transition to a post-capitalist society – and as providing the models and techniques to enable this transition. From 1924, 'Bolshevisation' was promoted on the basis that direction from Moscow was crucial to the sustained independent existence of the new international revolutionary movement, and that it was the only way of instilling the resoluteness without which all transformative and conflictual instincts would have quickly fallen victim to the assimilative potential of dominant political cultures.

The Bolshevisation campaign put in place a culture of mimicking the supposed style of the Russian communists. Would-be leaders consciously developed inner-party splits, as if by repeating the actions and style of Lenin, in thoroughly different circumstances, a revolution as dramatic as 1917 might in due course be conjured. Such devices recall the rituals of priests and shamans, rather than the actually revolutionary approach of Lenin and his comrades.

It is ironic that the main effect of Bolshevisation was to move the left in many countries away from the virtue which had characterised the Bolsheviks themselves, and laid the basis for their success: an attentive focus on the specific characteristics of their own situation – as seen, for example, in Lenin's early surveys of the development of capitalism in Russia. Instead of repeating this approach, in ways which matched the varied national and regional circumstances in which left-wing forces were trying to develop, the Bolshevised left instead repeated the gestures and rhetoric of specifically Russian practice, wherever they were. They did this even to the extent of attempting to introduce the urgent new telegraphic phrases and acronyms reshaping Russian political language into the daily life of such locales as small Scottish pit-head villages, northern English work-towns and Welsh mining communities: 'little Moscows' grew up in a few places – including the Vale of Leven, Chopwell and Mardy. Enthusiasts conceived of the Russian revolution as a blueprint, a fundamentalist script to be followed in its every detail.

Bolshevisation had the effect of establishing attitudes dismissive of the value of democratic process throughout the international communist movement. The perspective was that countries everywhere would soon see fundamental economic crises. As these arose, the powerful bourgeoisie would consolidate their power through using the repressive apparatus of the capitalist state: the police, the military and the secret services. Councils or soviets had to be put in place to break this power. Perry Anderson described how revolutionary communists believed that the resulting conflict would not permit a gradual process of change: once the bourgeois state and capitalist economy were ruptured, 'the ensuing social upheaval must rapidly and fatally pit revolution and counter-revolution against each other in a violent convulsion'.[13]

Although a number of small alternative and independent Marxist currents continued to exist, the alacrity with which large numbers of left-wingers from scores of countries agreed to work in line with the expectations and requirements of Lenin's party is very striking. Reaction to the first world war played a major role in this willing embrace of the new politics. Many radicals were attracted by communism's insistence on the need for a bold new start, and the setting up of parties to take forward socialist politics in a determined and resolute way, untainted by the failures and compromises of the Second International. In discussing the general mood of intellectuals and artists after the war, the art historian Michael Remy noted how the slaughter of millions of soldiers on both sides had led to widespread disenchantment with the hitherto sacrosanct values of flag, fatherland, family and religion. This view was widely shared in the wider population: 'How could any of these vainglorious concepts still be extolled when they had been used to justify such monstrous mass killings? Indeed, how could one still accept those philosophies and beliefs which failed to condemn it?'[14]

The first world war engendered a sense of futility, of belonging to a culture and society without credible values. A nihilistic mood took hold among substantial sections of the population – a feeling that little now mattered or made sense. For other radically minded people, communism was a way of regaining a sense of progress and meaning: here was a new politics that had not been part of the pre-war landscape, and which rejected (or had only a contingent, tactical relationship to) such constructs as nationalism and religion. For many people, internationalist class politics seemed more grounded and stable than nation-state allegiance – not least, as Hobsbawm describes it, given that at least ten of Europe's states after the first world war were either entirely new or had 'so changed from their predecessors as to have no special legitimacy for their inhabitants'.[15]

Leninism, uncompromised, was therefore able to quickly extend its appeal beyond the context of Russian autocracy in which it had been formed. As the only large group of socialists who had actually campaigned effectively against the war – in that they had overthrown a government committed to pursuing it, and had then withdrawn their country from the slaughter – Bolshevik arguments about the importance of party organisation and discipline quickly gained credibility.

## A LITTLE DANCE: LENIN'S HOPES

The attractions of Bolshevik culture were itemised by the writer Victor Serge as:

> a capacity for conviction; a unity of thought, action and life; personality, not individualism; social awareness; energy, capacity for sacrifice and hunger for victory ... superior intellectual training.[16]

Young people were flattered by the sense that they were 'people of a special mould', and were attracted to 'a party of a new type' which would put internationalism at the centre of its organising principles.[17]

Twentieth-century communism thus formed as a movement that saw national borders as contingent, and not as 'real' boundaries within which the identities and allegiances of its adherents should be constructed and constrained. The successful Russian revolutionaries generated optimism and excitement. Busy as they needed to be with pressing domestic concerns, here they were, pushing energy and resources into the development of communist politics in other countries. Many left-wingers saw such commitment as selfless, and as deserving a positive response and matching effort.

In late 1917 and early 1918, Lenin felt confident that the new revolutionary state would inspire widespread enthusiasm. At the same time, Bolshevik leaders knew how fragile the new state was. Their main hope was that it would survive long enough to be an inspiration to other countries' revolutionaries. Their earliest decrees were as much programmatic as legislative. Mindful of the inspiration that he and his comrades had drawn from the Paris Commune of 1871, Lenin danced a little dance in the snowy garden outside his office on the day which signalled that the new Soviet state had lasted longer than the Commune.

Until the early 1920s, Soviet attitudes were dominated by the hope and expectation that there would be 'events in the West'. Lenin in no way believed that the Russian revolution could sustain itself. The idea had been that revolution in Russia could serve as a trigger or catalyst on the international stage.[18] Trotsky would later recall that:

> all calculations at the time were based on the hope of an early victory of the revolution in the west. It was considered self-evident that the victorious German proletariat would supply Soviet Russia, on credit against future food and raw materials, not only with machines and articles of manufacture, but also with tens of thousands of highly-skilled workers, engineers and organisers.[19]

The perspective that the revolution was not conceived in a narrow national framework shaped Lenin's ripostes to the Mensheviks, who continued to warn that the Russian revolution had been premature and therefore could not possibly realise the goals it proclaimed. As good Marxists, the Mensheviks pointed out all the evidence that Russia was being pulled into chaos, thus proving that the revolution had been forced before its proper time. The Bolshevik counter was that the Russian proletariat was taking a lead, and showing that socialists could conquer and retain state power, at least for a while, even in the most adverse circumstances.

The Bolsheviks also looked east, encouraging campaigns against imperialist rule, and offering support to national liberation movements across Asia, Africa and Latin America. Their belief was that this would help to change the balance of forces between those who had ruled the world and their 'subjects'. In due course, communism would directly resource the people of China, Vietnam and many other countries in establishing unified, independent states.

Lenin's contribution was centrally important on this question, as on so many others. As Terry Eagleton has argued, despite his critical

attitude to nationalism, Lenin was 'the first major political theorist
to grasp the significance of national liberation movements': he recognised that national liberation was a question of radical democracy, not
chauvinist sentiment: 'In a uniquely powerful combination, Marxism
thus became both an advocate of anti-colonialism and a critique of
nationalist ideology'.[20]

The Bolsheviks' rhetorical support for emerging nationalists in
oppressed countries was confirmed by their actions in government.
For example, soon after taking power in 1917, they exposed the secret
Sykes-Picot agreement to parcel out the Middle East between France,
Britain and Tsarist Russia that had been made in 1916. And the
Bolsheviks went beyond calling for people to throw off their imperialist shackles in other empires: they also voluntarily renounced the
special concessions Russia enjoyed in China. As Pankaj Mishra notes:
'Lenin's actions were seen by many Asians ... as nothing less than
"an extraordinary and incredibly super-manic promulgation of a new
international morality"'.[21]

The Comintern set up communist parties across Asia, and in 1920
organised the Congress of the Peoples of the East in Baku, Azerbaijan,
which was attended by nearly 2000 delegates from Persia, Armenia,
Turkey, Georgia and elsewhere. And it also worked to establish and
link up with newly forming international anti-colonialism organisations to promote the anti-imperialist agenda. This approach drew
many emerging nationalist leaders toward communism, including a
young anti-colonial activist from Indo-China who was working in
Paris, Ho Chi Minh.

Nevertheless, Comintern anti-imperialism did itself involved some
ranking of countries, and this led to a degree of condescension towards
colonial peoples. For example, at the September 1920 Congress of the
Peoples of the East, whose delegates included many Muslims, the
atheist Comintern leader Zinoviev made highly cynical use of the term
'jihad' in seeking to encourage rebellion against imperial powers. The
Congress was a key initiative in attempts to create alliances between
communists and Muslims; attempts which were shaped by distances
and misunderstandings, but also significant 'points of contact'. These
included egalitarianism, the value placed on abstention from conspicuous consumption, and common opposition to western imperialism.[22]

Russian internationalists sought to use the potential for revolution
in the east primarily as a way of undermining the rulers of Western

Europe, which they still regarded as the centrally important task. In an August 1919 memo to the Central Committee, Trotsky argued that:

> we have up till now devoted too little attention to agitation in Asia. However, the international situation is evidently shaping up in such a way that the road to Paris and London lies via the towns of Afghanistan, the Punjab and Bengal.[23]

The Bolshevik perspective was that Western capitalism would be decisively weakened if it was cut off from its colonies, which provided so much cheap labour, raw materials and opportunities for super-profitable investment. But colonised countries were seen as a 'secondary' sphere, which meant that less attention was given to 'correct' strategy there, as compared with Western Europe. Whilst focusing on the precise formulae required for working-class movements in every European country, the Comintern was more relaxed about the ways in which the anti-imperialist movement might be related to the struggle for socialism in Asia itself. Whilst the push in Europe was to establish communist political leadership, the Comintern was comfortable with Chinese and Indian communist parties working in support of, and subordinating their interests to, their own 'anti-imperialist' bourgeoisie.

This had a significant consequence. Within a few years of the Comintern being founded, the old 'stages' theory came back in. In China and other colonised countries, Lenin's successors primarily encouraged nationalist movements which were seeking bourgeois democratic revolutions. The old perspectives of Russian social-democracy were re-established, through an insistence that the immediate task was the removal of imperialist domination. The argument was that national liberation would then allow the expansion of capitalism and democratic rights, and thus provide the best conditions for the self-organisation of the working class, so that, in due course, the socialist horizon might come into view.

## NOTES

1. Stephen Kotkin, *Stalin: Paradoxes of Power, 1878-1928*, Allen Lane/Penguin, London 2014, p145.
2. Savas Michael-Matsas, 'Lenin and the Path of Dialectics' in Sebastian

Budgen, Stathis Kouvelakis and Slavoj Zizek (eds), *Lenin Reloaded*, Duke University Press, London 2007, p102.

3. Other political forces also identified the moment that their national opponents were deep in war as precisely the moment to strike. For example, Irish republicans organised their rising and declared national independence in Dublin in Easter 1916.

4. Willie Thompson, *The Left in History*, Pluto Press, London 1997, p48.

5. The phrase quoted is from Karl Kautsky, 'Preface', *Terrorism and Communism* [1919].

6. During the 1840s, the term 'communist', as G.F. Hudson puts it, 'had come to have a slightly "sharper" and more "uncompromising" connotation than the word socialist'. Hudson says that, according to Engels, the part of the working-class movement that was convinced of the necessity for a total social change called itself communist, whereas 'socialism' was claimed by 'the most multifarious social quacks, who by all manner of tinkering professed to redress, without any danger to capital and profit, all sorts of social grievances'. G.F. Hudson, *Fifty Years of Communism*, Penguin, Harmondsworth 1971, pp4-5.

7. The first and founding Comintern Congress was held in Moscow in March 1919. Initial finance came from foreign currency, diamonds and other luxury goods confiscated from the Russian nobility following the 1917 revolution. The valuables were sold by Comintern agents in Germany and elsewhere.

8. Karl Kautsky, *Terrorism and Communism* [1919].

9. Leon Trotsky, 'Preface to the reissue of this work' in 'Results and Prospects', *The Permanent Revolution and Results and Prospects*, Red Letter Press, Seattle WA, 2010 [1919].

10. Massimo Salvadori, *Karl Kautsky and the Socialist Revolution 1880-1938*, New Left Books/Verso, London 1979, pp236-7.

11. February 1919 editorial, quoted in Arpad Kadarkay, *Georg Lukacs*, Blackwell, Oxford 1991, p208.

12. In 1926, when Labour began to purge communists from its ranks, around one fifth of CPGB members were also active Labour Party members.

13. Perry Anderson, *Arguments within English Marxism*, Verso, London, 1980, pp194-5.

14. Michael Remy, *Surrealism in Britain*, Ashgate, Aldershot 1999.

15. Eric Hobsbawm, *The Age of Extremes*, Michael Joseph, London 1994, p138.

16. Victor Serge, 'Mexican Notebooks', *New Left Review*, July-August 2013 [1941].

17. The quotes are from Joseph Stalin, *On the Death of Lenin*, 1924.

18. As Moshe Lewin comments in *The Soviet Century*, Verso, London 2005, p288: 'The prognosis was not confirmed, but at the time there was nothing absurd about it'.

19. Leon Trotsky, *The Revolution Betrayed*, 1936, Chapter Two.

20. Terry Eagleton, *Why Marx Was Right*, Yale University Press 2011, p217.

21. Pankaj Mishra, *From the Ruins of Empire*, Allen Lane, London 2012, pp194-5. Mishra is quoting Benoy Kumar Sakar.

22. For a good overview of these relationships, with many helpful pointers to further reading, see Ben Fowkes and Bulent Gokay, 'Communists and Muslims: the years of alliance', *Twentieth Century Communism*, 5, 2013.

23. Trotsky, quoted in Neil Davidson, *How Revolutionary were the Bourgeois Revolutions?*, Haymarket Books, Chicago IL 2012, p246.

# 9. Not catching modernity's promise

## HOW STALINISM DEVELOPED: RUSSIAN ISOLATION AND ITS CONSEQUENCES

Confidence that revolution would extend to the west soon faded. A managing strategy was needed until things changed. Lenin's last statement on the 'strange situation' was to shape communist internationalism for decades:

> What concerns us is not the inevitable ultimate victory for socialism. It is the tactics we must follow [in the meantime] to prevent the anti-revolutionary states of the West from crushing us.[1]

1923 saw the decisive defeat of a series of attempts at instituting revolutionary communism in Europe. Short-lived attempts to set up Soviet regimes in Hungary and parts of Germany had been crushed with unforgiving savagery. In Italy, Mussolini's fascist movement was able to succeed partly because of the counter-revolutionary support it attracted from an establishment that was responding to the 'two red years' of 1919 and 1920, when the trade unions and the left had attempted to base a revolution on factory uprisings. The mid-1920s also saw major setbacks for communists in contexts as varied as Britain and China.

These failures intensified Soviet isolation; and their resulting choices cannot be explained in terms of a moralistic account of communists 'betraying' the internationalism of 1917. By the mid-1920s, the decisive choice had been made. The tension between the two strands making up the dual policy of the Soviet government – the encouragement of world revolution and the pursuit of national security – had been resolved: the second strand had established a clear claim to priority.

First articulated by Nikolai Bukharin, the doctrine of 'socialism in one country' was soon identified with the increasingly dominant figure of Stalin. It gave a clear aim to a ruling group in beleaguered circumstances. As Hobsbawm notes, given that the revolution had failed to 'give a signal for a workers' revolution in the west', the dominant tasks of the Bolsheviks had to be 'the economic and cultural development of a backward and impoverished country, in order to create the conditions both for survival against foreign attack and for the construction of socialism in an isolated, if gigantic, country'.[2]

This kind of choice is recurrently faced by radical political movements. Once they gain a measure of power and some stability seems possible, they face two broad options: to consolidate the relatively limited gains achieved to that point, or to push on in order to more fully realise the ambitions that have motivated their heroic efforts so far, even at the risk of losing what has been achieved. The emerging Soviet bureaucracy went for the option of 'what we have we hold'. As E.H. Carr wrote: 'the rank and file, if not the party intelligentsia, needed the stimulus and inspiration of a finite goal not set in the remote future, and dependent for its realisation not on incalculable events in faraway Europe, but on their own efforts'.[3]

What form should those efforts take? Communists had little guidance. Marx had not matched *Capital* with worked out proposals for the future socialist economy. Those wanting to build it would have to be pioneers.

During the revolution, Lenin's own uncertainties had been evident. At the historic Congress of Soviets in October 1917 he may have struck an optimistic note and been rewarded with enthusiastic applause. But even as Lenin was addressing the victorious comrades, declaring that 'we shall now proceed to construct the socialist order', not one of them knew how they were going to do so.

In Western Europe, socialism had in large part developed as a way of giving voice to the interests of industrial workers. In Russia, socialists would need to develop industry themselves, and thus generate the proletariat who would then support their government. Optimists hoped that declaring socialism would make policy choices straightforward, and that 'people's goals would be obvious', along with the ways to organise work and provide resources to realise those goals.[4]

Not so. Instead, communists were pushed into particular economic policy approaches by events as they occurred: they were making their history not under circumstances they themselves had chosen, but under the given and inherited circumstances with which they were directly confronted.[5] From the summer of 1918, improvised approaches which were later given the title of 'war communism' were brought in as part of an effort to defend the Soviet state against both foreign powers and domestic opponents. A key element of this system was the direct requisitioning of food from the peasantry, in order to supply the Red Army and the workers in the factories. Physical force became the major mechanism of economic coordination. Food was rationed on class preferential lines. Soldiers and skilled workers, and then party members and approved intellectuals, did best out of this.

'Making a virtue out of a necessity' had never been a Bolshevik watchword. But now, in a kind of war-induced hallucination, some party members began seeing war communism not as a set of temporary controls and unfortunate emergency measures, but as a possible economic model for the future. Trotsky proposed militarising the workforce, and subordinating trade unions to state control, declaring that 'labour in general – society in general, if necessary – could do with a taste of the bayonet'.[6] Directing workers in an authoritative way, requiring compliance and a preparedness to use extreme coercion – this communist formula is worth reflecting on for those who equate 'being Bolshie' with oppositional and sectional trade union militancy.

The context for such proposals was the disorganisation of the ground on which the Bolsheviks had taken power. Many workers who had supported the revolution were now in the Red Army, or held government positions. The party's social base had crumbled through the civil war and wars of intervention, as urban populations had fallen sharply. As Bukharin wryly observed, Bolsheviks were trying to make proletarian revolution in the face of 'the disintegration of the proletariat'.[7] They had to recruit former Tsarist military officers to the Red Army. In an effort to keep an eye on the dubious new recruits, the basis was laid for a paranoid aspect of the Stalinist culture to come: Trotsky created the role of the 'commissar' to control these 'untrustworthy elements'. This 'double-administration' device was quickly extended into industry, with politically vetted workers appointed to supervise the 'bourgeois experts' kept on from the previous times.

Communist ambition became detached from the working-class constituencies to which the Bolsheviks had previously related. The communists' sense of purpose led them to conceive of the 'new man', an imaginary future Soviet citizen, in whose interests present actions were to be taken. A few years previously, in 1917, Bolsheviks had represented massive social movements for change. Now the party turned into a mechanism for appointing people to positions of responsibility in a fragile state that it was determined to strengthen and consolidate. With their weak appreciation of democracy, and given the autocratic context which had shaped them, the Bolsheviks now further downgraded the importance of persuasion and accountability.

'Voluntarism' developed – the expectation that change would result from the will of the political agent. People were seen either as happy expressions of that pre-existing will, or as recalcitrant barriers to what was expected to happen. Such an outlook results partly from the desire for a better future, and this has recurrently caused revolutionaries to assume that, once the resistance of the classes who are to be dispossessed of property, power and status is broken, all will be well and the citizenry will rejoice in the new order.

Such optimism is always unfounded. The years following the revolution provided plentiful evidence that the Bolsheviks had overestimated popular desire for change. Far from welcoming the fact that they had become the focus of revolutionary expectations, peasants fiercely opposed requisitioning, and this generated a second level of the civil war. Bolsheviks used increasing violence to extort what little grain had been grown. Nature also added its pressure to the terrible situation: in 1921 a drought triggered serious famine, in which millions of peasants died.

## SERIOUSLY AND FOR A LONG TIME

Partly in response to this, the party changed tack. Lenin brought in the New Economic Policy, 'seriously and for a long time'. From 1921 the NEP re-introduced some elements of a market system to exist alongside state control of the more important sectors of the economy. This helped lay the basis for some economic revival, and increasing living standards. Picking up – though without acknowledging this – on some of the policy proposals which the Mensheviks had been promoting, the Bolsheviks now allowed peasants to sell some of their grain for private profit – though only after they had met their quotas for the state distribution system. More generally, there was a partial restoration of capitalist activity, although only within government-determined limits.

A recurring debate ever since has been whether this was a tactical retreat from the centralised approaches which communists were presumed to favour, but which they could not carry out in the face of armed opposition from peasants; or whether the NEP represented the emergence of the kinds of sensible and incremental policies that serious socialists had always wanted to pursue, which had become possible now that things were settling down after the unwanted pressures of foreign subversion and royalist counter-revolution.

Alongside the Bolsheviks' debates over such questions, new flagship programmes were still being promoted. But collectivisation would now rely on volunteers: Lenin bent the stick back, away from coercion. He now urged the gradual, merger of small private farms into large collective enterprises, on the basis of the agreement of the participating peasants, and proclaimed socialism as a system of 'civilised co-operation'.[8] Gosplan, the new economic co-ordination agency, anticipated the eventual dominance of centralised national planning, but at first had a strictly limited remit: Lenin's slogan 'communism is Soviet power plus electrification' signalled the need to focus on well-defined, deliverable programmes, rather than grander, utopian visions of the 'ism'.

The logic of NEP increased the scope for capitalist-type activity. Before long, a social layer of peasants began accumulating resources, such as livestock, machinery and buildings, and started employing other, poorer, peasants. New petty capitalists and traders sometimes showed off the fact that they were making a profit through acts of conspicuous consumption (one reason they had some money to spend was that Bolsheviks had placed limits on capital investment). These 'NEPmen' generated resentment. Concerns then arose amongst Bolsheviks that these developments could lay the basis for a challenge to workers' power. Some linked this risk to the social pluralism that was emerging, with 'non-party' people increasingly able to participate in the political system.

Against this backdrop, in summer 1923, a wave of strikes broke out. The fact that these were happening in a 'workers state' opened fraught debates. Different groupings took shape around a 'triumvirate' of the increasingly dominant leaders, Zinoviev, Kamenev and Stalin, who favoured NEP, and a loose opposition in which Trotsky and Yevgeni Preobrazhensky were key members. Polemics began about whether it was possible to 'plan through the market' or whether plan-

ning was about 'overcoming the market'. Pat Devine has summarised
the central arguments about industrialisation:

> If the country was to industrialise, it needed a surplus for investment.
> As the Soviet Union was unable to rely on help from abroad, due to
> the capitalist countries' boycott, this necessarily involved restricting
> consumption. Should this fall on the urban working class or the
> peasantry, and how rapid should be the pace of industrialisation be? [9]

Discussions within the party and amongst technical experts were
wide ranging, detailed and well considered. As later observers
have commented, the Soviet industrialisation debates of the 1920s
offered 'many anticipations of issues later familiar in development
economics'.[10] Significant figures favoured an incremental transition to
socialism during which market relations would continue, particularly
in farming. Pitched against them were those who advocated a much
more rapid industrialisation. The make-up of groupings in favour of
one policy course or another shifted and changed over time. Zinoviev
and Kamenev, for example, supported a conciliatory approach towards
peasants in 1924. But from 1925 to 1927 they attacked Stalin and
Bukharin for pursuing that very same policy.

Ordinary party members also changed their views and allegiances,
as they chose to follow one or other of the leading figures. Wings of
the party developed, and people found it expedient to note who was
allied with whom, and what they were arguing at particular times, for
future use in disputes and arguments.

Bukharin was a key spokesman for the view that accommodating
to the needs of the countryside was essential to Bolshevik survival
in what was still an overwhelmingly peasant country. His policy was
aimed at increasing agricultural productivity. The resulting surpluses
would then resource a rising curve of steady industrialisation. As well
as food for urban workers, a prosperous peasantry, 'enriching itself',
would supply cotton, wool and leather as raw materials for industry.[11]
Purchasing power in the countryside would create a growing market
for manufactured goods. This would enable both the private and state
sectors to 'grow into socialism' in mutually beneficial conditions of
market relations and civil peace.

In contrast, a Left Opposition continued to promote the need for
world revolution, alongside rapid industrialisation, and argued that

peasants should be organised into collectivised farms. The opposition showed its strength in a big demonstration – and was then suppressed – late in 1927. Its leaders, which now included Zinoviev and Kamenev as well as Trotsky, were expelled from leading committees, and in some cases from the party itself. (Trotsky was exiled and then expelled from the Soviet Union in 1929. The other leaders, whether or not they now presented their position as having been a mistake, almost all perished in the purges of the 1930s.)

Then, in an unexpected development, and to the opposition's surprise, Stalin suddenly moved to adopt its policies. This turn was partly in response to the failure of NEP to persuade the peasants to sell enough food to the cities, and demands from peasants for better terms of trade. After reintroducing grain requisitioning in 1928 and 1929, in 1929 the Central Committee decided to abandon NEP. There was now to be a 'Left Course' of industrialisation, linked to and based on an accelerated and forced collectivisation of the land and farms. Agricultural surplus had to be extracted in order to fund the rise of industry. This change of policy towards the countryside went alongside a policy of accelerated economic growth and infra-structure development, whose goals were set out in the first Five Year plan, adopted in 1928.

Stalin adopted these 'left' policies for very different reasons from those informing Trotsky when he had proposed them. A major ambition in Stalin's 'great break' was the consolidation of the ruling group which he now headed. Large-scale reorganisation of social relations would help underpin this. This meant changing the balance of blocks of social forces. Whole groups were to be made less important – the peasant-employers or 'kulaks' – while others would be made more important – peasants organised into collective farms, and industrial workers. Some social categories of people were to be grown – Soviet trained specialists – and others were to be reduced – 'bourgeois experts'. This would happen through extending and denying rights, opening up and closing down opportunities, providing and taking property – and by killing and execution.

Stalin pursued this social engineering at a faster pace than the once 'irresponsible' Trotsky had ever suggested. A key slogan of the time volunteered that 'nothing is impossible for a Bolshevik'. In the resulting mashing of Marxism, as Boris Groys recounts, 'any reference to facts, technical realities or objective limits was treated as "cowardice" and "unbelief": it was thought that will-power alone could overcome anything that the bureaucratic, formalistic eye perceived as an insurmountable obstacle'.[12]

At the beginning of 1930, within the space of a few weeks, around half of all Soviet peasants – sixty million people across a hundred thousand villages – were 'collectivised', their households reorganised into collective farms. This was a determined and brutal way of dealing with the tensions and contradictions between the lifestyles and aspirations of the peasants, and the ambition of the country's new political leadership, which was determined to push modernisation and industrialisation.

To justify such steps, Stalin contributed one of his rare 'theoretical' notions to the 'science' of 'Marxism-Leninism' which the party was now codifying (and fossilising). This was the view that, as societies headed towards the establishment of socialism, the class struggle would become more intense. This was a direct attack on Bukharin's conviction that the main threat from the organised forces of counter-revolution in Soviet Russia was now over, and that it was now possible to build a lasting civil peace, which meant that more consensual ways forward could be found.[13]

By contrast, Stalin argued the need to 'advance full steam ahead along the path of industrialisation – to socialism, leaving behind the age old "Russian" backwardness'.[14]

## THE CONTRADICTIONS OF SUCCESS

The First Five Year Plan, completed by 1932 – within four years – saw rapid employment growth. Mary McAuley summarises some of the social achievements:

> Hundreds of thousands, even millions of peasants and industrial workers, society's poor, had obtained an education and moved up to office work, to positions of authority, and management ... there were factory directors who in 1917 had been apprentices, there were women who had escaped from the drudgery of home and sweat shop, and become engineers, architects, doctors and NKVD officials.[15]

Members of this remarkable cohort began running the new nationally planned economy, delivering massive infrastructural projects

– including the Moscow Metro, new roads, canals, cities, factories and industries. The world they produced was represented to the public, both domestically and internationally, in the striking, innovative magazine *USSR In Construction*.[16]

Stalin was deeply committed to 'catching up' with the west: his desire for personal power was linked to this, and he may have convinced himself that the first goal depended on the second. Success built credibility. As Isaac Deutscher reflected in 1960, from having been one of the world's most backward and poverty-stricken nations, 'in many respects closer to India and China than to the west', the Soviet Union rose 'within the lifetime of a single generation', to become the world's second industrial power. The percentage of Soviet workers employed in modern industry rose from about ten per cent at the outset of the Stalin era to nearly fifty per cent by 1959.[17]

Such positive assessments of Stalin's industrialisation drive were by no means limited to card-carrying communists, or dissident Western Marxists. Winston Churchill's later judgement of Stalin was that 'he got the country armed with a plough, but left it with nuclear weapons'.

This progress was not achieved in an orderly way, but in a haphazard, brutal and destabilising fashion. It frequently looked as if the Soviet economy was heading for crisis. Big drives to confiscate grain led to widespread starvation and degradation. In Ukraine, with its relatively better-off peasantry, there was significant resistance to collectivisation and requisitioning. There was regular criticism of the rapid pace and helter-skelter character of Stalin's approaches, and these came by no means from 'usual' oppositionists'. In August 1932, the former Moscow party leader Martemyan Riutin, the son of peasants, took the brave step of publishing a critique of the reckless speed of industrialisation and the terrible and destructive effects of collectivisation. He wrote a document that directly identified Stalin as the author of these policies, and called for the destruction of both Stalin and his leadership group. Interpreting this as a call for his assassination, Stalin demanded that Riutin be executed, but members of the Politburo, including the Leningrad party leader Sergei Kirov, objected. Riutin and associates were merely expelled from the party and banished from Moscow. (In 1937 he was executed in the purges.) William Taubman, while acknowledging that his comment 'sounds like an oxymoron', argues that such protests suggest that a 'moderate Stalinism' was possible – that 'some Bolsheviks who had backed using force and violence up to 1929 now tried to draw the line'.[18]

Many of the 'moderate Stalinists' of 1932 would have cause to regret not having moved decisively against Stalin's leadership at this moment. Most of them were to perish in the purges. Stalin resented criticisms from those he had promoted, and he was not prepared to accept open debate about how to proceed, preferring to win his position through repression. As he consolidated his power, bureaucracy usurped all hope of democracy; the short-term effectiveness of hierarchy displaced the value of equality; and edicts requiring conformity in science, the arts and intellectual life took the place of critical debate about all pressing issues.

Alongside these developments at the top of the party, there was a cultural shift throughout Soviet politics. Organising tens of thousands of inexperienced new party members for major development projects wasn't easy: things went wrong – and that needed explaining. Leaders at all levels now began characterising ordinary people thought to be responsible for the most minor lapses of effort and attitude as 'saboteurs'; and this became a convenient way of attacking political opponents or members of national minorities. For some, the notes which they had made during the factionalising of the 1920s now proved useful: selectively quoted, they could serve to defend one's own position – and to attack other people.

The repression was ratcheted up after December 1934, when Sergei Kirov was shot in his Leningrad office. The murder of this long-prominent and popular Bolshevik leader may or may not have been arranged by Stalin (as many have argued), but he certainly put the event to good use. A mania developed for identifying 'enemies of the people'. Resulting 'purges' were widespread, with the NKVD arresting 'spies', 'wreckers' and 'traitors' in successive and terrifying waves of repression.

From the mid-1930s, all the arguments which had animated the Bolshevik government in its early years were now 'decided' and buried through terror. No reasoned consideration determined the positives and negatives in the debates between Stalin and Bukharin, Preobrazhensky and Zinoviev: these were 'resolved' by the crude dispatch of many of the left's most remarkable intellects to the unmarked grave. Stalin eventually executed almost every nationally-prominent Bolshevik participant from the revolution of 1917, alongside a large number of foreign communists living in Moscow. Through this baroque and murderous turmoil, women and men were brutalised, humiliated and destroyed. Some were cynically tricked into hoping against hope that the promises of their torturers might be kept: that, if they confessed, their families would be spared; that if they confessed, they might live to see their loved ones again. The cellars of the NKVD's headquarters, the Lubyanka, were a long way from the hopes and promises of the Enlightenment.

The repressive nature of Stalin's regime meant that the 'success' of the Soviet drive to industrialisation was wholly tarnished and discredited, not least because of its condemnation of millions of people to a life of forced labour, and this judgement came to be shared by many communists.[19] During the worst years of Stalinism, prisoners arrested through the purges were transferred to mines and forests across the Soviet Union, where they faced a gruelling and degrading time. Many camps were in remote places with severe weather conditions against which prisoners were not protected. Some of the worst were in Kolyma, in the far east of the country, an enormous area with the coldest temperature in the northern hemisphere, 'so desolate and isolated that in 1927 there were only 7,580 inhabitants in an area five or six times the size of France'.[20]

The scale of the terror that resulted from 'the Stalin system', both in Russia, and in later variants under Mao and elsewhere, cannot be downplayed by anyone concerned with progressive politics. There can be no 'bleaching language' employed as a way to 're-describe mass murder'.[21] It may therefore seem unnecessary to even note the debates about its actual scale. A lower estimation of the numbers of those exiled, imprisoned, sentenced to forced labour or killed through the repressions of Stalinism could seem to be a downplaying of what happened. But even the most modest figures that all must allow provide the basis for damning judgement of Stalin's rule. As Moshe Lewin concludes, 'we are left with quite enough horrors to condemn what needs to be condemned'.[22]

The numbers incarcerated in the gulag system grew rapidly from 20,000 in 1928 to around a million in 1934. Thereafter, 'turnover' meant that there were normally about one million people being held at any one time, though the population peaked at 2.5 million in 1952. Anne Applebaum, a very careful sifter of the evidence, concludes that:

Between 1929, when the camps first began to expand, and 1953, when Stalin died ... some 18 million people passed through the system. In addition, a further six or seven million were sent not to camps but into exile. In total, that means that up to 25 million people had some experience of arrest in Stalin's Soviet Union, or about 15 percent of the population. Add to that the POWs who worked in the system, and the numbers grow even higher, to a total of 28.7 million.[23]

Applebaum calculates that between 1929 and 1953 around ten per cent of prisoners died in the camps of the Gulag and in the exile villages: she gives a figure of 2,749,163 people.[24]

The mass murder of Soviet citizens that took place under Stalin is understandably put forward as a major, and historically evidenced, argument against anyone who wants now to propose Marxist political projects. But those who want to equate communism with Stalinism face a range of difficulties. One is that:

[many] victims of Stalinism were [themselves] communist revolutionaries who protested against bureaucratic travesties and the degradation of Soviet democracy. In order to stabilise his regime, Stalin was to kill more communists and socialists than his absolutist predecessor, the Tsar.[25]

Just as there were many communists opposed to Stalin inside the Soviet Union, there have always been Marxists and liberal communists who have completely condemned the whole system. But it also has to be recognised that far too many have sought to excuse or even deny what happened.

## ASSESSING STALINISM: MORAL CHOICES IN 'THE AGE OF EXTREMES'

People on the radical left have had to return again and again to the issue of Stalinist atrocities: the crimes, the deaths and the corruption of the movement's animating ideals. In order to sustain their arguments in the face of such a terrible record they have taken different positions.

One shameful response has been simple denial, through such

grotesque assertions as that the 'claims' of Stalinist terror are fabricated by the enemies of socialism, and amount to little more than counter-revolutionary propaganda. This refusal or inability to recognise simple truth was often wheeled out as a 'communist' argument before 1956, and loyal supporters went through contortions to marshall 'facts' in line with such arguments. This view is not heard as frequently today as it once was.

A more familiar stance is to explain Stalinism as 'a lesser evil'. Here it is accepted that 'abuses' did take place, but argued that these must be judged in the context of the wider positive achievements: 'you can't make an omelette without breaking eggs'. The decision to use terror is seen as arising from a desire to start, accelerate or short-circuit social processes which had not been delivering what they should: force was a way to impose a broadly positive political direction. Its 'expense' in terms of human suffering, and the way it corroded the morality of the revolutionary cause, then becomes downplayed or forgotten. In spite of it all, so the argument goes, the political direction was correct.

This argument can be summed up as 'wrong things were done, but for the right reasons'. This approach assesses Soviet communism as a kind of wager. In Slavoj Zizek's account of the rationale, 'the present terror will be retroactively justified if the society that emerges from it proves to be truly human'.[26] In a more prosaic version of this thinking, Stalin becomes Russia's moderniser, forcing through essential indus-trialisation, albeit at enormous cost.

Here communism can be understood as highlighting classic moral choices that were keenly felt by many men and women during the 'age of extremes' that constituted the twentieth century. As Neal Ascherson puts it, the options were experienced as:

> whether to sacrifice a society's today for a 'brighter tomorrow', whether to ally with the lesser evil to overcome the greater, whether to shed innocent blood as the price of breaking humanity's chains.[27]

The moral framework which results from such choices allows people to view issues as if things can be balanced out: people witness appalling destitution, waste and murder, but discount these against their vision of a positive future. People recognise that awful acts are being carried out, but judge these as historically necessary steps on the path to better times – or as 'excesses' of a kind bound to happen in a currently imperfect world. The challenges and contradictions in this stance shaped the moral culture of a movement which derived its strength from ethical principles, but was prepared to stand back from 'operationalising' those principles in particular circumstances.

This willingness to suspend moral judgement must be understood as linked to the idea that people are means to an end. On the basis of envisaging future people, beautiful ones, who are not yet born, good people could explain to themselves the unfortunate short cuts they felt obliged to take. In a poem which communicates the communist mind-set, Bertolt Brecht stated that 'we who wanted to prepare the ground for friendliness could not ourselves be friendly'.[28]

Another way of responding to Stalinism's crimes is to focus blame on one current of communism, and insist that it is not the true representative of the tradition: the problem is 'Stalinism' rather than communism. This argument is given some credibility by the large numbers of Marxists who were killed by Stalinised Marxist regimes, and the existence of long-term communist projects free of repressive elements, but it runs the risk of not fully recognising that Stalinism came out of a communist way of thinking that contained within it the seeds for potential dictatorship.

An extreme form of the approach that seeks to focus blame as narrowly as possible is the personalisation of the issue so it becomes the responsibility of an individual figure: Stalin was 'evil', a monstrous cynic who knew that people were starving, that large numbers of innocents were being sent to the Gulag, and that the condemned at the show trials were innocent.

It *is* crucial to weigh the personal role of Stalin. But 'evil' will not do as a characterisation of the wider phenomenon known as Stalinism. And it will do even less as an explanation. To define something or someone as 'evil' is not so much to explain it as to give up on the possibility of explanation. 'Evil' repositions the things we fear and oppose into a zone of inexplicability.

From the 1950s, an increasing number of communists sought to shape a new formula for their politics. They attempted to take their distance from Stalinism, and – while giving critical support to the Soviet state in spite of the way in had developed – to keep their main focus on problems of inequality and oppression in their own countries. This is an example of a wider political practice whereby people seek to overlook a particular flawed expression of a general set of grand ambitions in which they want to continue to believe. Communists' critical defence of the particular expression of their politics in the Soviet Union was a way of staying loyal to their overall programme and hopes. People could be fiercely opposed to 'aspects' of what was going on but believe none the less in the originating impulses of the Soviet project – and in its potential for renewal.

## HERETICS AND BUREAUCRATS

Important analyses of the sources of Stalinist arrogance have been offered by many who have made the heretical effort, attempting to stay true to the general hopes of communism, whilst criticising and moving away from the particular forms in which they were currently expressed. One of the best-known efforts of this kind is represented by the work of Trotsky, from the time of his defeat in the inner-party struggles in the Soviet Union, through his years of exile up until his murder in 1940. It will always be important to consider Trotsky's incisive analyses of 'the revolution betrayed'. But his high profile has obscured the thinking of other anti-Stalinist oppositionists.

Christian Rakovsky, for example, was an important Left Opposition figure who at the same time disagreed with Trotsky on key issues. For Trotsky, the revolution's degeneration was mainly to do with Russian backwardness, the numerical weakness of the working class, the isolation of the new state and its encirclement by capitalists. For Rakovsky, the danger was inherent in the position of the working class as the new directing class. The potential for bureaucratisation and corruption 'would continue to exist ... even if ... the country was inhabited only by proletarian masses and the exterior was made up solely of proletarian states'.[29] Rakovsky identified what he saw as the 'professional dangers of power', which resulted from the existence of different degrees of preparedness and competence to lead, govern and organise – caused by uneven levels of political culture, understanding and commitment.

Even this reality did not necessarily lead to bureaucratisation in a negative sense. Whether this happened or not depended on a range of other variables. A degree of modesty was one, for, as Rakovsky stated, 'no class has ever been born in possession of the art of government'. Historically, 'there has always been a lack of harmony between the political capabilities of any given class, its administrative ability, and the judicial constitutional forms that it establishes for its own use after the taking of power'. Exploring how bureaucracy arises, Rakovsky argued that 'when a class takes power, one of its parts becomes the agent of that power': 'this differentiation begins as a functional one. It later becomes a social one'.[30]

The result of this is that the bureaucracy – the directing layer in the economy, the party and the state – ceases to be part of the class and constitutes itself on the basis of a new order, becoming 'a new social category'. The necessary response is 'a long and delicate process' of political education for the dominant class.[31] Such themes were echoed and developed in the work of Antonio Gramsci, who also recognised that inherent tendencies towards bureaucratisation were built into socialist politics – and needed to be consciously limited from the outset.

Victor Serge also developed similar arguments. In his first-hand accounts of how the rising bureaucracy squandered the radical potential present at the beginning of the revolution, Serge argued that the mistakes and flaws which Bolshevism wove into its political fabric came from turning lamentable necessities into virtues. But he did not see Stalinism as arising inevitably from communism. In 1937, he summarised the 'decoupling' position:

> It is often said that 'the germ of all Stalinism was in Bolshevism at its beginning'. Well, I have no objection. Only, Bolshevism also contained many other germs – a mass of other germs – and those who lived through the enthusiasm of the first years of the first victorious revolution ought not to forget it. To judge the living man by the death germs which the autopsy reveals in the corpse – and which he may have carried with him since his birth – is this very sensible?[32]

## NOTES

1. Vladimir Lenin, 'Better Fewer, But Better', *Pravda*, 4 March 1923.
2. Eric Hobsbawm, *How to Change the World*, Little, Brown, London 2011, p285.
3. E.H. Carr, 'The Dialectics of Stalinism', *Times Literary Supplement*, 10 June 1949.
4. A. Katsenellenboigen, quoted in Alec Nove, *The Economics of Feasible Socialism*, Allen and Unwin, London 1983, p33.

5. The famous phrase comes from Marx's *Eighteenth Brumaire of Louis Bonaparte*, published in 1852.

6. Leon Trotsky, *Terrorism and Communism*, 1920. As Victor Serge pointed out, the book's title risks being misunderstood: 'Trotsky does not defend what is usually meant by terrorism, but does demonstrate the unconditional necessity for the working class to prove its strength and its ability to use all the severities of war, in those revolutionary periods when its only choice is to win or die': 'Twice Met', *International Socialism*, 20, spring 1965 [1938].

7. Nikolai Bukharin, Seventh Party Congress, March 1918.

8. Lenin, 'On Co-operation' [1923]. This phase of policy is usefully summarised by Moshe Lewin, *The Soviet Century*, Verso, London 2005, pp299-300.

9. Pat Devine, 'Reviews', *Twentieth Century Communism*, 2, 2010, p240. Devine is reviewing Maurice Dobb, *The Development of Socialist Economic Thought*, Lawrence and Wishart, London 2008.

10. Phil Leeson, 'Development economics and the study of development' in Leeson and Martin Minogue (eds), *Perspectives on Development*, Manchester University Press, Manchester 1988, p6.

11. In a speech to Moscow party activists in April 1925, Bukharin argued that peasants should pursue their direct and immediate economic interests; argued that this would be positive for broader efforts to build socialism; and opposed more 'leftist' attitudes: 'accumulation is needed in the peasant economy ... Even now certain remnants of war-communist relations can be found in our country, which are hindering to our further growth. One of these is the fact that the prosperous upper stratum of the peasantry, and the middle peasants, who are also striving for prosperity, are currently afraid to accumulate. This leads to the position where the peasant is afraid to buy an iron roof for fear that he will be declared a kulak; if he buys a machine, he makes certain that the communists do not see it. Advanced technology has become a matter for conspiracy ... Overall, we need to say to the entire peasantry, to all its different strata: enrich yourselves, accumulate, develop your farms'. Translated by Francis King. Material at http://www.korolevperevody.co.uk/korolev/obogash-chaytes.html. Accessed 1 May 2017.

12. Boris Groys, *The Total Art of Stalinism*, Verso, London 2011, p60.

13. Stephen Cohen, *Bukharin and the Bolshevik Revolution*, Oxford University Press, Oxford 1980, p203.

14. Joseph Stalin, 'A Year of Great Change', *Pravda*, 7 November 1929.

15. Mary McAuley, *Soviet Politics 1917-1991*, Oxford University Press, Oxford 1992, pp3-4. NKVD was the acronym of the People's Commissariat for Internal Affairs. The Cheka later became GPU and then OGPU.

16. The journal *USSR In Construction*, founded in 1931, was published in

several languages. It celebrated and promoted industrial and economic achievements.

17. Isaac Deutscher, *The Great Contest*, Oxford University Press, London 1960, p2.
18. William Taubman, *Khrushchev*, Simon and Schuster, New York NY 2003, pp76-7.
19. Maurice Cornforth, *Communism and Philosophy*, Lawrence and Wishart, London 1980, p206.
20. John Glad, 'Foreword', Varlam Shalamov, *Kolyma Tales*, WW Norton and Company, London 1980, p8.
21. This charge is levelled at the 'new communists' Slavoj Zizek and Alain Badiou by Alan Johnson, *World Affairs*, May – June 2012.
22. Moshe Lewin, *The Soviet Century*, Verso, London 2005, p4.
23. Anne Applebaum, *Hoover Digest*, 1, 2005.
24. Anne Applebaum, *Gulag*, Penguin, London 2003, p520.
25. Tariq Ali, *The Idea of Communism*, Seagull Books, London, 2009, p48.
26. Slavoj Zizek, 'Introduction', Maximilien Robespierre, *Virtue and Terror*, Verso, London 2007, pxiii.
27. Neal Ascherson, 'Raging towards Utopia', *London Review of Books*, 22 April 2010.
28. Bertolt Brecht, 'To those who come after us', written around 1938.
29. Christian Rakovsky, 'The Professional Dangers of Power', *Selected Writings on Opposition in the USSR 1923-30*, Allison and Busby, London 1980 [1928].
30. For discussion of Rakovsky's perspectives, see Gus Fagan, 'Introduction', Christian Rakovsky, ibid.
31. Rakovsky, op cit.
32. Victor Serge, writing in 1937, quoted by Peter Sedgwick, 'Translator's Introduction', Victor Serge, *Memoirs of a Revolutionary*, New York Review Books, New York NY, 2012, pxxx.

# 10. 'Popular Fronts' and the war of position

## LEARNING FROM DEFEAT

At the end of the 1920s, taking their cue from the Comintern, communist parties in most countries had adopted a sectarian position known as 'class against class': they were very unwilling to work in alliance with social-democratic parties, which they saw as objectively serving the interests of the class enemy. But from the mid-1930s this attitude began to change, partly because of the overwhelming need to unite against the threat of fascism, and partly because it had become ever more clear that working-class take-over in countries outside the Soviet Union was not on the cards for the foreseeable future. It was therefore necessary to adapt communist positions to find ways of bringing about change within capitalist societies at the same time as working out new strategies for wider system change. It also became clear that the Soviet Union was going to continue for some time to be the only communist country, and 'internationalism' often now became understood as being synonymous with the interests of the Soviet state.

The shift to a less sectarian form of politics was pioneered in France. Right-wing anti-parliamentarian riots in Paris in 1934 shocked communists into working with other parties to defend democracy from the fascist and far right threat. Given these threats, the new priority was to defend the context within which it was possible to express left politics, not to push left politics to the degree that others on the centre and right might turn to an authoritarian option. As support for fascism grew in the 1930s, collaborative initiatives of different forms, and on different scales, were developed in a number of countries.

The major event which had spurred communists in this direction was the Nazi takeover of power in Germany in 1933. It would have been a rejection of every living impulse in Marxism had communists failed to react fundamentally to the rise of Adolf Hitler. As the Hungarian communist Georg Lukacs said: 'the experiences of the struggle against fascism [had to] lead the democratic left to criticise its own previous practice'.[1]

It was now recognised that the German Communist Party, which had a large membership and substantial support, had made a number of self-defeating mistakes in the lead-up to the Nazi take-over. Their overarching belief that socialism could only come through insurrectionary revolution had meant that their considerable constituency of members and voters had not participated fully in the democratic structures of the Weimar republic, set up after the war. As Donald Sassoon puts it, their weight had been subtracted from Weimar democracy rather than added to it.[2] Before 1933, the party's main target had been the social-democrats, who were seen as blocking the road to revolution.[3] But now, after a final flurry of continuing self-delusion, communists finally recognised that Hitler's rule was catastrophic. The party was suppressed almost immediately, and its activists were killed or thrown into prison camps, as part of a wider wave of repression against left-wingers and trade unionists.

Divisions had weakened the left and allowed the Nazis to build their strength. Working-class unity was therefore now the goal, as a basis for alliances of 'all progressive forces' around jointly-agreed programmes. These would not propose socialism immediately, but aim for limited and realisable goals. Within this – and in order to do this – communists had to learn to connect to people's actual views and feelings, rather than dismissing these as 'reactionary lies' or 'false consciousness'.

At the Seventh Congress of the Comintern, in 1935, the shift to a popular front strategy was agreed. (It should be noted that part of the context for this was the Soviet Union's need to defend itself from attack by Germany and hence to find allies internationally.) This shift was partly made possible because, although the Comintern had sought the imposition of a general model, it had in fact always been refracted through a variety of social conditions and perceptions. Over time, these had inevitably produced different approaches, reactions and outcomes. The Comintern had never been as monolithic as some historians have argued; nor did its constituent parties always wait for a signal from Moscow before taking independent initiatives.

In the mid-1930s, recent experiences and initiatives in a number of different countries now found expression in the new politics, which also recognised communist parties as legitimate players in a wide variety of national political contexts. Reminding delegates that Lenin had written positively about 'national pride', Georgi Dimitrov, the Bulgarian communist leader who was a leading proponent of the new approach, argued that:

> proletarian internationalism must, so to speak, 'acclimatise itself' in each country in order to sink deep roots in its native land. National forms of the proletarian class struggle and of the labour movement in the individual countries are in no contradiction to proletarian internationalism; on the contrary, it is in precisely these forms that the international interests of the proletariat can be successfully defended.[4]

Nazism, like Italian fascism, had connected to and articulated a sense of national humiliation after the first world war. Rather than compound that sense by promoting 'anti-national' politics, the left's task was to itself connect to the anxieties and frustrations that could be articulated in reactionary nationalism, and then channel them in progressive ways. This would involve telling *progressive* national stories. It was time to counter the caricature of the radical left as servants of a foreign power and alien ideology.[5]

The movement now increasingly saw itself as the most consistent defender of 'bourgeois democratic' values. Communists also promoted national liberation as a 'democratic' cause for oppressed countries, mixing class anger with popular desires for independence. This formula was highly attractive to emerging leaders in the colonised countries, who sought freedom, and, in the process, to overthrow the national elites who colluded with the imperial powers.

Suggestions that communists should focus their energies on proposing democratic reforms, at least in some circumstances, were not new. But in the late 1920s, these had been knocked down as 'rightist deviations'.

By 1934, a few leaders, including the Italian communist Palmiro Togliatti, who was living in exile in Moscow, recognised that fascism had in large part been mobilised as a way of resisting the 'threat' of workers' revolution. Particular capitalist interests had supported

fascism in order to smash labour movements, in what could be understood as a pre-emptive strike. A critical evaluation of communism's
early record in Italy and Germany might conclude that the result of
its assertive agitation had been to provoke effective opposition from
the right, with utterly disastrous results for the workers' movement
and internationalist hopes, and for those large sections of the population who would suffer murderous oppression under fascism, including
Roma people, gays, and Jews.

Following Togliatti's lead, communists identified fascism as the
politics of the most reactionary elements of the bourgeoisie, and
distinguished these sections from others who remained committed to
democratic processes. Appeals for alliances were based on the view
that there were deeply progressive resources within bourgeois culture.
There was recognition that the values, procedures and cultures of
liberal democracy were a powerful and necessary tool in the struggle
against what had now become the main enemy: a fascist and anti-
democratic form of capitalism. Substantial sections of the bourgeoisie
were themselves casting aside bourgeois legitimacy if their interests
so required, as in Italy, Germany and Spain. This created political
space for the left to take the banner. Communists would now follow a
new political formula: they would be democrats, genuinely allied with
all other democrats, against the fascists. Communists now once more
sought to harness commitment to democracy to a determination to
replace capitalism, rather than seeing democracy as a bourgeois diversion from that goal.

This Popular Front approach was a re-centring, if not a fundamental re-founding, of the communist movement. It was now a key
tenet that communism needed to incorporate democracy in order
to counter fascism, and to pre-empt further reactionary backlashes
to the rising power of the working class. Making the revolutionary
party the best defender of bourgeois democracy would be a base for
further progress. Democratic process and language could underpin,
and deliver, the socialist programme: there would be a strong relationship between the content of the politics and the form of its
delivery.

From the start, opponents of communism criticised this new
approach. Right-wingers presented the Popular Front as a duplicitous cover for the real intent of communism, which they believed
remained undemocratic and repressive: Marxists were seen as using

new language to manipulate and fool people. This argument was developed further after the second world war, when the US and West European powers provided substantial support and assistance to non-Marxist social-democratic parties in order to oppose the communists, and sought to make 'freedom' and 'market society' into interchangeable terms.

For some who saw themselves as being to the left of the communists, such as Trotsky's followers, the turn to bourgeois norms of political practice was evidence of 'sell-out'. For them, the Popular Front was the abandonment of revolutionary politics, which could only be expressed in a commitment to build counter-institutions of dual power opposed to the structures of parliamentary democracy.

Eighteen years on from the Russian revolution, Popular Front approaches did indeed amount to a recognition that the 1917 model was not universally applicable. Different strategies were needed for left advance in other national contexts. This recognition led towards the idea of diverse 'national roads' – including 'parliamentary roads' – to socialism.

The change of strategy soon yielded positive results. In France, a broad left-wing coalition supported by communists won the general election in 1936. Although in the end it held office for scarcely a year, it was able to introduce a range of progressive measures, which set the standard for postwar settlements across Western Europe; these included paid holidays, a forty-hour week, collective bargaining rights, increased wages and greater state control in the economy.

Popular Frontism showed that alliance-building could be an effective form of politics, and a good way to win support and define issues. In Togliatti's later summation, such an approach would be centred on the 'policy of the working class in struggle for democracy and socialism', with the capability of the Communist Party consisting 'in knowing just how to isolate the most reactionary groups, even in the bourgeoisie, through an extensive and flexible system of alliances, convergences, neutralisations, and so on'.[6]

The fact that communism's goal was to transcend current social relations did not mean that the appropriate strategic approach had to be head-on confrontation. Patient and pragmatic attempts to persuade and win support were more likely to succeed. After all, those who seek to make politics only with those with whom they are in agreement on every aspect of programme and tactics are doomed to be lonely.

During the 1930s, many liberals were attracted to Popular Front politics, for overlapping and sometimes contradictory reasons: for some, an association with communism gave their own politics a dangerous edge, while others thought they would be able to 'tame' communists; for most, the fundamental challenges of the time suggested that communism was a necessary defence against the all too real threat of fascism, and thus a way of guaranteeing liberalism.[7] The usual meeting place between communists and liberals was in 'front organisations'. This phrase is often taken to mean that communists were hiding themselves, disguising their presence to cynically draw in unwitting potential sympathisers. Communists were cast as latching on to popular causes for secretive, nefarious, Leninist, ends. In fact, communists increasingly saw honesty and preparedness to learn from others as necessary starting points for the delivery of social change. When this was legally possible, they almost always operated openly, seeking to show how people holding to different ideologies could campaign successfully together on the issues where their concerns and goals overlapped.

In 1936, with Italy and Germany already living under fascist rule, the European democratic crisis deepened when Spanish fascists led by Franco declared war on the democratically elected Popular Front government.[8] This was the start of the Spanish civil war. The Popular Front government had only a very narrow majority, and Spain was a new democracy, and this made the government's position very fragile. Germany and Italy supported Franco from the beginning, and contributed substantially to his military effort, including through the supply of weapons and troops. Franco's nationalists army quickly took control of a swathe of northern Spain, and by March 1937 had extended control down the west of the country.

The Spanish Communist Party had already helped to establish grassroots Popular Front committees to support the government, and as precursors of more advanced and extended forms of democracy. Now it rallied workers' militias to fight against Franco's forces. At national level, it participated in government, but it refrained from claiming the most important positions, concentrating instead on maintaining the unity of republican forces. It supported private farmers who were land owners, and rejected what it saw as the adventurist radicalism of the anarchists, with their calls for takeovers of land and the setting up of agrarian collectives. Communists argued that the immediate task was not to bring about a socialist revolution, but to defend the democratic parliamentary republic. The party grew rapidly during the war, from 250,000 members at the end of 1936 to nearly 400,000 by June 1937. Half of this membership served in the Republican army, meaning that communists constituted around a third of the government troops fighting against Franco.

All this was in line with the Comintern's 1935 position on the importance of communist support for democratic rights and for a radical left version of nationalism, articulated within a wider internationalist framework. Spain was seen as the battleground between progress and reaction, between democracy and fascism, and between decency and the threat of barbarism. It quickly became the focus for an impressive movement of international solidarity.

Communists from many countries gained credibility and moral authority across the left and liberal spectrum through their campaigns in support of democracy in Spain. This included organising international brigades of volunteers to fight in support of the elected Spanish government; wider solidarity campaigns in support of the republican war effort; cultural initiatives; and campaigns against the 'non-interventionism' of the British and French governments: communists demonstrated how this supposedly 'hands-off' position – which included an embargo on supplying arms to a legitimately elected government – amounted to objective support for Franco, given that he was being so heavily supported by Germany and Italy.

## RETHINKING COMMUNIST PRACTICE

As the movement was reshaping itself in the mid-1930s, one of its greatest leaders was finishing important work – though in utter isolation, and with no impact at the time. Antonio Gramsci, the imprisoned leader of the Italian communists, had set himself the task, among many other things, of understanding why his party had been unable to prevent the rise of fascism in Italy, and to think seriously about how communists might conduct politics in societies where civil society was more developed than in Russia, and where revolutionary rupture was not an immediate prospect.[9] After the second world war, selections from his prison notebooks – which were smuggled to Moscow for safe keeping after his death – were published in many editions and languages and became very influential on the communist and wider left.

Gramsci was a founder member of the Italian Communist Party (PCI). He was elected to its central committee at the founding congress in January 1921, and then spent time in Moscow representing Italy at the Comintern headquarters. After Mussolini took power in 1922, he persuaded the party to adopt the policy of a united front. He was elected to parliament in 1924, aiming to try and help defeat fascist authoritarianism and introduce elements of democracy into his country. Later the same year, he became leader of the party. In 1926 he was arrested by the fascist government in spite of the parliamentary immunity that should have protected him, and thereafter he spent the rest of his life in prison, save for his last eighteen months under military guard in a Rome clinic, terminally ill. He died in 1937.

Gramsci's politics were formed in the era of revolutionary Leninism and the big strikes and occupations which took place in Milan and Turin during and after the first world war. During the 'two red years' of 1919-20 he was very involved in the factory councils that developed within the major industrial enterprises in northern Italy, seeing them as the potential building blocks for a revolutionary challenge similar to that of the soviets. But the movement was contained in the big cities of the north, and eventually defeated. The government put troops into the factories before the argument that capitalism should be overthrown could take hold. It was the fascists who then took over Italy, not the communists.

Gramsci's political insights derived from reflecting on why all this had happened furnished the elements for a potentially more effective left political strategy (largely promoted at first through the efforts of his close comrade Togliatti, main leader of the Italian Communist Party after Gramsci's arrest, who drew heavily on Gramsci's work). Gramsci and Togliatti saw that the defeat suffered by the factory occupation movement had involved strategic failures; workers had been led to the brink of a violent conflict which they did not have the political resources to win.[10] Gramsci's efforts to understand why the factory councils of Italy had not achieved the same success as the soviets in Russia led him to a broader consideration of the social and cultural differences between the two countries:

> the determination which in Russia was direct and drove the masses into the streets for a revolutionary uprising, in central and western Europe is complicated by all these political superstructures, created

by the greater development of capitalism. This makes the action of the masses slower and more prudent, and therefore requires of the revolutionary party a strategy and tactics altogether more complex and long term than those which were necessary for the Bolsheviks in the period between March and November 1917.[11]

As the Marxist writer Jack Lindsay would later state, this was 'the beginnings of an analysis that makes possible a successful struggle in advanced industrialised countries', and provided the basis for understanding that democratic decision-making is both valuable in itself and consistent with revolutionary politics.[12]

One of Gramsci's most important insights was that the dominant classes in society rule through the means of hegemony, and the use both of coercion and of strategies to win consent. One aspect of hegemonic rule is the promotion by the dominant classes of their own understanding of how the world works, so that they try to make this the natural common sense of the whole society. The task for the working-class party is to construct what might be termed an alternative hegemonic alliance and an alternative common sense, so that the working class can emerge from its subaltern position to assume the leadership of the whole of society. This was a very different proposition from either simple electoral politics or notions of revolutionary takeover. Gramsci remained committed to the idea of a transformative social revolution, and was clear that this would require 'confronting in the final resort the repressive apparatus of the bourgeois state'.[13] But he saw that progress towards this goal would involve a long-term 'war of position' through intellectual and cultural advance and building up support for radical change, rather than 'a war of manoeuvre' in the form of an uprising. A key task was to understand the significance of molecular social processes for the prosecution of revolutionary strategy over an extended period of time.

The concept of hegemony means rethinking the kind of struggle necessary in complex societies, where rule is maintained through consent as well as coercion: socialists have to reflect on and contest the cultural means by which a ruling class establishes, consolidates and extends its leadership and domination, steering society in directions which suit its own interests but are presented as the interests of all groups. Under capitalism, workers' active participation in capitalist social structures and processes makes the task of developing an alternative hegemonic project particularly difficult. Developing radical politics cannot simply be a matter of removing a veil so that those oppressed can cast off indoctrination and instantly see things clearly. Ideology is interwoven into and constitutive of day to day life. Working towards a new settlement is therefore really challenging. As Gramsci stated:

> there must be a 'political hegemony' even before assuming government power, and in order to exercise political leadership or hegemony one must not count solely on the power and the material force that is given by government.[14]

Gramsci was very important to the political activist and cultural studies pioneer Stuart Hall, who drew on, and developed, many of the Italian's ideas in his own work. In the 1980s, Hall listed some of the implications of the concept of hegemony that had helped him understand Thatcherism's project to establish a new hegemonic settlement. This had involved:

> the struggle to contest and disorganise an existing political formation; the taking of the 'leading position' (on however minority a basis) over a number of different spheres of society at once – economy, civil society, intellectual and moral life, culture; the conduct of a wide and differentiated type of struggle; the winning of a strategic measure of popular consent; and, thus, the securing of a social authority sufficiently deep to conform society into a new historic project.[15]

Gramsci's understanding of political change also involved an expanded conception of the state, which he saw as being open to popular pressure: this was one of his many partial breaks with 'Leninism'. In discussing the changing relationship between the state in the narrow sense and in the wider context of civil society, he recognised that force and consent are never separated but are always interrelated.[16]

Partly because of his more expansive approach to politics, a great deal of Gramsci's work is concerned with culture. Some have suggested that this was an unfortunate and imposed necessity, resulting from his isolation in prison. But this does not account for the consistency with which Gramsci applied himself to cultural topics: nor does it do justice to the specificity of his thinking about cultural issues, 'which is above all remarkable for its refusal to divide culture from history and politics'.[17] As Terry Eagleton writes, for Gramsci: "'Marxist criticism" signified not primarily the interpretation of literary texts but the cultural emancipation of the masses'.[18]

Education of others, and of oneself, was crucial political work. If communists were to succeed they needed analysis that would enable them to create the preconditions for progress in a world dominated by hostile power, and to sustain support for radical change for decades ahead; they also needed historical understanding, the capacity for critical thinking, cultural sensitivity and a high ethical awareness. For Gramsci 'organic intellectuals' would play a key role here: these were thinker-activists who were fully part of the working-class movement but who, through membership of the party, could achieve the critical distance from the pressures of daily living and ruling-class ideology that would enable them to think strategically and find the ways ahead.

Some of these insights returned in significant ways to the Menshevik critique of Bolshevism. And they were being developed at the same time as the growth of the Popular Front understanding that communists needed to develop forms of leadership that were different from the Leninist model of 1917. Instead of willing a revolution into being through applying a correct line, the job was to seed and feed progressive impulses. For the Popular Front activists this meant working to defend democracy in broad organisations, and accepting the accountability and discipline that came with that. Gramsci's ideas were to become very important for the PCI in the period immediately after the second world war, when, having played an important role in the partisan movement's defeat of fascism, defence and extension of the new Italian democracy became central to its programme.

## THE TEST OF WAR

Following the defeat of the Spanish republic in April 1939, the threat of war loomed over Europe. Then, in August, after it had failed in its efforts to persuade other governments to join in establishing a security alliance against Hitler, in a surprise move the Soviet Union signed a non-aggression pact with Nazi Germany. This most spectacular of 'zigzags' alienated many of the supporters the Comintern had gathered through the Popular Front years. It was a clear example of the Soviet state putting its own defence above all other interests, and the situation was made worse by its characterisation of the war, when it finally broke out in September, as one of inter-imperialist rivalry. Communist parties the world over duly signed up for this analysis, however, and at first opposed the conduct of the war. Eventually, in June 1941, the Nazi invasion of the Soviet Union brought the Soviet Union into the war, and after this its valiant battles succeeded in generating huge sympathy for the Russian people, and the Soviet Union began to re-establish its position as the key force opposing fascism. From January 1943, when General Zhukov's soldiers inflicted a major defeat on the invading German armies at Stalingrad – a turning point in the course of the war – the Soviet Union's moral prestige grew ever stronger. Its conduct of the war also re-established the regime's legitimacy in the eyes of Soviet people themselves, while membership of communist parties around the world grew rapidly.

Communists' support for the Soviet war effort, and their full participation in the military campaigns of the Allied powers was, of course, a long way from the revolutionary defeatism of Zimmerwald. If that had fed into the revolutionary communism of the early 1920s, the war against Hitler now became the armed expression of Popular Front politics. 'Stalingrad' inspired underground resistance throughout Nazi-occupied Europe. Along with Churchill and Roosevelt, 'Uncle Joe' Stalin became one of the three leaders of the Allied forces.

During the second world war's last campaigns the Red Army marched into, liberated from Nazi rule, and established control over most eastern and central European countries. After the war, the Western allies recognised most of these areas as falling within a Soviet 'sphere of influence', and accepted that aspects of Soviet governance and economic management would be implemented there. Finally, the Bolshevik revolution had spread far beyond Russian borders – but it had happened through imposition, not through Leninist revolutionary communist uprisings. Instead of the revolution being saved by international revolutionaries seizing power in their own countries, inspired by the events of 1917, socialism in one country was to be defended by the creation of a buffer zone of communist satellites.

In some nations the postwar years did see communists making their own revolution: by 1949 the Chinese party had built on its decisive contribution to defeating the Japanese to win a successful struggle to control the country. In Yugoslavia and Albania, communist-led forces had achieved liberation from the Nazis without any direct contribution from the Red Army, and after the war they established independent communist governments.[19] Here, initially, Soviet guidance was welcomed, though there were always reservations on both sides. As Tito was well aware, Stalin was displeased that Yugoslav partisans had taken power without his say-so.

As Russian forces advanced towards Berlin in 1944 and 1945, local resistance movements grew rapidly in France, Italy, Greece, Czechoslovakia and Poland; and in many areas communists were in the fore of these struggles.[20] These were people's movements that linked socialism with the national struggle against Nazism, and in many cases their role in the resistance led to increased support for communist parties. The Italian Communist Party had achieved considerable popular support and high moral standing when, in August 1943, it declared that 'the communists are fighting alongside Italians of all persuasions on the road to peace and freedom in order to save the *patria* from ruin'.[21] In 1944, Togliatti declared that communists were:

> taking up and making our own the banner of national interests, which fascism has dragged through the mud and betrayed ... when we put ourselves at the head of the fight for the liberation of Italy from the German invader, we are in the line of descent of the real and grand traditions of the proletarian movement.[22]

As Ernesto Laclau reflected:

> one can see the history of the left ... as an attempt to create a frontier in terms of class, which went beyond all national boundaries. That attempt failed. It failed in 1914, and it failed later on with communism. In the end the national fact has always predominated over the class division ... the leftist movement which was successful in Italy at the end of the Second World War was a movement of national liberation ... successful because [it] combined the element of class identity with a plurality of other elements [and in particular, Italian nationalism].[23]

## TOGLIATTI RETURNS FROM MOSCOW

As the war ended, communist leaders in Western Europe insisted on the continuation of cross-class alliances with the forces of democracy. Italy provides the key example. In March 1944, Togliatti, returning from the Soviet Union after an eighteen-year period of exile, announced the 'svolta di Salerno', a turnaround of policy set out in a speech in the Italian coastal city. Italian communists were told that socialism was not on the agenda. The priority was the unity of all democratic forces for the restoration of Italian democracy after the long period of fascist rule: this required national unity, the expulsion of the Germans and the defeat of Italian fascists. Communists would build a strategically strong mass party, act responsibly and prevent the resistance from becoming embroiled in a devastating post-liberation civil war.

Communists were to respect the alliance-based government already in place and support its efforts to steer Italy out of the fascist period. The party's key objectives were to secure multi-party democracy and freedom of speech, press and religion. On that basis, it would then pursue a programme of thorough-going social reforms and promote regular participation of workers and their organisations, with a commitment to national independence and the rejection of war and power blocs.[24]

Towards the end of the war, Allied leaders had agreed treaties and protocols at Teheran and Yalta which meant that western Europe was ceded by Stalin to a postwar sphere controlled by the US and Britain. This effectively excluded Italy, and the rest of western Europe, from any possibility of establishing socialism. Whether or not Togliatti welcomed this division of powers, the position he adopted in any case tied in with some of the ideas he had been already been developing under the influence of Gramsci. The PCI's aim was to establish a progressive democracy, and to constantly enlarge its sphere and power, so that the country would be able in future to withstand any attempted coups against it, whether by the USA or from internal forces. Togliatti now 'conceived of communist politics in terms of the progressive unification of politically organised masses of people around a definite historical project'.[25] A Constituent Assembly setting up a new system of government to replace the fascist apparatus would agree the framework within which this project might develop, and democratic values and practice would now be integral to Italian communism.

There was opposition to the new approach from some of the more traditional comrades. But most party members and supporters saw Togliatti's approach as a logical continuation of the resistance struggle.[26] And their spirits were maintained when it became clear that Togliatti's line did not mean giving up any right to independent action. For example, when the American Allied commander declared that the 1944 summer offensive was over and ordered Italian resistance fighters home for the winter, communist leader Luigi Longo responded that the partisans would remain at their posts in the mountains and continue to fight.

Some on the left maintain that Stalin's acceptance of a western sphere of interest held things back, and that militants in France and Italy should have pushed for revolution at the end of the war, and organised insurrections. But this is to ignore objective realities, and to overestimate the level of support for revolutionary politics in those countries.

Togliatti's 1944 'turn' was no sell-out. But more nuanced criticisms and observations about the new position are possible. In particular it could be seen as signalling the beginning of the postwar Italian communist habit of making a virtue of necessity. As Claudio Pavone has commented, Togliatti often presented as 'victorious initiatives' what were in fact defensive actions: 'this was to be among his more lasting contributions to the party's mentality'.[27] Togliatti could also have pushed harder for the removal of fascists from leading positions within the police, armed forces and security services; and there was also a degree of self-deception in taking Italy's post-war constitution at face value.

Communists in other West European countries followed similar strategies to the Italian party. In France, those young communists who argued for attempting to seize power were advised by party leaders that British and American forces would intervene and suppress such adventures. Through discipline and obedience they came to adopt the line that the reconstruction of France was a revolutionary objective. Such perspectives seemed to promise real political change. In the French general election of November 1946, the PCF emerged as the party with the most seats – 169 – and the highest percentage of the vote – 29 per cent. The French communist leader Maurice Thorez became deputy premier in the new socialist-led coalition government. Approaches established through the Popular Front years seemed to be taking effective form.

## NOTES

1. Georg Lukacs, *The Historical Novel*, Penguin, Harmondsworth 1981 [1936-7], p333. Lukacs had been farsighted on the issues covered in this

chapter. A paper he had drafted for the Hungarian Communist Party advocated the formation of alliances with non-proletarian forces in order to work for democratic gains. This was a clear statement of Comintern policy as it would be from the mid-1930s. Unfortunately for Lukacs, he wrote his theses in 1928, just before the 'class against class' period, when such perspectives would be knocked down as 'rightist deviations'. 'The Blum Theses', *Tactics and Ethics 1919-1929*, Verso, London 2014 [1928], pp227-53.

2. Donald Sassoon, *One Hundred Years of Socialism*, Fontana, London 1997, p37.

3. One 'class against class' slogan of the KPD was: 'Wer hat uns verraten? Sozial-democraten!' ('Who has betrayed us? The Social Democrats!'). For a collection of detailed studies of the KPD from the first world war to the catastrophe of Hitler's seizure of power, see Ralf Hofrogge and Norman LaPorte (eds), *Weimar Communism as Mass Movement 1918-1933*, Lawrence and Wishart, London 2017.

4. Georgi Dimitrov, 'The Fascist Offensive and the Tasks of the Communist International', *Selected Speeches and Articles*, Lawrence and Wishart, London 1951, p102. This was the main report delivered at the Seventh Comintern Congress, 2 August 1935.

5. In Britain, this misrepresentation was pushed by George Orwell, whose lazy insult was that communist internationalism was nothing but a displacement of patriotism from one's own country to the Soviet Union: his late novels, incorporating this theme, were promoted by the USA during the cold war.

6. Palmiro Togliatti, 'On the History of the Communist International', *On Gramsci and Other Writings*, Lawrence and Wishart, London 1979 [1959], p232.

7. Stephen Spender's *Forward From Liberalism*, Left Book Club/Gollancz, London 1937, illustrates this position.

8. There were significant differences in political style, programme and character between the Italian National Fascist Party, the National Socialist German Workers' Party, or Nazis, and Franco's Spanish 'Nationalists' or 'Falangists'. There were also sufficient similarities to justify using the term 'fascist' to describe them all. Paul Preston's books on Spain provide carefully judged accounts: see, for example, *Revolution and War in Spain*, Routledge, London, 2001, and *The Spanish Holocaust*, HarperCollins, London 2012.

9. For a clear overview and guide to Gramsci's work and ideas, see Roger Simon, *Gramsci's Political Thought (third edition)*, Lawrence and Wishart, London 2015. Other useful commentaries include Antonio A Santucci, *Antonio Gramsci*, Monthly Review Press, New York 2010; and a recent book by the anthropologist Kate Crehan, *Gramsci's Common Sense*, Duke University Press, Durham NC 2016. Key writings include Antonio

Gramsci, *Selections from the Prison Notebooks*, Quintin Hoare (ed), Lawrence and Wishart, London 2005; Antonio Gramsci, *Further Selections from the Prison Notebooks*, Derek Boothman (ed), Lawrence and Wishart, London 1995; and Antonio Gramsci, *A Great and Terrible World: the pre-prison letters*, Derek Boothman (ed), Lawrence and Wishart, London 2014.

10. In his political biography, Aldo Agosti notes Togliatti's agreement, early in 1920, with the verdict of the Turinese branch of the Italian Socialist Party on contemporary events: 'the current phase of class war in Italy is the phase that precedes either the conquest of political power on the part of the revolutionary proletariat ... or a dreadful reaction on the part of the property-owning class and the governing caste'. *Palmiro Togliatti*, I B Tauris, London 2008, p13.

11. Antonio Gramsci, *Selections from Political Writings 1921 – 26*, Lawrence and Wishart, London 1978, pp199 – 200.

12. Jack Lindsay, *The Crisis in Marxism*, Moonraker Press, Bradford on Avon 1981, p5.

13. Quintin Hoare, Introduction to Antonio Gramsci, *Selections from Political Writings 1921-1926*, op cit, pxxii.

14. Antonio Gramsci, *Prison Notebooks, Volume One*, Joseph A Buttigieg (ed), Columbia University Press, New York 2011 [1929 – 1930], p137.

15. Stuart Hall, *The Hard Road to Renewal*, Verso, London 1988, p7.

16. Anne Showstack Sassoon, 'Hegemony and Political Intervention', in Sally Hibbin (ed), *Politics, Ideology and the State*, Lawrence and Wishart, London 1978, p12.

17. Geoffrey Nowell-Smith, 'General Introduction' to *Antonio Gramsci: selections from cultural writings*, Lawrence and Wishart, London 1985, pp12-14.

18. Terry Eagleton, *Walter Benjamin or Towards a Revolutionary Criticism*, Verso, London 2009 [1981], p94.

19. In Yugoslavia, significant war time support to Tito came from the British Special Operations Executive. There would later be cold war debates about whether the choice to back Tito's partisans rather than the monarchists had resulted from communist influence within the SOE, and in particular from the influence of James Klugmann. In fact, the decision to primarily resource Tito came from a straightforward military assessment: his forces were the most effective anti-Nazis. For an excellent biography of Klugmann, see Geoff Andrews, *The Shadow Man*, I B Tauris, London 2015.

20. There is no desire here to overstate the role of communists: there were anti-Nazi fighters across the political spectrum. But it is important to correct the continued downplaying and denigration of the communist element in the resistance. An example is Patrick Leigh Fermor's view that 'the only communist contributions ... were their attempts to disrupt the

resistance for postwar political ends': *Abducting a General*, John Murray, London 2014 [1966/67], pp75-6.

21. Long headline to article in *L'Unita*, 4 August 1943, quoted in Claudio Pavone, *A Civil War*, Verso, London 2013 [1991], p12.

22. Palmiro Togliatti, 'The Communist Policy of National Unity', *On Gramsci and Other Writings*, Lawrence and Wishart, London 1979 [1944], p 39.

23. Ernesto Laclau, 'Hope, Passion, Politics', *Soundings*, 22, winter 2002-03, p83.

24. Lucio Magri, *The Tailor of Ulm*, Verso, London 2011, p51.

25. Donald Sassoon, introduction, Palmiro Togliatti, *On Gramsci and Other Writings*, Lawrence and Wishart, London 1979, p8.

26. Pavone, op cit, pp432-4.

27. Claudio Pavone, quoted in Alessandro Portelli, *The Death of Luigi Trastulli and Other Stories*, State University of New York Press, Albany NY 1991, p110.

# 11. Cold War, Khrushchev and 1956

## WHICH SIDE ARE YOU ON?

As the second world war ended, communists could be justified in feeling optimistic. The Soviet Union was enjoying great moral prestige. Acting through local allies, it was set to play a key role in most Eastern European countries. Decolonisation was beginning in Africa and Asia, creating scope for Moscow to increase its international influence. Left-wing parties were widely supported in Western Europe: the communists were the biggest political force in France, and were working with others in a cross-party government; and in Italy, too, communists were helping to shape the new post-fascist Italian constitution.

Hungary, Czechoslovakia, Romania, Bulgaria, Poland and the eastern regions of Germany, all of which had been liberated from the Nazis by Soviet forces, were now widely (albeit often reluctantly) accepted as being part of a Soviet sphere of influence. New state structures were set up and local communists were moved into key positions within them; they were to be known as 'people's democracies'.

Hobsbawm writes that these were deliberately *not* set up as communist regimes, but as multi-party systems with mixed economies.[1] Within a few years, however, the non-communist parties in these countries had been squeezed from positions of power, and their scope for any independent activity had been reduced to a minimum. From 1948 onwards, there was no possibility – if there had been before – of open elections in Eastern Europe. With the possible exception of Bulgaria, any free and popular vote in Eastern Europe would have evicted the communists from power, and the Soviet leadership was not prepared to countenance this. In spite of all this, those in charge of the East European states continued to present them as 'peoples' democracies'. The self-designation may have been based on the claim that governments which act in the interests of the many are thereby and automatically democratic; but, in fact, it is an essential element of democracy that there is a regular and properly inclusive electoral process in order to decide who holds governmental power.[2]

Single-party dominance resulted from arrangements which had been determined in discussions held under Soviet tutelage. They were based on clunky and schematic 'Marxist-Leninist' conceptions of politics. Representatives of Czechoslovak anti-fascist parties, for example, met in Moscow in March 1945. They agreed that the country's government would be a 'national front' coalition of six parties. Parties which had collaborated with or supported the Nazi occupation were barred from participating in the new republics.

At first, the communist perspective was that there should be no immediate move towards socialism. They were committed to operate as part of 'a bloc of the working class, peasants and farmers, small urban bourgeoisie, the intelligentsia, and that part of the democratic bourgeoisie which wants to carry out the National Front programme'.[3] However, as political disputes developed within the coalition governments, and even where 'the proletariat' was not necessarily the numerically largest class, as in Romania or Bulgaria, it became clear that communists would, as representatives of the 'leading' class, necessarily and unquestionably have the leading role in decision-making.

The setting up of the Eastern European buffer zone was both a response to, and a contributory cause of, the rapid onset of the cold war, which was deeply entwined with developments in both the spheres of influence. Once fascism was defeated, there was a swift reversion to the situation before the second world war, when the Soviet Union had been regarded by the west as a threat. But now that its prestige had increased so much – to the extent that there were seen to be 'two camps' in global politics – it was regarded as even more of a threat than it had been before. The division of Europe which took place in the late 1940s now looks as if it was inevitable, but it did not seem so at the time, at least to many of socialist temperament. The historian E.P. Thompson would later reflect that:

> in 1944 all of Europe, from the Urals to the Atlantic, was moved by a consensual expectation of a democratic and peaceful post-war continent. We supposed that old gangs of money, privilege and militarism would go. Most of us supposed that the nations of West and Southern Europe would conduct their anti-Fascist alliances towards some form of socialism. Most of us (including many of the commu-

nists of those countries) supposed that the nations of Eastern Europe would be governed by some form of authentic socialist popular front.[4]

Whilst they *were* concerned to establish a buffer zone of allied countries around their borders, the Soviets were also war-weary, and did not have their eyes on any further geographical expansion. But dynamics of division and conflict were promoted by the USA and its allies in the western sphere of interest. Episodes which have been defined as evidence of the Soviet Union's repressive and aggressive nature were often reactions to American provocations. President Truman's 1947 programme of aid to Greece and Turkey was an explicit attempt to undermine communist support in those countries. The 1948 Berlin blockade was a response to the decision of the USA, France and Britain to extend currency reform in the zones of Germany which they occupied into west Berlin, which was in the Russian zone. This initiative was certainly aimed at destabilising and undermining the Soviet position in Germany which had been agreed between the allied powers as the Nazis were defeated. Once Truman pledged support for 'free people anywhere in the world' against the 'totalitarian regimes' of Soviet communism, which he misrepresented as being of an essentially destructive and expansionist nature, the cold war really got underway.

The Marshall Plan, which began operation in April 1948, offered financial assistance from the USA to European countries ravaged by the war, but this was on condition of state and market liberalisation. One of the central aims of the plan was to counter any potential communist successes in Europe, the threat of which was greatly exaggerated – partly because the American definition of communist behaviour was very wide. A second aim was the expansion of US economic interests: under the terms of the Plan, American companies were to be allowed to operate in European countries on favourable terms, and the dollar was to be given prime status as a trading and reserve currency. As Jean-Paul Sartre would judge: 'under its pacific externals, it was the beginning of a policy of "pressing back"' against the Soviet presence in Europe'.[5]

The effect was to push Stalin towards the assertion of even fuller control of Eastern Europe, destroying any limited scope there might have been for looser arrangements and variety in political trajectories there. Stalinists purged the more independently-minded and 'nationalist' cadre in all East European parties, and developed a model of suspicious policing in place of political engagement. Such travesties of socialist principles fed the dynamics of the cold war, and gave plenty of evidence to American and West European political scientists that their 'pluralist' systems were vastly superior, and indeed were the only proper and legitimate form of democracy.

With the Soviet Union now regarded as a threat to civilisation, western governments began to see all communists as actual or potential agents of a hostile foreign power. This fear was not wholly unfounded, given that communists were so loyal to the Soviet state, and that the logic of the cold war drove people into adopting positions within its terms. As is well-known, a small number of communist party members did in fact become spies for the Soviet Union – and this was then seized on as conclusive evidence that communism represented the enemy within. Once its logic was set in motion, acts on both sides continually fed the development of cold war oppositions. The ground for Popular Front politics disappeared fast: in Western Europe and the USA it became ever more difficult to articulate nationalism and communism together. In May 1947 French and Italian communist party representatives were summarily removed from their respective coalition governments, and the response of communists was to move towards ever more firmly expressed fundamental solidarity with the Soviet Union. The sense that all other political forces were against them sparked defensive bonding; there was a feeling that 'if ... the Party had collapsed in despair, all protests and all hopes would have collapsed along with it'.[6]

'Totalitarianism' became a key concept in the cold war intellectual contest. This was an ideological construction that used evidence of Stalinist repression to portray the concept of democracy as having no place within the anti-capitalist left. Hitler and Stalin were seen as the same, as 'evil twins', and the whole of the left became associated with the idea of a state-sponsored closing down of democracy. Liberal democracy was presented as the only possible alternative to totalitarianism, and communists were repositioned as opponents of democracy. Totalitarian theory emphasised structural and phenomenological similarities between Nazism and Stalinism, and defined both systems as being based on terror, and the drive for total control. Both were seen as using indoctrination and brainwashing to secure mass support, as presiding over police states, and as seeking control over all aspects of society and economy. Neither could tolerate any opposition from within civil society.

As a framework for understanding the real social dynamics of the Soviet Union and other communist countries, 'totalitarianism' obscured more than it illuminated. It did include an important critique of politics that seek to suppress distinctions and distances between state and society. But, overall, the concept exaggerated the power of the state and the ability of leaders to prevail, and cast the mass of people as unthinking dupes of the system. This was ironic, given that one of the key claims made by critics of totalitarianism was that it deprived people of their individuality and agency. The theory also lacked a sense of historical specificity, or of social forces, and this made it incapable of understanding how changes might occur within such societies. This had the perverse effect of depriving its supporters of insight into effective means of contestation.

The concept was, nevertheless, effective in its aim of creating an anti-communist common sense in Western Europe and North America. It took the idea of democracy – the moral resource that had been developed in the fight against Hitler – and turned it around so that it became a weapon to be deployed against the very forces that had provided the greatest material contribution to the war effort against the Nazis.

Although Christian Democracy was probably the biggest bene-factor from the concept of totalitarianism, within the left it served to strengthen social-democrats, who increasingly defined themselves through a cold war alignment of capitalism and democracy. The material basis that underpinned this position was postwar economic growth, which made it possible for working-class majorities to learn to love the free market. By the 1950s, living standards were rising for ordinary people in capitalist countries, with welfare state provision complementing slowly but steadily increasing wages, and access to new consumer goods. The ideology was promoted that 'democratic freedom was inseparable from, and indeed depended on, the freedom of markets and profit-making'.[7] The quest for self-determination, personal freedom and democratic participation was conflated with opportunities to go shopping. Social-democracy's emerging 'Atlanticist' pro-Americanism – in combination with its articulation of a widely-held desire to move on from the 1930s and the war, and its

contentment with the role of the market and business in building up
the economy – was granted by 'totalitarianism' the status of a moral
stance.

## KHRUSHCHEV'S SECRET SPEECH

The dynamics of the cold war were considerably reshaped during
the remarkable events of 1956. In February of that year, the new
Soviet leader Nikita Khrushchev made a 'secret speech' to his Party's
Congress, 'revealing' that the 'pathologically paranoid' Stalin (who
had died in 1953) had been responsible for a range of crimes including
mass arrests and deportations, and many executions without trial.
Khrushchev's aim was a controlled de-Stalinisation and the recovery
of the revolutionary myth that gave legitimacy to the system, while
sloughing off any sense that the crimes of the previous leader had been
in any sense a structural problem.

From the moment he sat down, debate began as to how a man who
had been on Stalin's team could now oppose what he had stood for.
Nevertheless, there were immediate positive consequences of the shift.
Most prisoners were released from the camps. During Khrushchev's
rule, about 20 million people were 'rehabilitated' – though most
achieved this status posthumously. The cultural accompaniment was
an uneven loosening of control over thought and expression: there
were some 'green shoots' of renewal in civil society and in the cultural
sphere, though society was still by no means liberal.[8]

Khrushchev's risk-taking resulted from his recognition that the
system enjoyed support and prestige, but modernisation was needed.
Although the country had lived through a period of extreme repression, the preconditions for modernisation were in many ways in place.
The victory over Nazism had enabled the Soviet state to refound
itself and win greater support among its own citizens. Patriotism and
communist values were articulated together. Soviet culture was shaped
and supported by a large intelligentsia, with many professional people
committed to socialism, and hopeful that it could be reformed as it
developed. Internationally, Soviet models for the planned development and industrialisation of agrarian economies were being adopted
by many newly-independent third-world countries.[9]

It seemed that an increasingly confident 'Soviet moment' had
arrived. This was expressed in what Nick Srnicek and Alex Williams

describe as 'a popular culture imbued with utopian desires'.[10] The view that communist economies were resilient, likely to continue expanding, and had compelling advantages over capitalist ones was shared across the political spectrum. The United Nations measured the Soviet Union's average industrial growth rate between 1948 and 1960 as exceeding ten per cent each year. The Soviet Union was seen in many quarters as a model that was capable of offering a real alternative to capitalist ways. The op-ed pages of European and American newspapers were full of 'anguished soul-searching', as columnists asked how a free society could hope to match 'the steely strategic determination of the prospering, successful Soviet Union'.[11]

In fact, the Soviet economy's expansion obscured fundamental problems – of which the country's leadership were all too well aware. Even as they promoted optimism, they lacked confidence in their own achievements, and were looking for new directions. The system's 'absolutist features' seemed to belong to another age, and were profoundly incompatible with the challenge of modernisation.[12] Management systems had not been updated since the 1930s, when Gosplan's 'balance method' had covered a few hundred products nationally. By the 1950s, the complexity of decisions had increased dramatically: the plan for a single enterprise might include as many as 500 separate indices.[13] It was simply not feasible for such a highly centralised state to process and co-ordinate the resulting mass of detailed tasks.

The resulting blocks in the system, and the wider problems of socialist planning, provided evidence for economists who believed that economies could not survive without markets. Ludwig Von Mises had argued since the 1920s that the market provided an essential function by acting as a kind of calculating machine: the choices that people made in a market economy ensured the most rational possible allocation of resources; and if you removed private property and worked against market logics through centralised planning, the calculating machine would break down.

For Soviet leaders seeking to disprove such capitalist doctrines, the positive growth their country had achieved was undermined by structural weaknesses. Francis Spufford describes these:

> For each extra unit of output that it gained, the Soviet Union was far more dependent than other countries on throwing in extra inputs: extra labour, extra raw materials, extra investment. The USSR got

65 per cent of its output growth from extra inputs, compared to the USA's 33 per cent ... This kind of 'extensive' growth (as opposed to the 'intensive' growth of rising productivity) came with built-in limits, and the Soviet economy was already nearing them.[14]

The surplus labour that had previously existed in the countryside no longer existed, and this meant that increasing output now required higher productivity per worker, rather than building ever more factories and moving new employees in from rural areas. As the centralised system failed to achieve intensive growth, discussion turned to economic reform, and to making planning more responsive.

Once established in office, Khrushchev made a number of major changes to party structures, some of them designed to decentralise leadership and therefore make it better able to respond to local economic conditions. These were unpopular amongst the apparatchiks. And Khrushchev also made some big mistakes in his large-scale agricultural experiments. In 1964, senior comrades, accusing him of 'amateurism' and 'dilettantism', used the international split with China as a pretext to remove him from office and to install Leonid Brezhnev as leader. But it was mainly to reassert the power and centrality of the bureaucracy that Khrushchev was retired. From that point on, the party leadership reverted to its old ways: but though the leadership became less quirky, it still did not manage to find solutions to the country's economic problems.

There *were* still some attempts in the mid-1960s to give enterprises real latitude and scope to replace administrative directives and orders with so-called 'economic methods'. Local managers gained more control over production, had some flexibility over wages, and could invest a proportion of 'profit' back into their own development funds. Decentralisation was extended so that particular factories and enterprises had more decision-making power than they would have with so-called 'centralised investment'.

But, however radical these attempts seemed to their initiators, Soviet attempts to overcome the limits of state planning 'foundered in bureaucratic paralysis'.[15] In Moshe Lewin's summary, all 'efforts to change the economic model were blocked by the political model, which was incapable of activating the nation's social and cultural reserves'.[16] Hierarchical structures meant that cadres lower down the pecking order sought advancement by seeking to please the higher authorities, rather than reporting on difficulties. This is always a recipe for problems, but Soviet society lacked the countering checks and balances that operate in liberal democratic systems and with economic competition.

## 'THROUGH THE SMOKE OF BUDAPEST': THE HUNGARIAN UPRISING OF 1956

Alongside these multiple challenges, there was a series of reactions and rebellions against the cold war settlement within 'the Soviet bloc', where post-war economic development was very slow and communist leaderships were rarely popular. No more than twelve years ever passed without a significant revolt somewhere in Eastern Europe, which almost always led to large-scale armed suppression of civilian protestors: strikes in East Germany in 1953; protests in Poland in June 1956; the uprising in Hungary a few months later; the 'Prague Spring' of 1968; and the forceful emergence of the independent trade union *Solidarnosc* in Poland in 1980. Some of these were sectional workers' strikes: others involved a strong nationalist element. Most were accompanied by modest but brave expressions of dissent by intellectuals.

As well as being a major event in itself, the 1956 Hungarian uprising generated considerable problems for the international communist movement. It began in late October as a governmental crisis triggered by visible divisions in the ruling party, which then began to widen to involve popular forces. While debates were still going on over pursuing a new course that would help build popular support for party rule, a big march and demonstration was held in support of reform, but this was fired on by state security police, killing many people. Three days of struggle followed between militant supporters of reform and Soviet troops who had been invited in by the anti-reformers still dominant in the government. The struggle quickly became an uprising against the government, and spread from Budapest to the rest of the country. After a few days the fighting died down – though not other forms of autonomous revolutionary activity – and a new (though still communist) regime led by reformer Imre Nagy took over.

For a short while, it looked as if the reforming government might remain in office: at the end of October the Soviet authorities announced that troops would be withdrawn from Budapest, and wider negotiations would begin about the presence of Soviet troops on

Hungarian territory. But this was not how things turned out. In the face of what the Soviet leadership saw as the new government's 'maximalist demands' for autonomy – which included the likelihood that Hungary would withdraw from the Warsaw Pact – and in (disproportionate) response to continuing local attacks on Communist institutions and leaders, the Soviet leadership decided to send in more troops and remove the Nagy government from office.

Bloody suppression followed: nearly 3000 people were killed, many thousands were wounded and 180,000 Hungarian refugees fled to the West. Nagy himself was executed, along with between 200 and 350 others (estimates are disputed).

The conclusions the Soviet leadership drew from the events in Hungary would ultimately prove self-defeating: encouraged by its success in reconquering Hungary, it now pursued a continuing policy of resting the stability of its empire on military force. As Eric Hobsbawm argued, once it became clear in the 1980s that Gorbachev was no longer ready 'to march or to subsidise', 'the immediate collapse of Soviet empire and influence was certain'.[17] More immediately, the morale, and the moral standing, of communist governance was massively reduced in all the East European countries, and the 'people's democracy' model further discredited.

The twin shocks of the secret speech and the bloody events in Hungary were big blows for international communism. There were divisions, dissidents and different forms of partial breaks from Stalinism. Some attempts to manage these issues saw Marxist leaders misrepresenting reality, and substituting vacuous wishful thinking for credible analysis. Even though it lost a quarter of its membership in the wake of the events of 1956, the British Communist Party leader John Gollan talked up the situation as potentially a 'great political turning-point', which could remove a 'temporary deformation' and lead to the renewal of the socialist system.[18]

Others opted for criticism rather than facile optimism, rejected key tenets of 'existing socialism', and set the direction towards what was to eventually become known as Eurocommunism. Recognising that developing new perspectives would require some autonomy from Moscow, Togliatti argued that the communist movement should be 'polycentric', with each party having scope and independence to determine its own political approach. By 1977, leading Italian communist Giorgio Napolitano was arguing that the events showed the need for an alternative model based on 'revolution as process'. The road ahead could not involve re-runs of 1917, but would instead consist in the 'deepening of democracy'.[19] Although it was true that the state in capitalist society operated so as to maintain the power of the dominant class, liberal democratic norms meant that it had to win the consent of subordinated groups and classes, and to make concessions, at least, to their demands. This characteristic of democracy had to be defended and used.

Alongside these developments *within* the movement, there were new breaks *from* communism. Factionalised but combative Trotskyist organisations positioned themselves to attract talented militants and young intellectuals who did not see Russian communism as an inspirational model; while a number of creative thinkers began to establish journals and networks comprising a 'New Left', which looked for new models of radical politics. These might be rooted in Marxism, but they had no desire to be part of the communist movement. In Britain, leading dissident communists Edward Thompson and John Saville founded *The Reasoner*, which later became a constituent partner of *New Left Review*, the foremost Anglophone left-wing journal of the 1960s. Stuart Hall was its first editor, later succeeded by Perry Anderson. This current, which itself had various strands, and which still continues to generate major debates and incisive analysis, began to develop an alternative socialism, distinct from both Stalinism and social-democracy. The New Left valued the autonomy of social movements, undertook a deeper consideration of culture than the left had previously achieved, recovered the analyses of a range of Marxists who had not been spokesmen for the official communist movement, and promoted the need to understand and tackle new aspects of capitalism, such as mass consumerism and technocratic managerialism.[20]

## NOTES

1. Eric Hobsbawm, *Interesting Times*, Allen Lane, London 2002, p180.
2. Both parts of this sentence draw on Jack Lively, *Democracy*, European Consortium for Political Research, Colchester 2007 [1975], pp35, 53. Lively is discussing arguments put forward by, respectively, C B Macpherson and Joseph Schumpeter.
3. Klement Gottwald, speaking in 1945, quoted in Jon Bloomfield, *Passive Revolution*, Allison and Busby, London 1979, p47.
4. E.P. Thompson, *The Heavy Dancers*, Merlin Press, London 1985, pp199-

200. Thompson believed that 'the division of Europe (for which I hold the rulers on both sides responsible) was a betrayal ... of democracy, of internationalism, of personal sacrifice. It turned all those famous victories [of the second world war] into a pile of shit'.

5. Jean-Paul Sartre, *The Spectre of Stalin*, Hamish Hamilton, London 1969 [1956], pp63-4.

6. Rossana Rosssanda, *The Comrade From Milan*, Verso, London 2010, p117.

7. Wolfgang Streeck, 'How will capitalism end?' *New Left Review*, May-June 2014.

8. William Taubman, *Khrushchev*, Simon and Schuster, New York NY 2003, pp648-9.

9. Eric Hobsbawm, *On History*, Weidenfeld and Nicolson, London 1997, p4.

10. Nick Srnicek and Alex Williams, *Inventing the Future*, Verso, London 2015, p138.

11. Francis Spufford, 'Red Plenty', *Guardian*, 7 August 2010.

12. Ronald Suny, 'Soviet Ice-Breaker', *New Left Review*, September-October 2005.

13. Maurice Dobb, 'Planning', in *The Development of Socialist Economic Thought*, Lawrence and Wishart, London 2008 [1972], p135.

14. Francis Spufford, *Red Plenty*, Faber and Faber, London 2010, p90.

15. Ronald Suny, op cit.

16. Moshe Lewin, *The Soviet Century*, Verso, London 2005, pviii.

17. Eric Hobsbawm, 'Could it have been different?' *London Review of Books*, 16 November 2006.

18. Kevin Marsh and Robert Griffiths, *Granite and Honey*, Manifesto Press, Croydon 2012, p187.

19. Giorgio Napolitano & Eric Hobsbawm, *The Italian Road To Socialism*, Lawrence and Wishart, London 1977, p30.

20. A growing literature on the New Left includes Lin Chun, *The British New Left*, Edinburgh University Press, Edinburgh 1993; Gregory Elliott, *Perry Anderson*, University of Minnesota Press, Minneapolis MN 1998; Michael Kenny, *The First New Left*, Lawrence and Wishart, London 1995; Oxford University Socialist Discussion Group, *Out of Apathy: voices of the new left*, Verso, London 1989; Steven Woodhams, *History in the Making*, The Merlin Press, London 2001.

# 12. The dialectics of 1968

## CZECHOSLOVAKIA'S PATH

During the 1960s, ideas of revolution and far-reaching social change started to come back on the agenda across the world. Most of the renewed enthusiasm did not come from the established left, though, whether communist or social-democrat. In many ways, both of these traditions were wrong-footed and disorganised by the new radical currents and social movements which now emerged.

In Eastern Europe there were some attempts to respond to the problems highlighted in 1956. Recognition that centrally planned economic management could lead to inefficiencies and stagnation resulted in limited experimentation around 'market socialism'. Though the Hungarian reform communist Imre Nagy was shot as a closing act of the suppression of the 1956 uprising, key elements of his 'Bukharinite' economic programme were implemented by his successor, Janos Kadar.

Kadar was given leeway to experiment with marketisation – 'goulash communism' – on the understanding that there could be no further challenges to Soviet authority over Hungary's position in the Eastern bloc. In an effort to build social cohesion, attempts were made to meet consumer needs and desires. Compulsory plan targets were abolished; managerial bonuses were linked to commercial results; and, in agriculture, delivery quotas were abolished. By May 1966, the Hungarian Workers' Party could declare that 'the development of an active role for the market requires that the laborious and bureaucratic system of centralised allocation of materials and products ... should give place to commercial relations'.[1]

This perspective led to Hungary's 'new economic mechanism' of 1968. Firms remained in state ownership, but were now expected to buy and sell on the open market, and to generate 'profits'. Such policies meant that, by East European standards, Hungary had a relatively broad range of consumer goods. Visiting Russians nicknamed it 'little America'.

Such experiments generated hope in other socialist countries that communism's social system could be combined with a political style that would secure popular support, and at last make it possible to refute the criticisms that Marxist government was necessarily repressive and undemocratic. The highpoint of this search for democracy came in Czechoslovakia, where a communist party in government officially converted to 'a tolerant pluralism'.[2] In January 1968, the new party leader Alexander Dubcek signalled moves towards a more liberal and democratic system. A Central Committee member declared that:

> it is necessary to eliminate everything that deformed socialism, everything that corrupted the spirit, everything that inflicted harm on the people and took from them so much of their trust and enthusiasm ... it is up to us ... to bravely set out towards uncharted territories and seek our own Czechoslovak socialist path.[3]

The aim was to link economic reforms such as those in place in Hungary to substantive political change and democratic reform – which the Hungarian leadership were not seeking. Dubcek's declared goal was 'socialism with a human face'.[4] The economist Ota Sik's proposals for market socialism began to be implemented, with decentralisation of economic decision-making, contractual supply arrangements, and incentives for individual enterprises, managers and workers. These raised a debate as to whether social ownership through the state and central planning were in fact crucial to socialism.

For a short, promising, period, it seemed that Czechoslovakia would originate a form of socialism that was centred on meeting people's needs but which also accepted that markets work better than centralised state control for calibrating production to demand, especially in respect of goods for personal consumption. This possibility created a fresh wave of support for socialism – and thus confirmed to the pioneers of neoliberalism in the West the urgency of their emerging project to discredit and defeat socialist politics. After all, even strong critics of communist orthodoxy were not dismissing socialism itself. For example, the Czech writer Ludvik Vaculik, in his dissident statement *Two Thousand Words that Belong to Workers, Farmers, Officials, Scientists, Artists and Everybody*, published in June 1968, accepted that the problem was not socialism 'as such', but that the socialist programme had fallen 'into the hands of the wrong people'. He called for 'faster and more comprehensive de-Stalinisation'.[5]

Censorship was abolished in Czechoslovakia, and some independent political organisations were established. The idea of multi-party elections began to be mooted. The Czechoslovakian party started to recognise that it had to work to win support and could no longer simply rely on imposing its policies. Mass popular organisations had a part to play in economic, social and political life. As Jon Bloomfield argues, such independent organisations 'could not continue as transmission belts for party directives. These bodies had to have their own autonomy and scope for activity ... there had to be more genuine discussion and debate in the press and media'.[6]

Many communists in other countries supported Dubcek's reforms. One Spanish communist leader Santiago Alvarez Gomez described the changes in Czechoslovakia as pointing to 'the type of socialist society which, given our concrete conditions and experiences, we think we must have in Spain'.[7] More and more left-wingers were enthusiastic about Dubcek's project, which, as Lucio Magri recounts, did not seek to undermine the socialist system, or to break off international alliances and links with the Soviet Union, 'but rather to make socialism politically less intolerant of dissent and less highly centralised in its management of the economy'.[8]

Leaders in Moscow thought differently. In August 1968, the Soviet Union invaded Czechoslovakia, enforcing the 'Brezhnev doctrine' that Moscow reserved the right to judge the socialist authenticity of other countries' governments, and if necessary to use tanks to block unauthorised developments. They took control of the country and imposed a reversal of almost all the measures instituted by the reformers, installing a conservative leadership in the party.

The suppression of the Prague Spring provoked greater divisions and distances within the communist movement than ever before. There was strong censure from communist parties in Italy, France, Britain, Austria, the Netherlands and elsewhere, as well as from – partly for their own reasons of state – the Yugoslavian and Romanian governments. Perhaps more significantly, the Soviet action in Czechoslovakia became a focus for increasing tensions between the USSR and China. From August 1968, Beijing began calling the Soviet Union a 'social-imperialist' state.

For many, the Soviet invasion of Czechoslovakia signalled the end of hopes for political reform from within in Eastern Europe and the Soviet Union. West European Communist Parties now increasingly turned their attention towards a politics of pluralism. The invasion made it imperative for people in the emerging Eurocommunist movement to examine the Soviet model much more critically than hitherto, and to finally end any attachment to the idea that it provided any kind of blueprint for the advance of socialism.[9] These critical reactions by Western communist parties were in many ways more politically consequential than the responses from Western governments.

The Spanish communist party provides a good illustration of the strength of feeling. The party was illegal, its exiled leadership dependent on Soviet funding, and its reputation shaped by decades of unswerving loyalty to Moscow. Nevertheless, its General Secretary Santiago Carrillo and other leading figures within the party openly criticised the Soviet invasion, and affirmed Togliatti's notion that divergence and diversity of opinion should be possible within the communist world.

As Richard Cross puts it, in many respects, the political current of Eurocommunism cohered in 1968, 'through the experience of shared opposition from within the communist camp to Soviet intervention in Czechoslovakia'.[10]

A range of thinkers, including the veteran Hungarian communist Georg Lukacs, who had managed to escape the fate of other members of Imre Nagy's government, were beginning to develop critiques of communist practice that stressed the importance of democratic process.[11] Lukacs recognised that democracy was crucial as a framework within which people's subjective identities, civic society and the state could be aligned. This was because – among other reasons – 'the socialist economy does not spontaneously produce and reproduce the men appropriate for it'. The function of socialist democracy was therefore 'precisely the *education* of its members towards socialism'.[12]

But, as Pauline Bren has described, the new Czech regime had no intention of encouraging anything to do with democracy or new ideas. Instead its policy of 'normalisation' aimed for suffocating social quiescence. The party leadership summarily brought to an end the brief period when the party had promoted a nation of eager, publicly active communists. 'Rather, it sought to create a nation of private persons joined in their mutual quest for the good life which, the regime insisted, could best be had under communism'.[13]

A loose protest movement emerged around Charter 77, initially the name of a dissident declaration published in 1977 and signed by a small number of critics of the government, including the playwright and future post-communist president Vaclav Havel. Although the policy of normalisation rendered these creative democrats almost invisible in their own country, amongst those who sought to amplify their arguments and profile in the West were many communists who supported Charter 77, and were among the most vociferous critics of the Czech government.

## UNKNOWN PLEASURES

'1968' also saw challenges to the establishment in North America and Western Europe. Increasing public dissent was legitimised by some establishment politicians promoting social liberalisation; examples of this trend in the British context include the limited decriminalisation of homosexuality in 1967, and the Theatres Act of 1968, which ended censorship on stage. A dynamic 'counterculture' was developing among the baby-boom post-war generation – among higher education students (whose numbers had increased substantially) and young working-class young people who were much more affluent than their parents' generation and were involved in a range of vibrant new subcultures. An exciting sense of change was promoted through television, music, new magazines and papers. There was marked shift away from deference: this was a new generation that would shake up the old establishment culture.

Revolutionary communist impulses were also part of the events of 1968: there were large demonstrations, red flags and chants of 'Paris, London, Rome, Berlin – we will fight, we will win'. There was a big surge in working-class militancy and a worldwide wave of anti-imperialist activity. American imperialism, particularly in Vietnam, looked vulnerable. This was a time of optimism for the left, and some even believed that 'pre-revolutionary situations were looming in the homelands of capitalism'.[14]

1968 can, however, be also seen as a moment which fundamentally undermined the prospects for communism. The most radical young people – those who were putting themselves at risk by opposing repressive systems in Czechoslovakia and Poland, and opening up fissures in the social structure which would twenty years later widen decisively – were not calling for the resurrecting of Lenin, but for what were essentially 'Western' freedoms and rights. Protests in Paris and Prague may have been similar in their questioning and undermining of the legitimacy of the established social authorities, suggesting an equivalence between 'the communist establishment' and 'the capitalist establishment', but the targets and hopes of protestors were different in each context.

Even where Western counterculturalists declared they were Marxists, they wanted more anti-authoritarian forms of politics. This, in part, resulted from a wholly new phenomenon: the increasing influence of cultural figures from the USA within European radical counterculture, as part of the wider more general American presence within popular culture. This had been building up since the late 1950s: jazz, the beatniks, the growing popularity of writers such as Allen Ginsberg and Jack Kerouac. By the late 1960s, many radical young people, from LA to New York, and from London to Berlin, were fans of both Lenin and Bob Dylan, both Mao and Jefferson Airplane. The new generation was resistant to the work ethics which had been established through previous decades. The 'old left' often seemed to share 'square', authoritarian values: it was no more to be trusted than 'the man' running capitalist corporations or 'the pigs' policing protests and festivals: in fact, 'anyone over thirty', particularly one's own suburban parents.

New Left and Trotskyist groupings were often more attractive to the confrontational and rebellious moods of 1968 than the older parties, and they now gained support, continuing to attract young recruits well into the 1970s. For some, though, even these more radical left currents were themselves just copies of the older communist and labour parties: on this basis, for the first time since the 1930s, anarchist ideas achieved significant social energy. Mixed with the new, fresh and assertive styles in popular music, film and fashion, a radicalised, libertarian politics developed, to be expressed most vividly in Paris, in 'May '68'.

Activists on the barricades in Paris – the first to be erected in Western Europe since the second world war – were more likely to see official communist parties as blocks to progress rather than as its expression. Anti-authoritarian leftists argued that new forms of social organisation and political activity were now needed. The libertarian Daniel Cohn-Bendit, a German student who had been born in France during the war, and was denounced by De Gaulle as 'the most dangerous scoundrel in France', emerged as a figurehead whilst consciously promoting themes drawn from the radically democratic 'council communist' current which had operated back in the early 1920s. Alongside such arguments, the ideas and language of the Situationists also infused the May events. This was an avant-garde group that had formed in 1957 for whom culture was central to the understanding of contemporary capitalism, and who sought to overcome alienation and promote a cultural revolution based on the full realisation of the talent and potential of all individuals. For them, boredom was a political issue.

In spite of this flowering of iconoclastic creativity, President De Gaulle soon reasserted his authority; his party convincingly won the National Assembly elections he called in the aftermath of the May events. And the French Communist Party's dominance of the left also continued for a while, but it had started to lose support. In the end it was more the wiles of the future socialist president Francois Mitterrand that effectively undermined their position, rather than any Situationist happenings. But the fact that from the late 1960s they struggled to win new cohorts of young members certainly laid the basis for French communists' future decline. A sense built up amongst radical young leftists and their academic champions that the elite of the working-class movement had abandoned and betrayed those most exploited and attacked by the capitalist state.

If key 'soixante-huitards' felt antipathy towards communist parties and parliamentary socialists, the feeling was often mutual. The traditional left found the spirit of 1968 hard to digest. Even if they had wanted to, it was not clear how established parties might relate to and organise these strange new social movements, with their radical anti-authoritarianism and confrontational style. These novel forms of individual self-expression – and sometimes self-absorption – were features of what Herbert Marcuse described as 'a great refusal', a reaction against social constraints and established expectations.[15] If the generation of the 1930s had wanted regular employment and steady increases in living standards, the hippies and Situationists were now rejecting the boring routines of everyday life.

Where some dialogue developed between the old left and the new social movements, useful directions came out of the interplay. In the United States, for example, Students for a Democratic Society, starting from their critique of consumerism, recognised some of the central contradictions of commodity capitalism. Fredric Jameson has drawn attention to their insight that capitalism produced not only wave after wave of technological innovation but also 'new desires in a well-nigh infinite measure'. The SDS concluded that 'the gap between this plethora of new desires and the capacity of the system to satisfy them would prove to be the real Achilles' heel of this mode of production'.[16]

But the main position of the established parties of the left was that the unexpected new social movements risked disorganising the left. The Italian communist Giorgio Amendola wrote an article which quickly became notorious amongst young radicals. Amendola attacked 'extremist and anarchist positions that have appeared in the student movement', and called for 'revolutionary vigilance' against 'provocateurs'. The PCI's general approach was to 'reject all adventurism'.[17] In due course, this would extend to the PCI backing Christian Democrats in clamping down on disorderly student demonstrations, and praising police actions.[18]

Such moves created controversy. Many people argued that the future of the left lay in connecting to, integrating and learning from young people and their fresh and creative demands. Maria Macciocchi was one Italian communist who cautioned against mistaking the new revolutionary forces for 'enemies of the party line'. She saw problems in the way that, from the late 1960s, the PCI adopted see-sawing positions, shifting from 'the desire to absorb these new forces painlessly and mechanically' to criticising them 'for pulling against the long-established strategy of creating defensive alliances to maintain democracy'.[19]

I would argue that the misgivings and oppositions of the traditional left were well-grounded and prescient, though there were problems in the positions of both the established parties *and* the new movements. Marcuse's view that the working class in Western Europe and North America was 'hopelessly' integrated, and could not sustain a movement against capitalism was, in large part, to be proved true. But neither was the alternative momentum of student radicalism destined to realise the realm of freedom. As Sven Lutticken observes, 1968's 'heterogeneous combination of students, intellectuals, artists, bohemians and layabouts' created many things, but revolution was not one of them.[20]

A balanced assessment of 1968 would recognise that its excesses tended to undermine its potential. The counterculture, and particularly its ultra-leftism and provocations, were to a significant degree irresponsible and self-indulgent. Here were people who rebelled against 'the system' in the same way that flowers 'rebel' against the earth from which they grow and are nurtured.[21] 1968's rejection of social conventions and prohibitions was done, not 'in the name of some other pattern of ordering society', but 'in the name of the unlimited autonomy of individual desire'.[22]

## FROM THE COUNTERCULTURE TO CONSUMERISM

The counterculture's demands proved capable of articulation in two broad directions. The 1970s showed how its values could shape progressive movements, including feminism and anti-racism. These causes were linked to, but independent of, class struggle, and the resulting demands and issues defined important new frontiers and divisions for left politics.

But the hopes and desires of the new social movements could also be channelled towards a possessive individualism. Identity politics – the right to recognition for what we particularly are, with its generation of new democratic demands to meet particular needs – could be translated to become the right to consume in our own way. The conservative French thinker Francois Furet was not alone in regarding 'a new bourgeois progressivism' as the major legacy of the May events, and noting that 'the old sixty-eighters ... soon made their peace with the market, publicity and consumer society'.[23]

Alarm and disapproval shaped the earliest conservative responses to the hedonistic youth culture of the 1960s: in so far as these new trends could be understood, they were clearly irresponsible, opposed to traditional authority, and lacking deference and respect. For radicals in tune with the new moods, what better reason to endorse and promote them?

But, for all that it troubled and unsettled the establishment, the spirit of 1968 also made a contribution to the new generation's turn away from the collectivist outlooks and responsibilities of class-based organisation (though perhaps the traditional left's lack of comprehension of the new zeitgeist did not help matters). And although the counterculture did induct many people into radical politics, the right has managed to profit much more from 1968 than the left ever did. Capital proved itself extremely effective at co-opting 'free floating utopian impulses'.[24] In Hilary Wainwright's words, it was more nimble in 'responding to and appropriating the new energies and aspirations stimulated by the critical movements of the 1960s and 1970s than ... the parties of the left, for which these movements could have been a force for democratic renewal'.[25]

During the 1970s, countercultural values were busily reworked into forms of individualism entirely consistent with neoliberalism. It was not long before positive thinking, cults of self-worth and self-realisation, and *ersatz* optimism were commodified and turned into supplements to consumerism and successful careers. For many, the consciousness-raising and self-discovery of the 1960s and 1970s turned out to be stepping stones linking the 1950s 'get on' advice of Dale Carnegie to the remaking-of-self which is continually expected by neoliberalism. In time, the hippy desire for freedom of expression was – albeit roughly and incompletely – mapped onto the market individualism of the 1980s. In Goran Therborn's assessment, the general range of cultural transformations rooted in 1968, notwith-standing their progressive character, 'have since largely been absorbed by advanced capitalism, with the informality of high-tech industries, a surge of female CEOs, the mainstreaming of gay rights and same-sex marriage, the social figure of the "bourgeois-bohemian", and so on'.[26]

These issues have been explored by Luc Boltanski and Eve Chiapello, who have scrutinised 'the celebration of creativity, worker autonomy, anti-bureaucracy and non-hierarchical and non-linear organisational systems in post-fordist management theory since around the middle of the 1980s', and noted how these drew from forms of radicalism associated with '1968'.[27]

Making this point is not to regret or condemn the countercul-ture, but to state the need for a critique of its hijacking by processes of commodification. The rebellious students of 1968 were reacting against order and deference, and this had a progressive content; it was a stand against arbitrary authority, the inane oppressiveness of 'our elders and betters' telling us we should do as they say. But it also had an individualist content, and there was a failure to understand the importance of acting collectively, and the value of some measure of collective discipline. The rebellion against the tradition and authority of elders helped dissolve and undo the ties and responsibilities that had shaped and underlain working-class progress and culture.

Left and working-class traditions could certainly be conformist and lacking in ambition, and exhibited many other oppressive qualities, particularly in relationship to their embeddedness in patriarchal and imperial cultures. But there was also a positive core, and this was corroded as the spirit of 1968 infused some aspects of left-wing politics with a hedonistic libertarianism, which, as Perry Anderson comments, 'sprang from the same moral soil as ... unbridled neoliberalism in the casting off of all restraints, first of sex and then of greed, in pursuit of naked individual desire'.[28]

Not all freaks were revolutionaries, it turned out: many were the consumers of tomorrow. Impulses initially seen as threats to the establishment – individualistic acts of outrageous self-expression through radical lifestyle choice, the adoption of dissident styles – were reshaped and reworked into capitalist dreams of self-fulfilment through the unexpected twists and byways of consumerism. Bill Gates and Richard Branson – 'character masks' of capitalism over the last few decades – can be seen as true heirs of '1968' just as much as, and perhaps even more than, Tariq Ali or 'Danny the Red' Cohn-Bendit. The insubordinate and newly-passionate forms of entrepreneurialism associated with Gates and Branson took root in the culture of individuation.[29] The products and associated cultural forms they began to develop from the 1960s seemed to offer new freedoms and possibilities – but were soon turned into ever-more effective devices to stupefy and atomise us. The neoliberal culture that began to shape the world from the mid-1970s was to emphasise the importance of the individual consumer choices we make; it redefined politics as the art of maintaining the framework within which we can be happy shoppers.

It is important to balance these concerns and regrets with a recognition that many progressive currents emerged from the radicalism of the late 1960s. For some years after 1968, left and radical agendas flourished: large numbers of students became involved in activism; there was a development of innovative intellectual critiques of capitalism; many activists experienced the power and liberating effect of new movements such as feminism and black consciousness; the range of politics expanded to include personal issues and cultural life; there was enormous energy, imagination and creativity. New social antagonisms and new kinds of social subjects were constituted, and with this came 'new models of society, a new sense of what socialism might and should be about'.[30]

Emerging through a struggle against the sexism and arrogance that were all too present amongst student radicals and counterculturalists, new women's groups emerged in many European countries and in North America. The women's movement – which had learned extensively from black social movements – opened up discussion and action about many issues new to politics: sexism, sex and sexuality, patriarchy, motherhood, the socialisation of children, gender-stereotyping, and discrimination at work and in social and political life. Feminism became far-reaching and influential, as was its insistence that 'the personal is political'. Before long, the issue of women's liberation was generating a dynamic of change across society. Equal pay became a major issue, as seen for example in the 1968 strike by machinists at Ford Dagenham for equal pay, celebrated in the 2010 film *Made in Dagenham*; activists disrupted the objectifying display of the Miss World 'beauty pageants'; and women in hundreds of thousands of homes and workplaces acted on the view that being treated as unequal within the family was no longer acceptable. Women started to make connections between their own personal experience and the social forces that structured them, and to recognise that their problems were shared by large numbers of other women: they were not caused by their own, individual, personal inadequacy. They also began to test the authenticity and consistency of organisations and individuals purporting to represent progressive principles.

New understandings were expressed at the level of 'theory'. For example, criticisms of consumerism, and the resistance to contemporary forms of oppression, were promoted by the French radical philosophers such as Gilles Deleuze and Felix Guattari, whose strategic proposals called into question some practices of the communist left. For example, their arguments for 'scattered resistance', and for maintaining the autonomy of social movements, countered all calls to build hegemonic politics.

A further legacy of 1968 is the social space it helped to make for the lyric impulse, for example through promoting a widespread cultural desire to reconnect with nature. The development of the counterculture, and the varied dissident subjectivities it produced, created spaces within which some distance from, and attempted refusal of, consumerism remains possible.

In spite of such theoretical engagements, however, the radical left proved unable to sufficiently connect to large numbers of people, and to develop sustainable alternative cultural milieus and structures. Capital, meanwhile, found its ways to engage and rework some of the values and desires generated by the spirit of '68. Rock music was soon doing more to expand the balance-sheets of major corporations than to inspire a radical consciousness in its fans. The 1960s dreams of liberation were reworked into the contemporary terrain on which we have been constructed as modern consumers – though, as Jeremy Gilbert has argued, consent organised on this basis is often disaffected.[31]

Marcuse – who, as Gregor McLennan argues, combined 'unflagging respect for the plain truths of Marxism alongside heterodox thinking about social novelty and the economically ungraspable' – was one of the first to recognise these dangers.[32] He suggested that consumer society, by legitimating capitalism and partially meeting human needs in its particular ways, was preventing democracy's full realisation in the form of socialism:

Has not late industrial society already surpassed, in a bad form, the idea of socialism? ... of course, all the wealth, the technology, and the productivity of this society cannot match the ideas of real freedom and of real justice which are at the centre of socialist theory ... [but] developed industrial society has already won for itself much of the ground on which the new freedom was to have flourished.[33]

In this context, the challenge in Western Europe and North America was to develop a strategy for liberation from 'a relatively well-functioning, rich, powerful society ... liberation from the affluent society'.[34]

The spirit of '68 was complex and contradictory. It has been condemned both by social conservatives who dislike what they see as the excesses of permissiveness and by traditionalists on the left who regard it as at best a diversion from the real struggle and at worst as the emerging spirit of libertarian capitalism. I would argue that the impulses to throw off socially-imposed petty constraints, puritan inhibitions and oppressive attitudes were healthy and progressive. But for some, the spirit of the new age was little more than a licence to act for short-term gratification, an impulse all too easily commodified. The sense that personal freedom could somehow be bought was promoted over and above any sense of the social good: indeed it was promoted precisely in order to undermine any sense of the social good. On the other hand, the liberatory impulse helped create the context for the emergence of new social movements, and these in turn gave rise to new understandings about the nature of power and its operation through many different ways and in so many sites. The tragedy is that capital had access to far greater resources for the articulation of the new spirit than were available to the left. Both the left and right include conservative currents unable or reluctant to adapt to new moods. But in the last few decades it is the right that has been ruthless in attacking conservatism.

My own feeling is that there is a logic in radical politics which means it flourishes best when we consciously subordinate our own short-term individual interests to that of the *collectivity* or group, in the knowledge that this is the only way for our collective interests to be strong enough to counter the inequalities generated by the capitalist logic of possessive individualism. It is community-minded activity – rather than individualism, distinctive self-expression and independence from social control – that has the capacity to liberate.[35] Serious radical politics is not about people breaking rules or being rebels (though it is often this impulse – a reaction to the unjust norms with which we live – which first brings people into radical politics): it consists in establishing a new framework for society whose norms and rules properly reflect the interests of ordinary people; it involves finding ways to work together to bring about change – which requires a degree of consistency and seriousness. If the groups to which we belong – whether these are small campaigning groups, political parties, local authorities, states or international unions – are felt to be democratic, the idea of the collective good, which may require us to give up some of our own particular desires, has much stronger purchase.

Progressive causes imply a strong concept of being a democratic citizen, and of accepting and acting on the disciplines and restrictions that come with that. But in the 1960s and 1970s, it was difficult to maintain this position: freedom was too often interpreted as freedom from constraint, as a release from discipline, rather as the freedom to express a consciously chosen responsibility.[36]

## NOTES

1. Quoted in Bela Balassa, *Change and Challenge in the World Economy*, Macmillan, London 1985, p264.
2. Eric Hobsbawm, 'Foreword' to Stephanie Gregoire, *1968*, Hazan 1998, p8.

3. Josef Smrkovsky, 'What Lies Ahead', *Rude Pravo*, 9 February 1968.
4. Alexander Dubcek, 'Speech to the Presidium of the Communist Party', *Rude Pravo*, 19 July 1968.
5. George Theiner, preface to Ludvik Vaculik, *A Cup of Coffee with my Interrogator*, Readers International, London 1987.
6. Jon Bloomfield, *Passive Revolution*, Allison and Busby, London 1979, p12.
7. Quoted by Eusebio M. Mujal-Leon, in Rudolf L. Tokes (ed), *Eurocommunism and Detente*, Martin Robertson, Oxford 1978, p228.
8. Lucio Magri, *The Tailor of Ulm*, Verso, London 2011, p227.
9. Manuel Azcarate, 'What is Eurocommunism?', in G.R. Urban (ed), *Eurocommunism*, Maurice Temple Smith, London, 1978, p18.
10. Richard Cross, '1968 and After' *Twentieth Century Communism*, 3, 2011, p8.
11. Georg Lukacs, *The Process of Democratisation*, State University of New York Press, NY 1991 [1968].
12. Georg Lukacs, 'Lukacs on his Life and Work', *New Left Review*, July – August 1971.
13. Paulina Bren, *The Greengrocer and his TV*, Cornell University Press, London 2010, p207.
14. Gopal Balakrishnan, 'Future Unknown', *New Left Review*, March – April 2005.
15. Herbert Marcuse, *One Dimensional Man*, Routledge, Abingdon 2002 [1964].
16. Fredric Jameson, *Valences of the Dialectic*, Verso, London 2009, p266.
17. Discussed in Phil Edwards, 'Rejecting all adventurism', *Twentieth Century Communism*, 3, 2011. Amendola's article was 'The necessity to fight on two fronts', *Rinascita*, 7 June 1968.
18. Giovanni Russo, in Paolo Fila della Torre, Edward Mortimer and Jonathan Story (eds), *Eurocommunism*, Penguin Books, Harmondsworth 1979, p95.
19. Maria Antonietta Macciocchi, *Letters from inside the Italian Communist Party to Louis Althusser*, New Left Books/Verso, London 1973, p138.
20. Sven Lutticken, 'Cultural Revolution', *New Left Review*, May – June 2014.
21. See Alasdair MacIntyre's sniffy but valid disapproval of 'parent-financed revolts' in *Marcuse*, Fontana, London 1970, p89. Some of the thinkers most sympathetic to 1968 were also highly critical of self-indulgent, provocative and adventurist behaviour, on the basis that it would limit the movement, and lead to its fragmentation. These actually included Marcuse: 'if the New Left is to continue to grow into a real political force, it will develop its own *spirit de serieux*, its own rationality in its own sensibility; it will overcome its Oedipus complex on political terms'. *Counter-revolution and Revolt*, Penguin, London 1972, p51.

22. Eric Hobsbawm, *The Age of Extremes*, Michael Joseph, London 1994, p334.

23. Francois Furet, *The Passing of an Illusion*, University of Chicago Press, London 1999, p492.

24. Bertell Ollman, 'The Utopian Vision of the Future (Then and Now)', *Monthly Review*, July – August 2005.

25. Hilary Wainwright, 'An Excess of Democracy', www.opendemocracy. net, 24 February 2012.

26. Goran Therborn, 'New Masses?' *New Left Review,* January – February 2014.

27. Jeremy Gilbert, *Soundings* 45, summer 2010. As Gilbert states, 'a key historical question ... is that of how far the expression of such sentiments by "countercultural" figures was ever a genuine challenge to established relations of power, and how far it was merely an expression of the spontaneous ideology of the avant-garde of capital itself'. The book under discussion: Luc Boltanski and Eve Chiapello, *The New Spirit of Capitalism*, Verso, London, 2007 [1999].

28. Perry Anderson, 'The Vanquished Left', *Spectrum*, Verso, London 2005, pp303-4.

29. Editors' introduction in Manuel Castells, Joao Caraca and Gustavo Cardoso (eds), *Aftermath*, Oxford University Press, Oxford 2012. Marx used the concept of 'character masks' to refer to people who expressed, justified or apologised for the social relations of their day, in ways which disguised or obscured social contradictions.

30. Stuart Hall and Martin Jacques, '1968', *Marxism Today*, May 1988.

31. Jeremy Gilbert, 'Disaffected Consent', *Soundings* 60, summer 2015.

32. Gregor McLennan, 'Charting Radical Theory' *New Left Review*, Jan – Feb 2013.

33. Herbert Marcuse, *Negations*, Penguin, Harmondsworth 1968, pxviii. Marcuse pointed out elsewhere that '"consumer society" is a misnomer of the first order, for rarely has a society so systematically been organised in the interests which control production'. *Counter-revolution and Revolt*, op cit, p23.

34. Herbert Marcuse, 'Liberation from the Affluent Society', in David Cooper (ed), *Dialectics of Liberation*, Verso, London 2015 [1968], p176.

35. The '"freedom" which isolated individuals may acquire thanks to their position in society or their inner constitution regardless of what happens to others means in practice that the unfree structure of contemporary society will be perpetuated in so far as it depends on the individual'. Georg Lukacs, *History and Class Consciousness,* Merlin Press, London 1971, [1923], p315.

36. This distinction between different forms of freedom draws from Antonio Gramsci, in Joseph A. Buttigieg (ed), *Prison Notebooks*, Volume Three, Columbia University Press, New York 2011, p10. It is significant that

Gramsci was *not* one of the thinkers widely celebrated in 1968. His reputation grew a little later, during the time of taking stock and recognition that leftist frontal assault had once more not turned out to be a straight path to socialism: Gramsci's work found its reception when people needed resources to understand and respond to setbacks, marginalisation and defeat.

# 13. September in Santiago

## THE BATTLE OF CHILE

Five years after the Prague Spring, another attempt to realise left-wing values on a democratic basis was crushed, this time in Chile – a country in the American 'backyard' rather than the Soviet buffer zone. The horrors of Santiago illustrated a major danger lying in wait for all those seeking democratic socialism: the reaction of the enemy. In Chile, a democratically elected government attempting to challenge the power of capital was met with intransigence and counter-revolutionary measures, before being overthrown in a violent coup which was backed by the United States. This was a further illustration of capitalism's readiness to dispense with democratic 'niceties' if it believed its interests to be threatened.

In 1969 socialist and left groups, including the communist party, had formed the Popular Unity alliance, which narrowly won the 1970 election (though it did not have an overall majority). The Socialist Party leader Salvador Allende was elected as president, on 39 per cent of the vote. This seemed a confirmation of the Chilean Communist Party's strategy of legal participation in the electoral system – a position it held in common with most CPs in Latin America at that time. Popular Unity showed that that democracy, law and progress could be articulated together in a broad alliance across the left – and separated from coercion, force and privilege.

But during the short life of the Popular Unity government, increasingly serious attempts were made to destabilise the alliance – including through a campaign of right-wing terrorism and acts of murder. Popular Unity's growing support infuriated the reactionaries of the 'import-export coalition'.[1] This was made up of business leaders whose economic interests depended on meeting the requirements of foreign capital: they had been in renewed negotiations with American copper companies, offering generous terms for the exploitation of Chile's nitrate resources.

In July 1971 US copper mining companies were nationalised; and the government began using the radical but legally-based concept of 'excess profits' to claim compensation from foreign firms and domestic capitalists for what they had taken from Chilean people over the decades. This assertion of sovereignty attracted massive opposition from the American-backed right, and there were fraught debates amongst Allende's supporters about how to proceed. The communists, led by Luis Corvalan, urged a cautious approach, emphasising that Chile could and should take a democratic path to socialism, and mindful of the dangers of a reactionary counterattack. But some socialists and ultra-leftists urged Allende to push ahead faster. It is by no means clear, however, that any strategy other than wholesale capitulation to the plutocrats could have prevented the coup.

During Allende's first year, nearly fifty large industrial firms were nationalised, along with most of the banking system. Factories introduced co-management, bringing shop-floor representatives into the boardroom, and increasing workers' sense of dignity.[2] Six million acres of land formerly held by the large landowners were expropriated and became communal property. There was full employment, inflation was being brought under control, and wage earners received pay rises averaging 30 per cent.[3] The share of national income accruing to ordinary workers – both manual and 'white-collar' – increased. Popular Unity worked hard to ensure that the middle class were also securing benefits from their programme, though not at the expense of the proletariat, as had always previously been the case, but instead at the expense of the financial oligarchy and foreign capital. But in spite of this strategy – and in many ways because of its potential success – there was fierce reaction from the richest forces in the country – and from their international allies.

The concern was not that Allende was failing in his goal to take Chile in positive directions, with popular support: it was that he was succeeding in this goal. In 1971's local elections, Popular Unity increased its support, winning half of the vote and becoming the biggest political force in the country. Henry Kissinger worried that Chile looked like becoming a dangerous example:

a successful elected Marxist government in Chile would surely have an impact in the rest of the world, especially in Italy; the imitative spread of similar phenomenon would in turn significantly affect the world balance and our position in it.[4]

As Oscar Guardiola-Rivera has argued, Western statesmen were concerned that Allende was both 'a revolutionary and a democrat, an avowed Marxist ... who believed in law'. This was a combination 'too strange [and] too perilous to be allowed to appear possible from the viewpoint of cold war politics'.[5]

Leftist groups had been growing in Chile throughout the 1960s, drawing energy from the wider climate of generational revolt. They took inspiration from the Argentinean Che Guevara, hero of the Cuban revolution, admiring his bravery and refusal to compromise, even though some disagreed with his guerrilla-based model – the idea that the armed actions of small groups could kick-start revolutions. Che had unsuccessfully tried to lead revolutionary groups of this kind in Congo in 1965 and in Bolivia in 1966, where he was captured and executed in October 1967. But his militancy and scathing critiques of illusions about democracy brought a clarity and anger to left politics in Chile, something that young people saw as having been lost by the older 'Stalinist' parties.[6] Thus the Movement of the Revolutionary Left, or MIR, warned that there would inevitably be a violent confrontation, engineered by the ruling class and 'Yanquis', who had no respect for democratic rules. Allende saw the *Miristas* as misguided and adventurist, at the same time as recognising their bravery and recruiting some of its members as his personal armed guard. He maintained that a democratic transition to socialism was possible.

If this was ever the case, it was not in fact to be. The CIA proved MIR right: Chile joined the list of democratically elected but radical governments overthrown with the direct involvement of the United States. The build-up to the coup took the form of great pressure being put on the budget, and politically engineered scarcities. Allende had anticipated that wage rises would lead to increased demand, which would then prompt an investment boom. This never came; it was blocked by the US and their allies. A mismatch opened between the high hopes raised by the government's declarations, and increasingly difficult economic realities. A right-wing coup attempt at the end of June 1973, which was foiled by constitutionalist army officers, led only to more determined efforts by the reactionaries.

Their key objective came into focus; not just to prevent immediate losses, but to protect and defend the prospects of future multinational profits from the wider threat posed by the existence of a popular and successful socialist movement. Although there was financial assistance from International Telephone and Telegraph and Anaconda Copper – American corporations with large holdings in Chile, which they did not want to lose – the key reason the US government needed to make it impossible for Allende's elected government to function was the fear that Chile would serve as an example to other democratic and popular movements in Latin American and elsewhere.

By late summer 1973, a 'transport strike' was paralysing the country. This was actually a lorry owners' boycott, sponsored by the CIA as part of a campaign which the US President Richard Nixon had commissioned in order to 'make the economy scream'.[7] Well-funded propaganda campaigns portrayed Popular Unity's programme as a left-wing heist, a blatant robbery of savings and investment funds. With the middle class being encouraged to stage 'strikes' and close shops, the government found itself under siege. Ordinary conservatives were cynically pushed into supporting the most reactionary politics, including the murderous suppression of the left. The right spelled out their view: democracy reached its limits when a democratically-elected government started interfering with property rights. When the rule concerning the bourgeois limits of 'democracy' was broken, bourgeois democracy no longer needed to be respected.

On 11 September 1973, coincident with joint American and Chilean naval manoeuvres in the Pacific, Chilean air-force pilots dive-bombed the presidential palace. Aerial assault was followed by tank fire: Allende died at his post, holding an AK47 he'd been given by the Cuban leader Fidel Castro. The CP was driven underground. In yet another instance of murderous anti-communism in Latin America, right-wing fury was visited on the left and trade unions, extending repression far beyond the ranks of card-carrying communist party members. Over 40,000 people were tortured, executed or 'disappeared', and hundreds of thousands cast into exile.

## OPENING UP SPACE: THE ITALIAN RESPONSE TO CHILE

The events in Chile were the catalyst of political debate. For some leftists, the murderous overthrow of the democratic government conclusively destroyed the myth of legalism. The war-planes swooping down on La Moneda had confirmed their analysis: this would not have happened if only more people had joined them in confronting the rich pro-Americans.

In Western Europe, revulsion at Allende's murder helped create what Christopher Hitchens later described as 'a shift in which important elements amongst the conservative order, especially in Italy, decided not to identify themselves with authoritarian rule'.[8] Eurocommunists in that country saw the need and opportunity to respond to these developments: they had their own difficulties in overcoming the blocks they faced in the structures of Italian politics.

These structures were set around the Christian Democrats, who had been central to every post-war Italian government. *Democrazia Cristiana* had won its first overall majority in the US- and cold war influenced 1948 elections, and 'DC' had subsequently governed throughout the postwar period in a succession of centre-right or centre-left coalitions. The DC ascendancy had entrenched clientelism in Italy, especially in the south, where it had repurposed social institutions created under fascism for its own political advantage. The resulting corruption and political instability had made it difficult for government to tackle Italy's longstanding economic problems. And despite regularly winning around a quarter of the vote, as well as its record of efficient municipal government in Italy's 'red belt' regions, the PCI had effectively been excluded from power at national level.

By the early 1970s, the need to address these problems, together with the post-Allende mood, led to new ideas about how to advance the cause of socialism. Increasing numbers of non-communists felt that, without bringing the PCI into government, the country's underlying economic and political problems could not be solved.

Communist leader Enrico Berlinguer took note of the likelihood of increased support for the party. But there was to be no excited dash for power. As recounted by the Italian left-wing politician Altiero Spinelli, Berlinguer's reflections on the events in Chile centred on the judgement that Allende had not been able to sustain his democratic right to govern because 'the great mass of non-electoral power – the police, the civil administration, the judiciary, the holders of economic power: in brief, the Establishment – was against the elected government'. The conservative constellation of forces outside parliament was thus able to generate a successful challenge to the government:

Pondering this example [Italian communist leaders] came to the conclusion that a similar fate might befall an Italian communist government. Even if the communists and the socialists united, they would, so the communists realised, still be too weak to govern and resist the combined opposition of the parliamentary right and that large conglomeration of non-parliamentary power that would try to defeat a communist-led government. The next step in the Communist Party's reasoning was to say that, in order to come to power and exercise power with any chance of success, the party must come to an understanding with the Christian Democrats.[9]

Avoiding Allende's fate became a key concern. The communist aim was to help establish a unified national leadership founded on broad agreement between all those parties and groups who were committed to democracy and the political priority of meeting the needs of ordinary Italians. Working to keep the middle class on board with strategies for change thus became a key element of political strategy.[10]

This led to the adoption of an emphasis on preserving democracy, rather than on the anti-capitalist dimensions of class struggle: too rapid an advance of the left would expose Italy to reactionary backlash. Over the next few years, and despite increasingly good electoral results, the PCI refused to countenance taking power directly. Berlinguer would not move on the basis of a technical majority of 51 per cent. The initial level of support of less than forty per cent which had brought Allende to power had certainly not been enough to preserve the Chilean government. Berlinguer's position was that, unless radicals could get an overwhelming mandate, freely expressed in successive competitive elections, and sustained and strengthened over time, alongside serious and continuous political education, they simply would not be able to achieve the transformative changes which they wanted to implement.[11]

Berlinguer also argued that it was proper and crucial to relate to those who would not support a radical approach even when there was a convincing majority mandate. Through a 'historic compromise' with DC, the PCI would establish a unified bloc of democratic forces that would be strong enough to withstand the tensions generated by the coming to power of a communist party. Italy would then be spared the terrible divisions which had split Chile.[12]

In following this strategy, communists saw themselves as determined champions of the constitutional order, and on that basis moved
into *de facto* alliance with conservatives. From June 1976, when it won
34 per cent of the vote, the PCI gave its support – through abstention
from voting against – to a minority DC government and co-operated
with DC on a national programme of retrenchment and reform. This
'national solidarity' approach was consolidated in 1977, when the PCI
began to vote *for* the government instead of merely refraining from
voting against it.[13]

Radical leftists saw Berlinguer as having abandoned any serious
commitment to socialism. They mocked the communists for their
'fear of winning'. In fact, their patience and long-term perspective was
the mark of the Italian communists' seriousness. The final aim was
not for a permanent governing alliance between the left and conservatives: the historic compromise was a strategy of transition, an essential
step in the unblocking of Italian democracy, which would open the
way for a new situation in which the PCI could take its place as a fully
legitimate party of government. At this point, the DC's hold on power
could be ended.[14]

Fundamentally rejecting the confrontationist style of revolutionary
communism, the radical insight shaping the strategy was that profound
changes would only be possible if the party could avoid the prospect
of serious political polarisation.[15] As part of this, the PCI thought
it was important to maintain an open channel with the institutions
and culture of Catholicism, given that the majority of the population were Catholic.[16] Even in the party itself, Catholics outnumbered
atheists. In the mid-1970s, in the 'red' Emilia-Romagna region, the
PCI was the largest Catholic Party, simple arithmetic evidencing
that more Catholics were voting for the communists than for the
Christian Democrats. This situation had built up even as Pope Pius
XII had excommunicated believers who voted communist. By 1977,
Berlinguer could deny 'accusations' that the PCI professed atheism
and materialism. He described the party as 'lay and democratic, and
as such not theistic, atheistic or anti-theistic'.[17]

All this put the party in the position of seeking to control and
regulate working-class militancy. Although experienced trade unionists could understand the strategy, it created space to the left of the
communist party for those who wished to resist such discipline. The
PCI was showing its understanding of the dangers of moving too

soon, being premature, arriving before the preconditions were in place to establish and consolidate success. But its wisdom in this respect was so developed that some felt it could not see the opposite danger: of not moving at all.[18]

Nevertheless, key communists in other countries took the lessons of Chile in the same way as the Italians. Santiago Carrillo, now helping steer and steady his country towards post-Franco democracy, recognised the need for the proletariat 'to remain allied with the middle strata and not to become isolated'.[19]

It was not only socialists and communists that looked hard at the implications of Chile. For right-wing intellectuals and politicians it was a case study and laboratory for the new neoliberal ideas. Friedrich Hayek, an early apologist for the dictator of Chile and neoliberal pioneer Augusto Pinochet, thought it better to have a dictator who preserved 'the rule of law' than a democracy that ignored 'the rule of law'. As David Runciman pointed out, 'by the rule of law, Hayek meant above all the preservation of private property against the depredations of inflation'.[20]

## THE TEMPTATIONS OF ADVENTURISM

Whilst Berlinguer looked towards 'historic compromise' as the way forward for the left, small groups of determined leftists were clear they would never adopt such a strategy. Some groups of young people turned to what they called 'armed struggle' as a mark of their seriousness and determination. The most significant of these was in Italy, but there were others, such as the Red Army Faction in West Germany and the Weather Underground in the US.[21] Eric Hobsbawm judged that the fact that such groups enthusiastically proclaimed their connection with Marx did not conceal that 'they were pursuing strategies and policies which Marxist revolutionaries had traditionally rejected or distrusted'.[22]

Horrified and 'driven crazy' by their country's war in Vietnam, and by the systemic racism directed at black people, the Weather Underground's roots were in the anti-war campaigns of Students for a Democratic Society. After trying and failing to take over the SDS, the 'Weathermen' decided to reject legal campaigning, seeing themselves as 'communist cadre working for the violent overthrow of the government of the USA'.[23] Their isolation only further confirmed their feelings of anger, sectarianism and purism, and desire to punish: their initially positive motivation to fight oppression became warped and distorted into the terrorist option.[24]

Self-justification came from decontextualised readings of literature from national liberation struggles in Asia and Latin America, such as Regis Debray's 1967 book *Revolution in the Revolution?*. The idea that the 'small motor' of a guerrilla nucleus would be able to create the conditions for the 'big motor' of mass movements had already proved a suicidal fantasy in parts of Latin America, such as in Bolivia, where Che Guevara perished, and in Peru, where Luis de la Puente Uceda had failed to attract indigenous peasant support for his insurrectionary efforts in the central highlands, and was killed in 1965. That even Debray had recognised that the principles he set out were relevant only to 'certain regions of Latin America', and only 'in the long run', was hastily skipped over by would-be urban guerrillas in northern countries: tactics that had worked in the Cuban Sierra Maestra were highly unlikely to find any traction in New York's Greenwich Village, however 'radical' the counterculture there might be. One of its thoughtful former members has reflected on the Weather Underground's moral analysis:

> we felt that doing nothing in a period of repressive violence is itself a form of violence ... if you sit in your house, and live your white life, and go to your white job, and allow the country that you live in to murder people and to commit genocide, and you sit there and don't do anything about it, that's violence.[25]

In developing such perspectives, the Weather Underground drew on a selective reading of Herbert Marcuse's work. They believed that, by definition, any form of protest that was likely to be effective would not be permitted by the authorities: any state-sanctioned demonstration was thus automatically suspect. By allowing certain oppositional activities, the state was adopting a policy of 'repressive tolerance' (a term coined by Marcuse): it was providing a safety valve for dissent, which kept the opposition happy but presented no real challenge to those in power.[26] The true revolutionary would act outside the law, if necessary meeting violence with violence (this was not Marcuse's conclusion). The analysis of the Weathermen as they observed political and social trends from their hiding places and assumed identities, was not without insight: they accurately comprehended the frustrating reality that apparent gains often change into their opposite. For example, child-care facilities are campaigned for as a progressive demand, but once in place they can be utilised as a way of ensuring that women are available for low-paid work.

From the mid-1970s, some Weather Underground members began to critique and distance themselves from aspects of their earlier practice, recognising that violence can become a way, not of effectively expressing anger, recovering pride and agency and promoting a cause, but of enabling that cause to be discredited, marginalised, and defeated. Through this recognition, they were able to reject the tactics they had adopted, whilst staying loyal to the reasons they had adopted those tactics.

An understanding of 'systemic violence' and state repression was also key to the development of the Red Army Faction in West Germany (also known as the Baader Meinhof group), a far-left group espousing violent tactics that consisted of a few dozen actual members, supported by perhaps 1500 sympathisers. The group's development was partly due to fact that the Communist Party had been banned in West Germany since 1956, meaning that youth radicalism developed without the relatively stabilising effect of a legal CP; and the ban also lent credibility to the argument that the Federal Republic was a successor state to the Third Reich: formally democratic, but actually authoritarian. Ulrike Meinhof's articles for the magazine *konkret* compared 1960s West Germany to the Nazi regime, enabling readers to conceive of themselves as potential moral agents with a duty to act against the cleverly disguised totalitarianism in which they lived.[27] The death of Benno Ohnesorg, a demonstrator killed by police in 1967, seemed to confirm this view, as did the attempted murder of student leader Rudi Dutschke a year later.[28]

Having been galvanised into a more militant stance by state repression, and having seen how violent demonstrations provoked arrests and emergency legislation, Meinhof, Andreas Baader and the other RAF members adopted the 'strategy' of attempting to provoke the state into ever-more frequent and excessive acts of repression, on the basis that this would kick-start 'the masses' into effective revolutionary action. Their approach – 'the worse things get, the better our chances' – failed entirely. In the novelist Heinrich Boll's damning formula, the RAF's was 'a war of six against sixty million'.

Some radicals continue to express misplaced sympathy and romantic admiration for terrorist groups such as the RAF. But the RAF's criminal and counter-productive actions were an expression of powerlessness and frustration – a fact that Slavoj Zizek fails to foreground in his provocative and irresponsible suggestion of endorsement of Meinhof's 'insight' that 'in an epoch in which the masses are totally immersed in capitalist ideological torpor ... only a resort to the raw Real of direct violence ... can awaken them'.[29]

## CONTESTING THE STRATEGY OF TENSION – OR FALLING INTO THE TRAP?

This is not to say that all the left-wing 'urban guerrillas' of the early 1970s were entirely deluded or cut off from any significant social base. In Italy there were strong links between leftist armed groups and militant workers. The *Brigate Rosse* (Red Brigades, BR) – a revolutionary group committed to armed struggle – emerged from a milieu of widespread radical extra-parliamentary activity. This milieu was influenced by autonomism, a tendency which originated from the early 1960s around the journal *Quaderni Rossi*. It celebrated unofficial strikes in which advice from trade union leaders and the PCI was rejected; advocated forms of shop floor resistance which amounted to a refusal of work; explicitly rejected strategies of developing working-class hegemony; and argued that that the working class should resist capitalism independently – autonomously – from political parties and trade unions. Within the autonomist collectives critiquing what they saw as PCI reformism, some activists promoted violence as theoretically justified. As Alberto Melucci recounts, armed clashes with the police during demonstrations, and physical violence against their adversaries – including members of the Communist Party, who they regarded as traitors – became routine from 1977 onwards, and for many young people constituted their first step towards terrorism.[30]

The BR and other armed left-wing groups in Italy had more credibility than their counterparts in other countries because they were responding to actual right-wing repression: they were not imagining it or, even more mistakenly, trying to provoke it. In Italy, shadowy right-wing forces *did* plan to stage a quasi-military coup in response to an act of violence that they would carry out but then blame on the left. They envisaged a scenario in which the resulting destabilisation of the state would lead to a fascist take-over, assisted by sympathisers already embedded in the military and security services. Behind these undemocratic intrigues was a secret NATO organisation code-named Gladio, which had been established after the second world war as a 'deep-state' outfit whose aim was to prevent by means of military coup any communist takeover, democratic or otherwise, and, if that failed, to oppose the subsequent communist government through terrorism. (Similar outfits were also set up in a number of other European countries regarded as being part of the postwar western sphere of influence.) As Sebastian Losurdo records, in post-war Italy the possibility of a PCI/Socialist coalition coming to power by electoral means was regarded as so alarming that the US trained a secret underground armed right-wing force 'to commence operations in such an eventuality':

> Another element of the CIA's approach was a plan to foster and support secessionist movements in Sardinia and Sicily, and thus dismember any Italy that would vote a left-wing government into power in 1948. The 'danger' was abated by the use of CIA funding to encourage the defection in 1947 of a part of the [Socialist Party] to form a safely anti-communist Social Democratic Party, which was immediately accorded political respectability.[31]

Such secret forces and hidden politics indicate that a number of West European post-war political settlements were brought about through the exercise of great pressure rather than the 'normal' practices of democracy. Normality is always something that is constructed and worked for by particular social forces.

As the left grew stronger in Italy, the secret forces had no intention of sitting on their hands. They pursued a 'strategy of tension' aimed at creating a climate of fear and chaos that would pull people away from the left, and during the 1970s and early 1980s – 'the years of lead' – a series of attacks were carried out by right-wing terrorists: an early outrage was the bombing of the Piazza Fontana in Milan in 1969, which killed seventeen people and injured many more.[32] The BR formed partly in response to this strategy, with a view to resisting an expected right-wing coup.[33] But such groups were a minority response to these state-sponsored outrages. The reactionary provocateurs had misread the context. The mainstream left and workers' movement, with experienced anti-fascist resistance veterans at its head, responded with dignity rather than anger to the provocative massacres. They organised massive silent marches rather than responding violently as the bombers had hoped. Christian Democrats were appalled by the far right's violence, and people across the political spectrum were impressed with the left's disciplined actions. If the aim of the reactionary bombers had been to provoke the left in ways which would push mainstream conservatives towards the position that democracy should be ditched, they had failed.

In this context, the PCI did not seek a dialogue with the radical left constituency from which the BR drew support; and they felt compelled to distance themselves 'not only from the armed milieu, but also from all of those who might be looked upon as its supporters'.[34] Some commentators argue that this helped erode support for the PCI among young radicals. But the strategy of the PCI was to work to counter the possibility of 'an authoritarian solution' by further developing its collaboration with other mainstream political forces, on the centre left – and on the centre right.

## NOTES

1. Oscar Guardiola-Rivera, *Story of a Death Foretold*, Bloomsbury, London 2013, p45.
2. Peter Winn, 'Living the Chilean Revolution', *Radical History Review*, 124, 2016.
3. Gabriel Garcia Marquez, 'Why Allende had to die', *New Statesman*, 15 March 1974.
4. Kissinger to Richard Nixon, 1970, quoted in Guardiola-Rivera, op cit, p56.
5. Ibid, pp150-1.
6. Interviewed by a British communist journalist in 1962, Guevara set out his view on the likely course of attempts to advance 'democratically'. 'Let's take for example a country in Latin America where you've got some sort of democratic system and the communist party is legal. You work away, you've got parliamentary elections and you have a dozen communists elected to parliament, then you double and treble the number of communists and you continue on this policy by parliamentary means and it looks as if at the coming election you could have a big victory. Before that election comes, the regime cancels the system and you're finished'. When his interviewer pointed out that Latin American communist parties thought that there was in fact a possibility of democratic advance, Guevara's response was that 'the communist parties of Latin America are

*shit'*. Sam Russell, 'Moscow – Havana – Prague', *Twentieth Century Communism*, 3, 2011, pp160-1.

7. Nixon gave his instruction to the CIA director Richard Helms during a short meeting on 15 September 1970, also attended by Henry Kissinger. A facsimile of Helms's handwritten note of the meeting: http://nsarchive2. gwu.edu/NSAEBB/NSAEBB8/ch26-01.htm (accessed 3 June 2017).

8. Christopher Hitchens, '11 September 1973', *London Review of Books*, 11 July 2002.

9. Altiero Spinelli, 'How European are the Italian Eurocommunists?', in G.R. Urban (ed), *Euro-communism*, Maurice Temple Smith, London 1978, pp189-90.

10. Enrico Berlinguer's 'Reflections on the events in Chile' were carried in *Marxism Today*, February 1974.

11. Berlinguer's point on the need for strong electoral support echoes Ernst Wigforss, Sweden's social-democrat finance minister in the 1930s: 'when radical reforms are passionately opposed by powerful minorities, a bare majority is not enough: you need an overwhelming majority'. Swedish social democracy can be seen as anticipating Eurocommunism in this and a number of other ways.

12. Lawrence Garner, 'Enrico Berlinguer' in Robert A. Gorman (ed), *Biographical Dictionary of Neo-Marxism*, Mansell Publishing Limited, London 1985, p70.

13. John C. Campbell, 'Eurocommunism', in Rudolf L. Tokes (ed), *Eurocommunism and Detente*, Martin Robertson, Oxford 1978, p526.

14. Philip Daniels, 'The Impasse of Italian Communism', *Journal of Communist Studies*, Frank Cass, June 1989, p229.

15. Stephen Hellman, *Italian Communism in Transition*, Oxford University Press, Oxford, 1988, p21.

16. Aldo Agosti, 'A Man Between Two Worlds?', *Twentieth Century Communism*, 1, 2009, p165.

17. Bartolomeo Sorge, 'Will Eurocommunists and Eurocatholics Coverge?', in Urban, op cit, p268.

18. Fernando Claudin argued that 'if it is true that one of the lessons of Chile … is that a large majority conscious of its goals is necessary for a sure progress towards socialism, another no less true lesson is that the ruling-classes and their state machine will not sit idly by while the working-class bloc acquires that large majority – unless they are confident that the parties and trade unions that represent that bloc have no intention of changing any of the basic features of the capitalist system'. *Eurocommunism and Socialism*, New Left Books/Verso, London 1978, p116.

19. Santiago Carrillo, *Dialogue on Spain*, Lawrence and Wishart, London 1976, p187.

20. David Runciman, *The Confidence Trap*, Princeton University Press, Oxford 2013, p207.

21. The 'Angry Brigade' provided a British example of the self-defeating consequences of what a few misguided young leftists from a countercultural milieu might do in times which demand radicalism, but in which no effective strategy appears available.

22. Eric Hobsbawm, *How to Change the World*, Little, Brown, London 2011, p360.

23. Mark Rudd interviewed in the film *The Weather Underground*, 2002, directed by Sam Green and Bill Siegel.

24. How far away this option was from the Leninism of the early 1920s can be judged from the April 1922 'Rome Theses' of the Italian communists, already then fighting directly against fascism: 'the party must avoid harbouring ... the illusion that ... it is possible to bring about the awakening of the masses for struggle through the simple effect of the example given by a group of brave men launching themselves into combat, and attempting *coups de main* against bourgeois institutions'. The Party's 'Lyons Theses' of January 1926 'excluded' the view that 'a violent action by individuals or groups can serve to shake the working-class masses out of their passivity ... the activity of armed groups, even as a reaction to the physical violence of the fascists, only has value insofar as it is linked to a reaction of the masses or succeeds in provoking or preparing one'. Antonio Gramsci, *Selections from Political Writings 1921-26*, Lawrence and Wishart, London 1978, pp112, 370-1.

25. Naomi Jaffe, interviewed for *The Weather Underground*.

26. Ron Jacobs, *The Way the Wind Blew*, Verso, London 1997, p5.

27. In her preface to a collection of Meinhof's writings, the Austrian novelist Elfriede Jelinek states that 'it is tragic ... to find the tone of her work getting more and more apodictic, demanding and self-righteous, a tone that in the end tramples everything down, every possible objection, perhaps from desperation because her texts have so little influence, perhaps for private reasons; and then to have a brutally commanding tone set in that is already very like the pitiless barked commands we find in her later texts from the underground'. Ulrike Meinhof, *Everybody Talks About the Weather ... We Don't*, Seven Stories Press, New York 2008.

28. Isabelle Sommier, 'Revolutionary Groups after 1968', *Twentieth Century Communism*, 2, 2010, p75.

29. Slavoj Zizek, *First as Tragedy, then as Farce*, Verso, London 2009, p58. This position is quite different from the classical Marxist understanding that terrorism is a 'false option' which emerges from frustration with the ineffectiveness of reformism: it is not one or the other of these options that is needed, but effective revolutionary activity.

30. Alberto Melucci, *Challenging Codes*, Cambridge University Press, Cambridge 1996, p269.

31. Domenico Losurdo, 'Lenin and Herrenvolk Democracy' in Sebastian

Budgen, Stathis Kouvelakis and Slavoj Zizek (eds), *Lenin Reloaded*, Duke University Press, London 2007, p250.

32. John Foot, *Modern Italy*, Palgrave Macmillan, Basingstoke 2014, p72.

33. Sommier, op cit, p75. Sommier mistakenly implies that 'those on the left' supported this move to terrorism. In fact, the vast majority of the left opposed it as counter-productive adventurism. The issue of whether to support ultra-left terrorism was not a test of being on the left: it was an issue on which the left was split, with only a small minority being in favour: a bigger minority in Italy than elsewhere in Europe, but a small minority nevertheless.

34. Leo Goretti, 'Book reviews', *Twentieth Century Communism*, 4, 2011, pp235, 237. Goretti is reviewing Phil Edwards, *More Work! Less Pay!*, Manchester University Press, Manchester 2009.

# 14. Menshevism reloaded?

## EUROREDS: THE POLITICS OF EUROCOMMUNISM

The events in Czechoslovakia had convinced many that the Soviet model should be abandoned, while the overthrow of Allende's government had reinforced the sense amongst European communists that their politics could only succeed if explicitly recast to become attractive to a substantial majority of electors. Most West European communists now believed that the possibility of Marxist advance in western democracies depended on rejecting the democratic pretensions of the people's democracies and by extension the USSR. The late 1960s and early 1970s had seen a rise in the broad attraction of radical politics, and communists needed to find ways of working with the new generation of left activists. And from the mid-1970s the Spanish and Greek communist parties were emerging from periods of dictatorship and anti-fascist militant illegality; and their approaches involved 'increased sensitivity to democratic structures'.[1]

New strategies were already being tried in France, where in 1972 communists had joined socialists in promoting the *Programme commun*, a left alliance centred on proposed pay rises for organised workers and higher social spending. (However, Francois Mitterrand, the leader of the Socialist Party, proved the better strategist in this relationship. The Socialist Party soon became the more electorally popular element of the alliance, and by 1976 French communism was facing decline.)

These various but related currents cohered in the mid-1970s as Eurocommunism. Its proponents recognised that communism in power had failed to develop democratic procedures, and had relied instead on centralised bureaucracies and repression.[2] In contrast, democratic practice was central to Eurocommunists: they no longer dismissed liberal democracy as bourgeois. Not only did they accept that they needed to engage with processes such as freely contested parliamentary elections; they saw these as valuable and integral processes in their strategic route to power, and as part of the systems which they wished to institute in future. Speaking immediately after Brezhnev at a big meeting in Moscow in November 1977, Berlinguer told the Soviet leader and his audience that democracy was 'the historically universal value on which an original socialist society must be founded', and was the guarantee of 'all freedoms – personal and collective, civil and religious'. The state had to have a 'non-ideological character', and there had to be the possibility 'for different parties to exist side by side, and pluralism in society, culture and ideals'.[3]

Promoting advanced democracy, the PCI effectively dropped any notion of 'seizing' power. Instead, it looked to transform state and society through democratic reform. This was no sudden tactical turn, or a mask concealing unreformed desires to establish a Soviet Europe. Far from it. Of course Eurocommunists knew that most aspects of the Soviet record – in practice and in theory – now represented a handicap rather than an asset. Nevertheless, their renewal of communism in Western Europe expressed a tradition that had been integral to the movement from its roots in nineteenth-century socialism; after faltering in the 1920s and early 1930s this tradition had then been central to the subsequent fight against the Nazis. As described in chapter 10, the view that communists should be the best democrats had been established at that time. The task of left-wing partisans had been to create the greatest possible unity against the Nazis, and unity around democratic aims was understood as an effective and powerful tool in the struggle both for fighting fascism and promoting socialist politics. As Basil Davidson noted of anti-Nazi resistance fighters:

> they were stuck with their doctrine about revolutions having to impose a 'dictatorship of the proletariat' ... On the other hand, ringing through their daily experience like a peal of bells in full swing and clamour, came the absolute demand of the liberation fight. This was that democracy should prevail, and be seen to prevail. Success could only come from the voluntary participation of the masses of ordinary people in their own liberation.[4]

The 1944 'svolta di Salerno' had represented a continuation of Popular Front approaches, combining them with a real – patriotic – commitment to Italian development. After 1956, 'polycentrism' had marked a further move by the PCI towards rejection of the Soviet model.

The Italian new thinking in the 1970s drew from the practical experience of exercising political power at municipal and regional level, and doing so responsibly. Through the 1950s and 1960s, in 'the red region' of Emilia-Romagna, communist mayors and councillors had built a – largely – justified reputation for high standards of public management. By 1974, Bologna was being praised as 'efficient, democratic and relatively incorrupt' by the *New York Times*, and as 'the best-governed' area in Europe by *Newsweek*.[5] Communists extended their local government base in the mid-1970s, taking leadership roles in Rome, Naples and Turin as well as in the party's established strongholds. The PCI administrations were not adventurist: they exercised fiscal caution and sought respectability, and tried to avoid conflict with the Christian Democrat governments.[6] As Stephen Gundle commented, their political practice was shaped by 'profound realism'.[7]

For theoretical legitimacy, the PCI drew on a reading of Gramsci, whose work has been described in chapter 10. His concept of the 'war of position' underpinned the PCI's strategy of accepting the merits of parliamentary democracy and 'treat[ing] the state as a potential mechanism for national solidarity and socialist reconstruction'.[8] Gramsci's generous conception of the state also enabled Eurocommunists to promote an expanded conception of democracy. Whist valuing representative structures and electoral politics, they thought of themselves as 'fuller' democrats than the kinds of politicians who wanted its exercise limited to the rituals of voting and statecraft. For the Eurocommunists, democracy should be a feature of civil society, not just of the state. On this basis, democracy could be pursued through elections, within governmental structures, in municipalities and community organisations – and in places of employment.

The Italian party promoted these themes internationally, drawing on and feeding into the broader discussions taking place across Western Europe and North America. These emphasised the importance of ongoing participation within institutions and processes, and the meaningful inclusion of people based on their identities and interests. These developments enriched and deepened the concept of democracy, so that, instead of people thinking of it as 'an exclusive quality that a system of decision-making either has completely or lacks completely', it was seen as a matter of degree – 'of more or less, not all or nothing'.[9]

Through conferences, publications and public interventions, culminating with 1977's 'Madrid Summit', which brought together the leaders of the French, Italian and Spanish communist parties, Eurocommunism was shaped around the needs, realities and prospects of parties operating within modern, parliamentary, industrial states. This involved an increasingly explicit rejection of the '1917' model of revolution, and more layered and dynamic understandings of state structures than the movement had previously achieved. The view now was that the road to socialism in the West would require 'a protracted struggle to exploit the internal contradictions of the state', rather than the building up of a new monolithic and proletarian bloc that would 'oppose, contest and replace the unified capitalist state'.[10] Such perspectives led Eurocommunists to break with insurrectionary approaches to the winning of power. There was a move away from any talk of instituting a 'dictatorship of the proletariat'.

Eurocommunism was, instead, a kind of 'revolutionary reformism', aimed at the full transformation of society, but accepting and defending a wide range of democratic institutions and practices, including the legitimacy of electoral politics. The French communist theoretician Jean Elleinstein declared that 'communists are perfectly prepared to abide by the rules of parliamentary democracy and relinquish the levers of power if they lose the confidence of the public'.[11] The French party was always more 'workerist' than the Italian, holding to an idealised conception of working-class culture. A greater proportion of its members stayed loyal to traditional, even Stalinist, positions. Nevertheless, its leader Georges Marchais stated explicitly in the mid-1970s that: 'there is no democracy and liberty if there is no pluralism of political parties and if there is no freedom of speech ... it is clear we have a disagreement with the Soviet Communist Party about this question'.[12] The party also developed some recognition of the need for broader cross-class appeals, linking workers and new middle strata and beginning to connect more effectively to the women's movement.[13]

Confirming Eurocommunist trends in the Communist Party of Great Britain, Alan Hunt argued that:

socialism has as its goal the completion or realisation of the democratic project initiated by the bourgeois revolutions of the eighteenth and nineteenth centuries ... [This] involves not the smashing of bourgeois democracy but its completion, liberated from the undemocratic framework of capitalist relations. Political competition, representative government, political rights do not bear an ahistorical capitalist essence, but provide elements whose transformation makes possible the attainment of the socialist project.[14]

For a while, Eurocommunists appeared to be catching the potential of the 1970s. Their analyses were well-grounded and influential: many of their leaders and activists were impressive, highly credible individuals, able to reach way beyond their own followers. Drawing legitimacy and authority from communism's historical record, particularly in resisting fascism, Eurocommunism at the same time positioned itself as modern, in tune with new social dynamics, responding to and incorporating (to varying degrees) feminist, gay, anti-racist and green agendas, and promoting attractive cultural activities including festivals and some lively magazines.

Theoretical resources were offered by a new generation of academic Marxists. From Paris, Nicos Poulantzas, a Greek communist in exile, set out nuanced analyses of the character, evolutions of, and differences between, various forms of capitalist state power. He argued that 'a real permanence and continuity of the institutions of representative democracy' is 'an essential condition of democratic socialism'.[15] Poulantzas suggested combining the different political models of overthrow and rupture, reform and interstitial work – through an effort to democratise state structures 'from within' and through social movements exerting pressure 'from without'; and through respecting independent organisations in civil society as well as through winning elections.

Such analyses suggested how both direct and representative forms of democracy might operate simultaneously and be combined, and how there might be 'a gradual dismantling in social peace of a capitalist state constructed for class war, or a meliorist transformation of a market economy into its historical opposite'.[16] For Poulantzas, this meant rejecting simplistic notions that the state was 'either a reflection of the relations of production or a simple instrument through which the capitalist class achieved its ends', and instead recognising that it was, rather, 'the specific material condensation of a relationship of forces among classes and class-fractions'.[17]

Instead of being a monolithic bloc, the state operated as a complex strategic field, in which there were multiple and recurrent opportunities for progressive steps to be taken and defended. This made the state a potential site for revolutionary intervention, given that its various constituent elements had different, sometimes contradictory, interests.[18]

Eurocommunists also reacted against the way that the communist movement had, in an earlier period, set its ambitions in the grandest possible terms. The new view was that more modestly conceived immediate aims would generate an incremental, popular and effective practice. Communist parties adopted a politics that did not seek an immediate transition to socialism, but was centred on making interim advances against the monopolistic power base, in the interests of the people, and on establishing a government of alliances. These were variously conceptualised as '"forces of labour and culture" (Spain), "new historic bloc" (Italy), "union of French people" (France) and "broad democratic alliance" (Britain)'.[19]

This approach was expressed in economic policy. Italian communists supported 'productive' and 'enlightened' businesses, which they distinguished from the 'parasitical' classes. The PCI's economists began to revise their theory of profit, and now regarded it as a positive factor as long as it was directed towards production.[20] A sympathetic British Labour Party politician noted that since the 1950s the PCI had given no priority to the extension of public enterprise. It was certainly not automatically in favour of nationalisation, and valued the 'mixed economy'. The party's approach was shaped in part by a 'neo-Gramscian' recognition of the 'importance of gaining and maintaining the support of broad sections of the self-employed petty bourgeoisie, as well as that of workers in non-unionised small and medium enterprises'.[21] Berlinguer backed 'small and medium-sized [private] businesses – industries, artisan enterprises, merchants, peasant farms':

> in an industrialised country like Italy, it is advantageous to maintain private enterprise from all points of view ... planning establishes the frame of reference within which both the public and the private sector work ... socialism does not mean total socialisation of the means of production.[22]

In Bologna, a co-ordinated plan to develop trade and industry zones saw communist councillors working closely with local capitalists. According to the local communist mayor:

Private enterprise functioning on a profit-base is to have a place in this framework; but a private enterprise which will develop, not anarchically, but within a definite supply system. Private entrepreneurs themselves demand such a framework.[23]

Through such approaches, communists in Emilia-Romagna won support from many ordinary business owners, generating successful local economies composed of networks of medium, small and very small enterprises, with few large industrial concerns.[24]

There were also significant breaks from established forms of communist internationalism. Eurocommunists took up the themes of détente that had emerged within the blocs as a way of thawing the cold war, and – partly in response to their geographical location between the two 'superpowers' – adopted foreign policy positions which could no longer be reduced to solidarity with the Soviet Union. They were positive towards European institutions, and talked of 'regional dimensions' and 'convergence'.

## HEGEMONICS: TAKING DEMOCRACY TO ITS LOGICAL CONCLUSION

How did Eurocommunist formulae fit within the longer history of the movement? For the revolutionary communists of the 1920s, the craft and process of 'formal democracy' was irrelevant: at best a tactical option, at worst a con-trick, a diversion, a barrier. In Poulantzas's wry observation, in those days 'everything was "reformist" which did not lead to the creation of dual power and achieving the possibilities of a frontal clash with the state'.[25] Radical goals were seen as requiring violent means: being serious about socialist transformation meant 'bourgeois democracy' had to be dispensed with. There was a decoupling of democratic values and practices from the project to achieve the goal of socialism through the replacement of capitalism.

The Popular Front politics of the mid-1930s had seen democracy as a useful tool to help deliver and underpin the communist programme. But it was largely a means to an end. Now, however, Eurocommunists explicitly stated that democracy was integral to real socialism: rejection of democratic norms and values would compromise the programme and make it impossible to deliver. Even more significantly, for Eurocommunists socialism consisted precisely in the fullest possible extension and application of democratic methods and values.

There were always accusations from right-wingers that Eurocommunism was an attempt to deceive and lull electors by politicians who actually remained unreconstructed Leninists. Henry Kissinger was a great promoter of this myth, claiming that he could not believe that communists, 'through some magic ... have become democratic'.[26] West European communists countered this accusation of deceit with a simple argument: it was not true.

The suggestion that Eurocommunism made the CPs indistinguishable from social-democrats was trickier to dispute, however, especially given that the 1970s saw renewed efforts by many radical social democrats to push beyond capitalism – in Britain, Sweden and elsewhere. Berlinguer asserted that the key difference was that 'social-democratic societies are not moving towards the overcoming of capitalism'.[27] Marxists were no longer criticising social-democrats for their democratic zeal, but for restricting their ambitions 'within the bounds prescribed by the bourgeoisie'.[28]

Eurocommunists also linked formal political activity with mobilisation in workplaces and communities: they were not, as was sometimes claimed, excessively focused on parliamentarianism. There were big debates about the need to radically change state institutions, to develop new modes of political intervention in civil society as well as in the state, and to deepen democracy.[29]

Spanish leader Santiago Carrillo in particular continued to assert the possibility of justified armed uprisings if the ruling class should reject a democratic verdict against them. His experience during the Spanish civil war and over the decades since had made him well aware of the dangers of naive faith in democracy: the opponents of socialism and revolutionary change may spout democratic phrases, but if radical socialists show signs of succeeding – as happened in Spain in 1936 and Chile in 1970 – they will be first to drop the mask. The cost of naivety could well be the destruction of the left.

Nevertheless, whilst reserving the right to use violence against undemocratic counter-revolution, Eurocommunists stressed that sustained radical advance must be based on democratic mandates. Progressing through non-violent and constitutional steps was a way of building support, and of reducing the scope for political enemies to marginalise and attack the left.

Eurocommunists accepted that western capitalist societies had successfully developed certain forms of democracy and freedom – but also understood that these were societies built on exploitation.[30] In contrast, communist states had succeeded in abolishing particular forms of economic exploitation, but the resulting polities lacked democratic character or mandate, and did not allow or facilitate important individual liberties. In this context, Eurocommunism was based on the conviction that it was possible to have both freedom and socialism.

The new approach did not need to take sides in the old debate between reform and revolution. As Fred Halliday pointed out, it was now understood that these alternatives, once regarded as mutually exclusive, had not expressed 'some eternal polarity': that debate had been a product of the particular context of the early twentieth century, and the split between different factions of socialist movement during the first world war.[31] Instead of choosing between 'rhetorical maximalism and inept reformism', revolution was now conceived of as a process of incremental but thorough-going reform, during which those not initially on board for social change would be gradually won over to participate. Even though a few people were always likely to remain hostile to a potential socialist settlement, measures to create political hegemony in the interests of the majority, as well as education, would make it relatively easy to handle the remaining minority – and to do so without recourse to criminal acts of repression.

The understanding was that success in one step and stage would lead to others, and that the transformation to a different system did not have to be catastrophic. Revolution did not need to involve heavy civil war: decisive defeats could be inflicted on the old ruling class in other ways. Social transformation need not involve the total collapse of the old society and the 'promethean conjuring of something entirely unrecognisable in its place'.[32] Reform, and achievements from interstitial spaces, could lead to change quite as radical – and more securely grounded in social realities – as anything that might be achieved through overthrow, force and rupture.

Eurocommunism rejected the simple binary distinction between the sudden seizure of power or the reformist programme. As the mayor of Bologna stated, there would be no 'X-hour when capitalism ceases to exist and socialism begins', but rather 'varying lengths of transitional phase'.[33]

Theories and practices of gradualism and amelioration had previously been identified with the limited goals of social democracy, which was content to work within the horizons and 'common sense' of capitalism. But within the terms of the Eurocommunist strategy, patient alliance-building and the accumulation, defence and bedding in of reforms would constitute effective revolutionary work. This was connected to a whole wave of new attempts in the 1970s to establish more democratic forms of decision-making in workplaces, boardrooms and many other institutions.[34]

Eurocommunism can be seen as having forged a novel synthesis of communism and social-democracy. Strategically, it insisted that achieving socialism through the replacement of capitalism could only succeed through democratic methods and values. Socialism consisted precisely in the fullest possible extension and application of democratic methods and values, taking 'democracy to its logical conclusion'.[35] Socialists had to build on such practices as free elections by secret ballot, the separation of powers between different parts of the state and guarantees for the rights of individuals; it was wrong to reject these as a sham, as what Jacques Ranciere describes as the 'appearances under which and instruments by which the power of the bourgeois class is exercised'.[36] Recognising the need to win popular consent and to patiently build electoral support was only part of the new approach. Eurocommunists saw the '"advanced" task of the mature Marxist party' as being to win a broad and progressive series of gains within capitalist democracy through democratic collectivism.[37]

Leftists besotted with the particular forms and confrontational language of the revolutionary communist moment from 1917 through to the mid-1920s frequently ignore the extent to which Eurocommunism was recognised as a serious threat by the leading powers in the cold war. The shift to inclusive politics, alliance-building and preparedness to use the equipment of bourgeois political culture was not a betrayal of class struggle: it was a demonstration of communist determination.

## IF, POSSIBLY, PERHAPS ...

The fact that Eurocommunism failed, and that – particularly in the case of the PCI – it did come to involve a self-defeating accommodation to existing reality, does not mean that the ultra-leftists are correct. It is true that Eurocommunist parties were reshaped by the bourgeois culture around them more than they were able to transform it. But in large part this reflected the massive economic and social changes that were underway across Western Europe by the late 1970s, based on a complete restructuring of the economy. The deep conviction that communism needed to be democratic emerged during the period when state communism as an alternative economic system was becoming exhausted and disorganised. Whether different outcomes could have resulted had a democratising approach taken hold earlier, at a time when communism's economic model was still delivering growth, will now remain an unanswerable question. As the poet W.H. Auden wrote in the 1930s, 'history, to the defeated, may say "Alas", but cannot help or pardon'.[38]

By the 1970s, the organised working class – the central component in the alliance that Eurocommunists wished to create, the gravitational core to which all other social forces were meant to relate – was itself being knocked out of place, decentred and disorientated. Economic and social trends, sometimes promoted by powerful interests precisely for this purpose, were undermining the foundations of the membership-based organisations that underpinned the successful parties of the left, both social-democratic and communist: trade unions in manufacturing, mining and the public sector; working-men's clubs; tenants' committees – and the churches.

In Italy, industrial employment in PCI strongholds such as Turin continuously declined during the 1970s and 1980s.[39] The social compactness, stability, cultural integration and uniformity which had marked Italian urban culture before the 1970s were disorganised and disrupted, undermining the 'Emilian model' of local government. In the analysis of Rudolf Bahro, an East German reform communist and pioneer of green politics, Berlinguer's recognition of the strategic need to take account of the danger of right-wing counter-attack was achieved at a moment when the dynamic of class contradictions already had 'a declining potential for shattering the system'. Bahro argues that the consequential 'neo-reformism' and 'falling back into the old social-democratic gradualism' was perhaps unavoidable.[40]

The working class and its labour movement, supposedly well-integrated into west European society – and as analysts like Herbert Marcuse saw it, compromised by its consumerist enjoyments – was now being increasingly atomised and individualised. Collective attitudes, including class solidarity, and the institutions which espoused them, were in decline, regarded by many as 'old-fashioned'. Left-wing politics in all its forms had been substantially based on communities built around large numbers of workers coming together, daily, in factories, mills and large bureaucracies. The material dismantling of this model of employment would prove more effective in undoing the left than any amount of intellectual criticism.

For some years, however, Eurocommunists were a creative, energetic and successful force, engaging with existing power structures, making practical suggestions about current issues and highlighting new possibilities. They invested energy in, and made a real difference to, a wide range of projects and campaigns in local specific circumstances. In Alberto Melucci's assessment, the PCI, for over a decade from the mid-1960s:

> was the catalyst for expectations of change ... managed to garner the most immediate effects of the student and workers' movements ... increased its votes and membership, gained control of numerous local and regional administrations, renewed its cadres ... and recruited new supporters.[41]

Even where Eurocommunists were part of a small national organisation, without any significant electoral representation, they made major inputs into social movements and campaigns which did have real effect. Taking the Communist Party of Great Britain as an example, effective activity in the 1970s and even into the 1980s included work at all levels of many trade unions and in the Trades Union Congress; successive Communist Universities of London, which discussed and promoted the concept of the 'broad democratic alliance'; the accessible magazine *Marxism Today*, which enjoyed wide influence on the left, including in the Labour Party, particularly for its analysis of Thatcherism and changes in the forms and cultures of capitalism; support for and significant contributions to the feminist and anti-racist movements; positive activity in scores of local communities; and crucial input into national campaigns including the People's March for Jobs, the Anti-Apartheid Movement, the Campaign for Nuclear Disarmament, support for the miners' strike of 1984-1985 and protests against the Poll Tax.[42]

Some debates and arguments from these years mark missed opportunities in British left politics. One example will illustrate this. In the
1970s, a Eurocommunist minority on the CPGB's advisory Economic
Committee argued against overly confrontational and 'economistic'
trade union militancy.[43] They warned that short-term sectional gains
were diverting the left's attention from the fact that an effective
long-term backlash against trade unions was being prepared. These
'Gramscians' were positive about the prospect of a negotiated incomes
policy as part of a social contract – something also advocated by a
minority of trade union leaders, most notably Jack Jones. This would
be an opportunity for the labour movement to 'bid for hegemony by
offering to accept voluntary pay restraint in exchange for structural
reforms aimed at democratising the economy: within the enterprise
and workplace as well as at the macro-social level; in private companies as well as in the public sector; and with respect to major policy
issues, not just matters of day-to-management'.[44]

If such views had been more influential within the party, it is just
possible to conceive that, through a new alliance with other labour
movement leaders, the political and economic conflict of the 1970s
might have been resolved differently. Instead of trade unions being
blamed for the state of the economy, thus paving the way for the
dismantling of many workplace rights, they might have been able to
present a convincing alternative that could have seen off Thatcherism.
If, possibly, perhaps ...

There was engrained hostility on the left to any form of pay
restraint, however. This meant that what would today be seen as a
left-wing fantasy, but was then within the grasp of a united labour
movement and Labour Party – a national agreement between trade
unions and government over income levels, workers' rights and welfare
provision – was dismissed as a 'right-wing trap'. But in any case, the
social base for any strategy centred on the organised working class was
by now being eroded.[45] Furthermore, effective reactionary forces were
working on 'unhinging it from below'.[46]

Attempting an overall assessment of the Eurocommunist moment
in 1997, Willie Thompson argued that in the 1970s the communist
parties of the European democracies were moving to fill the political
space on the left as it was being vacated by their social-democrat counterparts moving to the right: 'apart from certain peculiarities of their
internal regimes and their fraternal links with the Communist Party

of the Soviet Union', the Eurocommunist parties were to all intents and purposes 'nothing other than left-wing social-democratic parties with some infusion from the new left'.[47]

In Italy, Eurocommunism took the party to a point where sharing governmental responsibility seemed a real possibility; and for communists to achieve this on the basis of a strong electoral mandate would have been a major development in cold war Europe. Togliatti's desire to develop for the PCI a different path to power from that followed by the 'people's democracies' seemed close to realisation.[48] In 1978 it looked as though the historic compromise might be expressed in a grand coalition that was being negotiated between the Christian Democrats and the PCI. Such a move was opposed from different positions, but what effectively ended it was the murder of the Christian Democrat leader Aldo Moro in May 1978 at the hands of ultra-left terrorists from the *Brigate Rosse*.

Thereafter, Eurocommunism followed what has become a recurrent path in the history of the left. In what was in many ways a replay of old Second International tracks, the focus shifted from programme and political content to a concern with process. There was an echo of Menshevism in Eurocommunism's concern about the danger of overstepping limits and provocatively driving the bourgeoisie into the camp of reaction, thus spoiling the chances of revolutionary change; and the historian André Liebich has identified wider resonances between Russian Menshevism and Eurocommunism. Both took a revolutionary line in relation to Western capitalism at the same time as calling for reforms in the Soviet Union. Both wished to develop a politics which was neither Bolshevik nor reformist. Both experienced a confusion of means and ends, in which adopting a commitment to democratic process became a route to dropping the goal of socialism, rather than being a means by which to realise the goal. And both Mensheviks and Eurocommunists put a great stress on the need to put preconditions in place before taking premature action.[49]

Although their historical roots in Leninism blocked them from acknowledging this, the approach of the Western communist parties in the mid-1970s to a wide range of questions – including the relationships between society, state and party – could be defined, 'without the slightest polemical provocation, as essentially "Kautskyist"'.[50] By 1980, Perry Anderson was clear that the heirs of the Third International in Europe were espousing policies that were 'increasingly convergent with

those of the parties of the classical epoch of the Second International':
for him, 'the continuity of the political ideas of Kautsky ... with those
of Berlinguer and Carrillo on the road to socialism in Western Europe
is now virtually complete'.[51]

The subsequent unravelling of Eurocommunism reflected still-
unresolved difficulties in developing effective left politics. These
had been reflected and expressed in debates between different broad
tendencies *within* Eurocommunism. In Fabien Escalona's account,
the respect of one tendency for existing forms of politics meant that
it enclosed its strategy within 'a classic conception of the gradualist
conquest of state power': 'the centrality of the electoral objective ...
tended to lead to the party's programmatic moderation, bureaucratisation and the absorption of its desires for change within the limits of
the capitalist state'.[52]

The alternative tendency, which was associated in the PCI with
Pietro Ingrao, was linked more closely with social movements; emphasised the aim of combining representative government with economic
democracy in workplaces; and maintained that any real socialist transformation of the state and the economy would necessarily involve
'moments of rupture', rather than any smooth procession of politics at
the governmental level alone.

In theorising this left-wing Eurocommunism, Poulantzas accepted
that focusing on representative democracy could reproduce the illusion
that the capitalist state is neutral. Conversely, excessive emphasis on
direct democracy and social movements could encourage the illusion
that it was possible to succeed without the state or representative politics. Poulantzas set out some of the dangers of shaping politics entirely
around social movements and rank and file control. He argued that if
representatives of the dominated classes made no effort to secure positions of power within the capitalist state, this would simply clear the
way for the capitalist powerful to reinforce their control. Instead, he
advocated participation within the different areas of the state and civil
power in order to intensify internal contradictions; this would help
to create the moments of rupture that would shape 'the democratic
transition to democratic socialism'.[53] In the most concise summary of
his late thinking, Poulantzas argued that the 'essential problem of the
democratic road to socialism' was to find ways to 'radically to transform the state in such a manner that the extension and deepening of
political freedoms and the institutions of representative democracy ...

are combined with the unfurling of forms of direct democracy and the mushrooming of self-management bodies'.[54]

Such thinking came from increasingly rigorous understandings of the workings of the capitalist state and political dynamics in modern society. But understanding the way things work does not mean that they will work for you. As Eurocommunists were beginning to bring the issues raised by their politics into clear focus, and figuring out the best way to proceed, the ground they stood on was rapidly disappearing.

This was largely because 'the other side' was far from giving up on class struggle. Internationally, the political right were developing the ideas and practices of neoliberalism: they were determined to restate the rights of shareholders and the rule of market forces, and to push back the gains that had been made by ordinary people and their political representatives since the 1940s.

In 1973 the Trilateral Commission was set up by an emerging group within US academic and government circles that would promote liberal economic policies and co-ordinate co-operation between the US, Europe and Japan. The Commission was a key initiator of the intellectual and political themes that would eventually come to be described as neoliberal: some of its ideas initially looked eccentric, but they would be 'common sense' within twenty years. Other organisations and networks soon joined in this project to secure greater operational freedom for advanced capitalism. In spite of rising oil prices and instability, there would be no retreat to protectionism and the defence of national currencies. A world politics for capitalism was the aim, to be achieved through harmonising economic policies and rules; building up supranational bodies to oversee the work of national governments in cutting real wages and reducing welfare spending; promoting the ideologies of individualism and consumerism; and – not least – doing away with contexts in which any future Allende or Berlinguer could get into power.

## NOTES

1. George Bridges, 'Western European Communist Strategy', in Sally Hibbin (ed), *Politics, Ideology and the State*, Lawrence and Wishart, London 1978, p127.
2. Stefan Berger, 'Communism, Social-Democracy and the Democracy Gap', *Socialist History*, 27, 2005, p13. Initially, Eurocommunism was

not a self-designation: the label originated with critics rather than proponents.

3. Quoted in Paolo Filo della Torre, Edward Mortimer and Jonathan Story (eds), *Eurocommunism*, Penguin Books, Harmondsworth 1979, p15.

4. Basil Davidson, *Special Operations Europe*, Gollancz, London 1981, p227.

5. Quoted in Max Jaggi, Roger Muller and Sil Schmid, *Red Bologna*, Writers and Readers Publishing Co-operative, London 1977, pp7, 30.

6. Simon Parker, 'The Modern Prince in the Metropolis', paper to the Alternative Futures and Popular Protest conference, Manchester, March 1996.

7. Stephen Gundle, 'Urban dreams and metropolitan nightmares', in Bogdan Szajkowski (ed), *Marxist Local Governments in Western Europe and Japan*, Frances Pinter, London 1986, p66.

8. Finn Bowring, 'From the Mass Worker to the Multitude', *Capital and Class*, 83, summer 2004.

9. David Purdy, 'Keywords: Democracy', *Perspectives*, Democratic Left Scotland, Dundee 2007.

10. Bob Jessop, *Nicos Poulantzas*, Macmillan Publishers, London 1985, p289.

11. Jean Elleinstein, '"The Skein of History Unrolled Backwards"', in G.R. Urban (ed), *Eurocommunism*, Maurice Temple Smith, London 1978, p77. Cold war ideologues maintained the suspicion that such commitments were not genuine: Rudolf L. Tokes fretted 'that a communist party, upon its defeat at the polls, might, with the help of the pro-communist volunteer militia, seek to remain in power and, if necessary, summon external assistance from like-minded foreign powers'. Introduction to Tokes (ed), *Eurocommunism and Detente*, Martin Robertson, Oxford 1978, pp14-15.

12. Georges Marchais, newspaper article in *L'Humanite*, 15 January 1976: quoted in Edward Mortimer, 'The French Communist Party' in della Torre et al, op cit, p135.

13. Jean Jenson and George Ross, *The View from Inside*, University of California Press, London 1984, pp334, 335.

14. Alan Hunt, 'Taking Democracy Seriously', in Hunt (ed), *Marxism and Democracy*, Lawrence and Wishart, London 1980, p1.

15. Nicos Poulantzas, *State, Power, Socialism*, Verso, London 2014 [1978], p261.

16. Perry Anderson, *Arguments within English Marxism*, Verso, London 1980, p196. Anderson is criticising the 'strategic conceptions' underpinning Eurocommunism, and their 'libertarian version' in the work of E P Thompson.

17. Nicos Poulantzas, op cit, p129.

18. Eileen Meehan, 'Nicos Poulantzas' in Robert A. Gorman (ed), *Biographical Dictionary of Neo-Marxism*, Mansell Publishing Limited, London 1985, pp346-7.

19. Bridges, op cit, p128. Bridges saw that this strategic conception was 'a

transcendence of the traditional formula "the working class and its allies" not just in the breadth of social forces referred to, but in the nature of their inter-relationship'.

20. Giovanni Russo, 'Il Compromesso Storico: the Italian Communist Party from 1968 to 1978', in della Torre et al, op cit, p83.
21. Stuart Holland, 'The New Communist Economics', in ibid, p228.
22. Quoted in Don Sassoon (ed), *The Italian Communists Speak for Themselves*, Spokesman, Nottingham 1978, p2.
23. Interview with Renao Zangheri, in Jaggi, op cit, pp193-4.
24. Gundle, op cit, p77.
25. 'Interview with Nicos Poulantzas', *Marxism Today*, July 1979. The interview was conducted by Stuart Hall and Alan Hunt.
26. Quoted in della Torre et al, op cit, p10.
27. Quoted in Sassoon 1978, op cit, p72.
28. Fernando Claudin, *Eurocommunism and Socialism*, New Left Books, London 1978, p73.
29. Anne Showstack Sassoon, 'Hegemony and Political Intervention', in Hibbin, op cit, p17.
30. In many places outside Europe, of course, the capitalist reality was that exploitation was *combined* with a fundamental lack of democracy.
31. Fred Halliday, 'Utopian Realism', in John Foran (ed), *The Future of Revolutions*, Zed Press, London 2003, p308.
32. Seth Ackerman, 'The Red and the Black', *Jacobin*, 9, 2012.
33. Interview with Renao Zangheri, in Jaggi, op cit, p200.
34. David Purdy, 'Keywords: Democracy', *Perspectives*, Democratic Left Scotland, Dundee 2007.
35. Rome declaration of the PCI and PCF, November 1975.
36. Jacques Ranciere, *Hatred of Democracy*, Verso, London 2014 [2005], p3.
37. Gregor McLennan, *Marxism, Pluralism and Beyond*, Polity Press, Oxford 1989, p89.
38. W.H. Auden, 'Spain', 1937.
39. Stephen Hellman, *Italian Communism in Transition*, Oxford University Press, Oxford 1988, Chapter 9.
40. Rudolf Bahro, *Socialism and Survival*, Heretic Books, London 1982, p72.
41. Alberto Melucci, *Challenging Codes*, Cambridge University Press, Cambridge 1996, p264.
42. For a detailed account of the CPGB from 1964 to its dissolution in 1991, see Geoff Andrews, *Endgames and New Times*, Lawrence and Wishart, London 2004.
43. Ibid, pp127-9 and 145-8.
44. David Purdy, 'The Wages of Militancy', July 2006: www.hegemonics. co.uk/docs/Incomes-Policy-Hegemony-1970s.pdf, accessed June 2016. See also Mike Prior and David Purdy, *Out of the Ghetto*, Spokesman Books, Nottingham 1979, discussed in Andrews, op cit, pp168-9. For the

formation of the intellectual networks that this work emerged from, see Andrew Pearmain, 'Dissent From Dissent', Chapter 6 of Evan Smith and Matt Worley (eds), *Against the Grain*, Manchester University Press, Manchester 2014.

45. In *Marxism Today,* beginning with 'The Forward March of Labour Halted?' in 1978 and concluding with 'Another Forward March Halted' in 1989, Eric Hobsbawm analysed the shifting class structure of British society, and the consequent rise of Thatcherism and the crisis of the Labour Party. Hobsbawm's intention was to help assess 'the situation of the labour movement realistically in the light of economic and social changes whose significance was often overlooked by the left'. 'The Forward March: Eric Hobsbawm in Conversation with Jonathan Rutherford', *Public Policy Research*, IPPR, September-November 2011.

46. Stuart Hall, 'Introduction: Thatcherism and the Crisis of the Left', *The Hard Road to Renewal*, Verso, London, 1988, p11.

47. Willie Thompson, *The Left in History*, Pluto Press, London 1997, p183.

48. Aldo Agosti, 'A Man Between Two Worlds?', *Twentieth Century Communism*, 1, 2009, p167.

49. Andre Liebich, *From the Other Shore*, Harvard University Press, Cambridge MT 1997, p4.

50. Massimo Salvadori, *Karl Kautsky and the Socialist Revolution 1880-1938*, New Left Books/Verso, London 1979, p13. On p68, Salvadori quotes an 1899 article by Kautsky which could have been readily quoted to bolster Eurocommunist strategy: 'our task is not to provoke catastrophes, but to avoid offering any pretext for such catastrophes and to act so as to win over the majority of the politically active masses'.

51. Perry Anderson, *Arguments within English Marxism*, Verso, London 1980, p196.

52. Fabien Escalona, 'The Heritage of Eurocommunism in the Contemporary Radical Left' in *Socialist Register 2017*, Merlin Press, London 2016, p110.

53. Bob Jessop, *Nicos Poulantzas*, ibid, pp130, 297.

54. Nicos Poulantzas, *State, Power, Socialism*, Verso, London 2014 [1978], p256.

# 15. The end of the old times

## THE ECONOMIC FUNDAMENTAL

From the end of the 1970s, the European left was in retreat. In Britain, France and even Scandinavia, social-democracy's post-war influence, which had been expressed in a consensus around the welfare state and the social benefits of 'high-wage' economies, was beginning to be effectively disputed from the right. At the same time, attempts to sustain twentieth-century communism faced growing and accumulated problems. These included ever-diminishing moral prestige, ongoing fragmentation and the failure to attract new young members in any significant numbers.

The most fundamental problems facing communist parties in power were in the field of the economy. The suppression of the Prague Spring had been followed by strict limits on experimentation not only in Czechoslovakia but in other communist countries too, even though new approaches were sorely needed: decentralisation, modernisation, initiatives to incentivise innovation and productivity, and democratisation.

The limited capacity of the state-planned economy to refresh itself had become increasingly apparent. At the same time, developments which were beginning to reshape the world-wide organisation of the forces of production, particularly the shift to informationalism and the intensive and expansive use of computer technology, entirely undermined communism's state-centred economic processes. Soviet managers had not responded positively to the first signs of this shift. The party-state apparatus of the Soviet bloc regarded research on the application of cybernetic thinking to the problems of socialist planning as a threat to the orthodoxies on which they based their legitimacy – and therefore did not allow it.[1]

By the time they did start to make half-hearted efforts to access computer technology, Soviet leaders found that Western powers were making determined efforts to withhold it from them. And when they finally did attempt to apply information technology to production and planning, they did so without adapting established management systems and cultures. As Slava Gerovitch recounts, the result was that technological innovation became a bureaucratic nightmare:

> Ever-increasing amounts of raw data ... generated terrifying heaps of paperwork. In the early 1970s, roughly 4 billion documents per year circulated through the Soviet economy. By the mid-1980s, after Herculean efforts to computerize the bureaucratic apparatus, this figure rose ... to about 800 billion documents, or 3,000 documents for every Soviet citizen. All this information still had to pass through narrow channels of centralized, hierarchical distribution, squeezed by institutional barriers and secrecy restrictions. Management became totally unwieldy.[2]

Such problems expressed the fundamental absence of democracy and openness. The possibility of rational economic planning depended on the flow, consideration and application of intelligence. Any bureaucracy faces difficulties in arriving at and handling the appropriate balances between 'free' flow and 'organised' flow of information, and deciding on actions to take. But in the communist countries, fear that significant freedom of flow could lead to the party losing control led to the flow itself being stopped.

This problem was not a new one: on a 1954-5 visit to the Soviet Union, the British communist Eric Hobsbawm had been struck by 'the sheer impracticality of a society in which an almost paranoiac fear of espionage turned the information needed for everyday life into a state secret'.[3] Over time, this led to increasing difficulties. As Hobsbawm saw, the deficiencies and flaws of the system eventually led to its breakdown: 'the system became increasingly rigid and unworkable, and especially because it proved incapable of generating or making economic use of innovation, quite apart from stifling intellectual originality'.[4]

The system did not facilitate people's active participation in decision-making. Sometimes they were actively blocked from taking part; more often, workplace and wider political norms confined them to an essentially passive role. Such a culture was the very opposite of the basis for any kind of socialist society, for, as Pat Devine argues, 'alienation can only be overcome, non-coercive human social relations can only be achieved, when people are autonomous, self-activating and self-governing':

> In the economic sphere, this requires political democracy, enabling people individually and collectively to be involved, on the basis of adequate knowledge and understanding, in deciding at the national level the strategic issues and priorities that set the broad outlines of the plan. It also involves industrial democracy, with workers participating in decision-making at the level of the enterprise.[5]

Soviet and Eastern Europe realities – with the possible exception of Yugoslavia, where forms of workers' self-management had been tried – were a long way from any form of industrial democracy. Instead, passivity and dodges shaped the daily routine of factories and offices: a common saying was 'they pretend to pay us, and we pretend to work'.

By the 1970s, genuine commitment to Marxist and communist principles was becoming rare even amongst party members. Just as liberalism had failed to deliver the promises of 'bourgeois democracy', it was now clear that Marxism-Leninism was failing to deliver the promises of 'socialist democracy'. In response to the crude statist ideology that had taken the place of what had once been a rigorous tool for critiquing capitalist ideology, some attempts were made to refresh and renew Soviet and East European Marxism. But those making such efforts openly were labelled as 'dissident', and effectively silenced.

These problems were in part a perverse effect of not separating the economy from society and politics: this meant that every problem was regarded as systemic. Every social tension was seen as the responsibility of the government, rather than as a problem in civil society; every economic hitch was seen as the responsibility of the overall system, rather than as a problem in the management of individual enterprises or sectors. The consequence of attempting to control everything was that you politicised everything. By trying to manage and determine every aspect of society, the communist states had turned every aspect of society into a potential form of protest. As Anne Applebaum correctly argues, this approach inevitably led to dissent: 'thus the system lays the basis for its own undermining and destruction'.[6] This in stark contrast to the market system, which offers a way of managing society that does not require every economic process to go through a political decision-making process. This is a major factor in the market's success: it is an institution which claims not to be one.

It was during this period of state socialism's difficulties that the neoliberal ideology was emerging to challenge both communism and social-democracy. Neoliberalism articulated an ideological conception of democracy that actively sought the systematic exclusion of economic questions from politics. The capitalist powerful now reclaimed – and expanded – what they saw as their right to pursue their private economic interests. The old argument that the health of liberal democracy depended on some degree of social and economic equality was attacked and marginalised. A new common sense was promoted. The state should stay out of investment decisions: these should be made by the private sector working in line with market forces.

At the heart of neoliberal ideology was its conception of individualism and individual choice. In capitalism, the push is to do well for oneself regardless of whether or not society as a whole is doing well. In socialism, by contrast, the conception is that one does well in so far as the society as a whole is doing well. The possessive individualist approach is defended – or excused – by neoliberals by the argument that the net and multiple effect of such individual effort will, in the long run, somehow, be good for society overall.

## GORBACHEV'S REMEDY

Mikhail Gorbachev, who became general secretary of the Soviet Communist Party in 1985, made a valiant attempt at renewal, introducing what were to be the last Soviet attempts at economic restructuring and democratisation. Twenty years on from the Prague Spring, influenced by Eurocommunism and market socialism, as well as the approaches that had been pioneered by Dubcek, the new leadership now attempted reform from the centre of the communist system.

Believing there was a basis for renewal and revitalisation, Gorbachev worked with reformers who opposed dogmatism, pioneering a new approach to political science, 'in which questions would be asked to which the answers were not already known'.[7] His new approach drew on concerns that had been raised by reformers within the party during the long Brezhnev 'era of stagnation', who had argued that democratisation was a necessary condition for qualitative improvements in efficiency.[8] From the mid-1980s, the combined programme of *perestroika* and *glasnost* ('reconstruction' and 'openness') sought to address the twin crises of economic dysfunction and political illegitimacy. The initial policy changes were responses to campaigns and dissident opinion around environmental issues. Writing in 1988, Lewin noted

> a large-scale public movement expressing disgust and horror at the ecological disasters and widespread pollution created as a by-product of the relentless concentration on massive industrial projects. Ecology is now a catchword, and the ensuing debates and actions are a genuinely public affair.[9]

From this relatively safe and tolerated starting point of ecological problems, wider concerns about the communist party's monopoly on power emerged: as the protesters gained in courage, they started to raise bigger questions, and with increasing success.

Trying to maintain the system whilst reforming it soon generated tensions. Gorbachev's appeals to Leninist norms looked increasingly odd; they were widely regarded as an attempt to engage 'believers' in the process of change. The rehabilitation of Bukharin in 1988 signalled a preparedness to dismantle centralised economic structures.[10] The party promoted an 'intensification' of democracy in order to eliminate 'the braking mechanism' which was hampering restructuring.[11] But the unintended effect of Gorbachev's policies was to set in motion the system's disintegration. A key dynamic was the response of ordinary citizens. Initially assuming the new slogans were just another round of state-orchestrated rhetoric, after a while people began to see genuine opportunities. Independent activity developed, in the arts, in professional life and – perhaps most significantly for a communist government – in the trade unions. Miners' strikes in 1989 were the most visible expression of this.

Gorbachev's own thinking also evolved as the situation developed, and he sought to engage and integrate some of the new independent forces through a new representative body, established in 1989. Though its name seemed familiar, the Congress of People's Deputies was a fresh development in Soviet politics: two thirds of the seats were open to competition on the basis of universal suffrage. This democratic reform opened up logics far beyond what had been intended. Although the electoral commissions remained in party hands, and in many constituencies only one candidate was nominated, some nomination meetings witnessed serious competition, and candidates were nominated to run against those proposed by the party apparatus.[12]

In Moscow, Boris Yeltsin, who had initially been promoted by Gorbachev, and had subsequently made a name for himself as a populist urging a swifter pace for reform, stood for election against an officially sponsored opponent. He won overwhelmingly. Elsewhere, important party secretaries lost to little-known individuals, or failed to get the required fifty per cent of the vote to take up their seats. Familiar co-ordinates were shifting, and long-established authority was being called into question.

The evolution of *glasnost* and *perestroika* was coupled with a new policy of non-interference in the affairs of neighbouring states, and this too led to surprising events. Small demonstrations began in East Germany in late 1987, the instigators hoping that their country could be transformed into a democratic socialist republic. From March 1988, there were large demonstrations for political change in Budapest. In August, on the twentieth anniversary of the Soviet invasion, there was a large march in Prague against 'the regime'. In September 1988, the Polish trade union based movement Solidarity, which had been founded in 1980 and had survived and even flourished during the repression that followed, was invited to take part in 'round-table talks' with the government.

In February 1989, the Hungarian CP renounced its 'leading role' and proposed multi-party politics. Three months later, Hungary opened its border with Austria, leading to increased pressure from East Germans to be allowed direct access to West Germany. Around 130,000 of them moved west by travelling through Hungary, even before the fall of the Berlin Wall.

In Poland, the June 1989 elections brought Solidarity to power. Dynamics of reform and revolt now widened. The autumn saw an accelerating flow of Hungarians and East Germans into West Germany. Leipzig became the focus of a rapidly growing grassroots movement. Numbers attending weekly demonstrations increased from around a thousand in September 1989 to 20,000 in the first week of October and 70,000 in the second. Slogans included 'we're staying', and 'we are the people'. The call was still for the socialist state to listen to its people and reform.

But then, in Berlin, in November 1989, during a televised live press conference, an East German politburo member announced that the wall was now open. Whether or not he quite meant to say what he did, the news spread: thousands immediately converged on the symbol of Europe's cold war division, which was physically dismantled as security guards first watched and then opened the gates. The West Berlin authorities handed out maps, Coca-Cola and spending money. By now the chants of 'we are the people' had morphed into 'we are one people': Helmut Kohl's agenda of German reunification would be implemented by October 1990.

The Czechoslovakian party fell following large street protests. The symbolic event of Hungary's shift to post-communism was Nagy's reburial: the June 1989 re-internment of the executed reform leader of 1956 was attended by large crowds. In Bulgaria, in November 1989, Todor Zhivkov was removed by reformers in a 'palace coup'.

In almost every one of these countries, as in Russia, much of the change was initiated by members of the communist party. It turned out that CPs were not monolithic after all. Each contained a reform faction. In Hungary the reformers were already dominant by the time of *perestroika*. In other countries – Bulgaria, Czechoslovakia and East Germany – there were soon successful struggles against 'hardliners'.[13]

Romania provided a rare example of violent overthrow, but even here, combining self-interest and principle, most former communist bureaucrats backed the ousting of Nicolae Ceausescu. His utterly bewildered look when he came onto the balcony of the Central Committee Building in Bucharest on 23 December 1989 to experience hostile chanting from the crowd in the square, instead of the expected adulation, remains a defining image of the period: television cameras had caught the moment of revolution.[14]

Early in 1990, there were elections to the Soviet republics. In March and May, the Lithuanian and Latvian soviets voted for their republics to be independent nations.

The Soviet Union now relaxed price controls, privatised much of industry and deregulated the financial sector. By April 1991, the state planning agency had been abolished, and Gorbachev was applying for the Soviet Union to be admitted to the International Monetary Fund and World Bank. In June, Yeltsin used his profile as mayor of Moscow to pursue a successful campaign to be directly elected as leader of the Russian republic.

At this point, a group of traditionally minded communists felt they could take no more. August 1991 saw an attempted overthrow of Gorbachev. Resistance to the coup was led by Yeltsin, who by now had left the Communist Party. His role in countering the coup further increased his popularity. Gorbachev, on the other hand, was fatally weakened. Emboldened by success, Yeltsin now issued a decree terminating the existence of the Communist Party. On 7 December 1991, Yeltsin and the heads of state of Belarus and Ukraine announced that the USSR was dissolved. Gorbachev resigned, not having a position to hold any more, and Yeltsin moved into the Kremlin, which was now the seat of government for the Russian republic, not the Soviet Union.

The end of the Soviet Union, the dissolution of the Russian Communist Party, the collapse of East European governments and the rapid reunification of Germany on Kohl's terms – these were not what most demonstrators for change, or people more generally, had wanted. Whenever asked, most had said they wanted reform of the system. A 1989 poll of Czechoslovakians had found that just 3 per cent wanted majority private ownership in the economy. In 1990, in a referendum asking Soviet people if they wanted to dissolve the USSR, 76 per cent said 'no'. In May 1991, an American poll found that 54 per cent of Russians wanted to keep socialism, 27 per cent would like a mixed economy, and only 20 per cent hoped for a free market economy. Alas: pushing for democratic change does not always lead to the result most people want.

Gorbachev's attempt to overcome the difficulties facing Soviet society had failed. As Immanuel Wallerstein commented, his remedy was 'in many ways a brilliant success', but, 'unfortunately, the patient died'.[15]

## THE COLLAPSE OF COMMUNISM AND RISE OF NEOLIBERALISM

The communist project of social transformation and construction had ended: it was worn out, defeated and discredited – the future fell 'appallingly backward'.[16] For most people, the first years after the dissolution of the USSR were a period of traumatic social dislocation. There was an economic slump, mass pauperisation, disorder and health and mortality crises.

The people who now were steering the former Soviet republics and eastern European countries grossly and recurrently misrepresented the likely effects of privatisation, abolishing price controls and ending welfare provision. Here was a neoliberal replication of Stalinism's shrug that the 'means justifies the ends'. 'Transition' debates over what institutions to set up, how to prepare companies for capitalism, and whether voucher or mutual-fund privatisation was to be preferred, were little more than a sideshow. It was resource grabbing by the emerging oligarchs that largely reshaped post-communist economies. By 2013, 35 per cent of Russia's riches would be in the hands of 110 people: the country was heading for the highest level of wealth inequality in the world.[17] For many people, the capitalist restoration meant social collapse, regression, degradation, demodernisation and humiliation.

The unsurprising reaction was – and still is – widespread nostalgia for the way things were. This takes varied and complex forms, and is a cultural and emotional phenomenon in response to current frustrations and realities, rather than a political basis for 'going back'.[18] Nevertheless, its broad characteristics are telling. Now entirely aware of the decades of repression he oversaw, people continue to insist on the positive achievements even of Stalin. A 2015 survey showed that 45 per cent of Russians thought the sacrifices made under Stalin were justified, 'given the speed of the economic growth during his rule'.[19] Similar views can be found in other formerly communist countries. In a 2015 poll 82 per cent of respondents in the former German Democratic Republic answered that life was better before unification: 'they said there was more sense of community, more facilities, money wasn't the dominant thing, cultural life was better and they weren't treated, as they are now, like second-class citizens'.[20]

In Bulgaria, Hungary, Slovakia, the Czech Republic, eastern Germany and the Baltic states, people who had been used to a sense that society was reasonably equal were unsettled by the growth of significant inequality. But the tools that might have provided a basis for a challenge were unavailable. Political analysis of class and inequality had been discredited precisely at the moment when class relations and the distribution of resources were being rapidly restructured in the interests of capitalist investors and marketeers.

The human costs of transition were hardly a cause for concern for Western politicians. Instead, they were presented as if they were the fault of the previous regime; and, while some of the developments were acknowledged as regrettable, they were seen as the justifiable by-products of steps that were necessary to achieve the greater good – arguments reminiscent of the 'omelette' justification for everything that went with Stalin's industrialisation drive from 1929.

The tools and style of communism now had very small purchase on new conditions and trends: capitalism and neoliberal globalisation were promoted as the spirit of the times. Attempts to sustain communist political discourse found themselves 'fundamentally challenged by material developments'.[21] The old left was being left behind.

The left in the western capitalist democracies was also on the defensive, as the postwar gains of social-democracy were gradually being rolled back. As Len McCluskey has argued, a key motivation for the radical backlash which took shape from the mid-1970s was not, as the neoliberals proclaimed, the economic failures of communism and socialism: it was more a question of reclaiming class power:

> it was about restoring what our rulers regarded as the proper social hierarchy, including getting the working class out of politics. Its main front was … attacking trade union power, destroying the main organisations through which the working class has found social expression.[22]

In many countries, including France and Spain, neoliberalism was first consolidated whilst social-democratic parties were in government. Starting in the early 1980s, most social-democrats gradually ceded ground to the neoliberals: public services have been denigrated, reduced, fragmented and marketised, and assets and functions outsourced and transferred to profit-driven businesses. Institutions and activities outside the market, from universities to voluntary organisations, have been targeted to bring them inside the market, or reshape them in line with competitive values. Alongside deregulation, there has been ruthless pursuit of profit by private enterprises, and the facilitation and celebration of this by politicians.

Social conservatives even re-appropriated some of the radical language that the left had developed in the 1960s and 1970s: this was an attempt to render extinct 'the words, phrases and gestures of human solidarity'.[23] 'Budget cuts' became 'savings'. Tax evasion became 'income protection' – something that 'smart' people do. Private employers became 'job creators'. The 1968 liberation language of freedom, choice and competition was used to 'oust solidarity, co-operative creativity and equality'. As Beatrix Campbell commented: 'the language of the marketplace appears not only to govern the economy, but life itself'.[24]

## THE LOSS OF A SENSE OF ALTERNATIVE?

With the collapse of the communist states, the sense of the possibility of alternative forms of communism was also thrown into crisis. More than this, the disappearance of communism seemed to disable all projects aiming at a social alternative. The existence of the Soviet Union and the wider bloc had allowed, at least, what the Chilean poet Pablo Neruda once called 'a way of comparing possibilities'.[25]

For those still determined to sustain progressive efforts, stated one clear thinker, 'the only starting point ... is a lucid registration of historical defeat'.[26]

Not everyone thought that the collapse of the Soviet Union was a negative development for left politics. Some Trotskyists believed that the removal of Stalinism might open the way for their version of communism. But Trotskyism as a programme – rather than simply as confrontational style – only ever made sense as a critical surplus to an actually-existing project: 'when the Soviet ship went down, it also capsized, willy-nilly, the row boats of dissenters paddling in its wake'.[27] To those who thought that 'the idea' of communism would not be sunk by the events of 1989-1991, Antoine Vitez restated what might be thought obvious truths for materialists:

> One cannot separate the idea from the material disaster; it does not float intact above the ruins. Ideas exist only in their incarnation; if the incarnation disappears, the idea itself is mortally wounded.[28]

Gopal Balakrishnan felt that:

> we may be in the midst of a deeper transformation that has scrambled the very phenomenon of agency, relegating classical partisanships to the status of more or less eccentric, ideological preferences.[29]

For Hobsbawm, this 'scrambling' involved a painful recognition that, in retrospect, the twentieth-century communist project could be seen as doomed to failure, 'though it took a long time to realise this'.[30]

Within such recognitions, the validity of Marxism also came into question, even for its most skilful exponents. Tom Nairn now characterised it as a 'Rhineland-based diversion of global history, mistaken for the mainstream during a prolonged period of warfare, genocide and democratic defeat', while its state-power structures 'were themselves accidents of uneven development'.[31]

Whilst left-wing intellectuals attempted to recalibrate their ambitions in the context of demoralisation and disorientation, the response of 'modernising' social-democratic leaders to the new situation was to pursue 'the third way'. This would be equidistant from the excesses of unrestrained market economies, and from undemocratic, wasteful 'statist socialism'. But this was a 'triangulation' in which one of the nodes was weak. The first – the market economy – was real, vigorous, dominant. By the 1990s, the second – bureaucratic planning – was non-existent, surviving only as a myth. Because of this, 'third way' politics was always a false construct. Kicking against the bogey-man of 'bureaucratic planning' was a way of justifying an ever more intimate embrace of market values: it was the final squeezing out of some value from anti-communism.

Even third-way concepts which appeared to recover some genuinely social-democratic notions turned out to be about promoting the common sense of neoliberalism. Enthusiasm for 'social enterprise', for example, embedded business-friendly concepts in voluntary organisations and charities.[32] Social-democratic leaders and think tanks promoted acceptance of the globalised neoliberal world as a 'given', and saw their task as adjusting what remained of the traditional labour movement to this 'new reality'.[33]

The third way was the form social-democracy took at a time when there was no living alternative to neoliberalism. Hobsbawm noted that 'with the fall of the Berlin Wall, capitalism could forget how to be frightened, and therefore lost interest in people unlikely to own shares'.[34] Robert and Edward Skidelsky, no radical leftists, saw that the social liberalism shaping western European welfare states after 1945 had suffered a *coup de grace* with communism's demise: 'in the cold war era, the West had to proclaim its own concept of the good life to counter the appeal of communism. This necessity was now gone'.[35] As long as there had been a chance that Soviet approaches might succeed, the onus had been on capitalism to outdo communism's achievements. But with the collapse of alternatives, free market fundamentalism became the only game in town. Communism, against which it had fought so hard, turned out to have been a condition of possibility for post-war social-democracy.

Many members of social-democratic parties did attempt to limit commodification and privatisation. The French Prime Minister Lionel Jospin's phrase 'market economy – yes: market society – no' reflected this. Others argued that leaders were doing what they could – 'the third way did represent an attempt to come to grips with real changes in the contemporary world, such as … growing individualisation' – and to progress whatever redistributive and just projects were practically possible in this 'actual' situation.[36] On such a reading, Tony Blair could be understood as having successfully settled potential opposition through business-friendly policies, and in this context had been able to invest in working-class communities: tax credits, housing programmes, new schools and child care provision. A more critical assessment was that politicians of the left arguing for their policies in terms of neoliberal values – competitiveness, labour market flexibility, choice – might very well be intended as a 'realistic' approach, but this was seriously mistaken: 'they are not only failing to put forward their own coherent alternative values; they are also contributing to the further consolidation of neoliberal values as the only possible world view'.[37]

## NOTES

1. Shivdeep Singh Grewal, 'Reviews', *Socialist History*, issue 22, 2002.
2. Slava Gerovitch, 'How the Computer Got Its Revenge on the Soviet Union', *Nautilus*, 9 April 2015.
3. Eric Hobsbawm, *Interesting Times*, Allen Lane, London 2002, p199.
4. Eric Hobsbawm, *On History*, Weidenfeld and Nicolson, London 1997, p309
5. Pat Devine, *Democracy and Economic Planning*, Polity Press, Cambridge 1988, pp76-7.
6. Anne Applebaum, interview in *New Statesman*, 9 December 2012.
7. Archie Brown, 'Obituary of Fedor Burlatsky', *The Guardian*, 30 March 2014.
8. Roy Medvedev, *On Socialist Democracy*, Spokesman Books, Nottingham 1977.
9. Moshe Lewin, *The Gorbachev Phenomenon*, Radius / Century Hutchinson, London 1988, p79.
10. Stephen Cohen, introduction to Anna Larina, *This I Cannot Forget*, Hutchinson, London 1993, p28. There had been calls for Bukharin's

rehabilitation in the 1970s, but Soviet leaders resisted these, partly on the basis that 'such a rehabilitation might serve to legitimise Eurocommunism'. Vernon Aspaturian, in Aspaturian, Jiri Valenta and David Burke (eds), *Eurocommunism Between East and West*, Indiana University Press, Bloomington 1980, p14.

11. Anthony Barnett and Nella Bielski, *Soviet Freedom*, Picador, London 1988, p58.
12. Mary McAuley, *Soviet Politics 1917-1991*, Oxford University Press, Oxford 1992, p97.
13. Michael Waller, 'Editorial to a Special Issue on Party Politics in Eastern Europe,' *Party Politics*, Vol 1, No 4, 1995, p476.
14. Eric Hobsbawm, *The Age of Extremes*, Michael Joseph, London 1994, p457.
15. Immanuel Wallerstein, 'The Curve of American Power', *New Left Review*, July – August 2006
16. This phrase is from George Barker's 1937 poem *Calamiterror*.
17. Credit Suisse report, *The Guardian*, 9 October 2013.
18. For detailed articles on communist 'memory and nostalgia', see *Twentieth Century Communism*, 11, 2016; and Kristen Ghodsee, *Lost in Transition*, Duke University Press, Durham NC 2011.
19. Nadia Beard, 'Stalin rises again over Vladimir Putin's Russia, six decades after his death', *Independent*, 24 February 2016.
20. Tariq Ali, 'The New World Disorder', *London Review of Books*, 9 April 2015.
21. Susan Buck-Morss, *Dreamworld and Catastrophe*, MIT Press, Cambridge MY 2002, p39.
22. Ralph Miliband Lecture, reported in *Morning Star*, 16 January 2013.
23. Felix Guattari, *The Three Ecologies*, Bloomsbury, London 2014 [1989], p29.
24. Beatrix Campbell, 'After Neoliberalism', *Soundings* 56, Spring 2014.
25. Pablo Neruda, *Memoirs*, Penguin Books, London 1978 [1974], p194.
26. Perry Anderson, 'Renewals', *New Left Review*, January – February 2000.
27. Russell Jacoby, *Picture Imperfect*, Columbia University Press, New York 2005, Chapter 1.
28. Quoted in introduction, Costas Douzinas and Slavoj Zizek (eds), *The Idea of Communism*, Verso, London 2010, pix
29. Gopal Balakrishnan, 'Future Unknown', *New Left Review*, March – April 2005.
30. Eric Hobsbawm, interviewed by Maya Jaggi, 'A Question of Faith', *The Guardian*, 14 September 2002. Elsewhere, Hobsbawm reflected that 'the USSR and most of the states and societies built on its model … have collapsed so completely … that it must now be obvious that failure was built into this enterprise from the very start'. *Interesting Times*, Allen Lane, London 2002, p127.

31. Tom Nairn, 'History's Postman', *London Review of Books*, 26 January 2006.

32. This was one of the critical insights on social policy promoted in the late 1990s by the Social Exclusion Network of the New Politics Network, a successor organisation to Democratic Left.

33. John Schwarzmantel, 'Introduction: Gramsci in his time and in ours', discussing the contribution of Jules Townshend in Mark McNally and Schwarzmantel (eds), *Gramsci and Global Politics*, Routledge, London 2009, p14.

34. Eric Hobsbawm, *How to Change the World*, Little, Brown, London 2011, p413.

35. Robert and Edward Skidelsky, *How Much is Enough?* Allen Lane, London 2012, p192.

36. John Schwarzmantel, 'Introduction', discussing the chapter by Will Leggett in McNally and Schwarzmantel, op cit, p14.

37. Editorial, *Soundings* 54, summer 2013.

# 16. The red and the green

For all the sharp differences between communism and capitalism, both of these rival systems failed to address – and indeed exacerbated – ecological problems. Each of them promoted intense industrialisation; each failed to register the environmental costs of economic growth; and each betrayed arrogance in assuming man's (sic) 'mastery' over nature. For these and many other reasons, there is no intention here to argue that the left tradition has the necessary answers to environmental questions. But, given the central importance of this issue, it is worth looking back to discover resources which can suggest some of the right directions on this issue. Environmentalists and the green movement have made most of the running in these debates, but the focus here is on arguments within socialism.

Many left-wingers have been disappointed that a movement which aimed to be both scientific and socially liberating could have been responsible for domineering attitudes towards the environment. On thinking through the issues, Alex Nove's response was that, whereas ecological degradation can be seen to result 'consistently' and necessarily from private profit-making, 'at least the model of a socialist planning system' implies that such degradation does not have to happen and can be planned out.[1] Brian Pollitt argued that the 'appalling' environmental record of Soviet planning did not reflect any specific property of planning mechanisms *per se*:

> it reflected, rather, the excessive priority given over many decades to high-tempo industrial growth regardless of its wider environmental impact. But such a negative historical precedent does not weaken the proposition that the state is manifestly able to perceive social costs – such as environmental degradation – that fall outside the concerns of economic enterprises which are ruled by ambitions to maximise profitability and/or productivity.[2]

Nevertheless, both socialist planning and capitalist markets have in practice worked on the assumption that the natural environment is a ready resource to be used in the course of production for human consumption, and could provide an inexhaustible 'sink' that would mysteriously and 'naturally' deal with the toxic 'by-products' of industry. This shared outlook of 'industrialism' was rooted in Enlightenment traditions, and evidenced the common origins of communist and bourgeois economic practice. Capitalist ways of degrading the environment resulted from exploitation for private profit. But communism, with its voluntarist arrogance, was at least as fixated on the goal of abundance, which would abolish scarcity and remove the material base for social conflict, and thus take away the need for all kinds of difficult policy choices. Both systems led to gross environmental destruction, which resulted from the 'extractivism' that was central to both capitalism and communism: 'communists, socialists and trade unions' were merely fighting for 'more equal distribution of the spoils of extraction'.[3]

The twentieth-century left proved unable to promote and implement ecologically sound politics. But, believing that this failure is not inevitable, an increasing number of activists have attempted to combine environmentalism and socialism.[4] To lend support to this effort there are a few flecks of inspiration from a small number of pioneers from the period of classical Marxism: the English writer, artist and craftsman William Morris; the zoology student Rosa Luxemburg; and the friend of Engels and Second International theoretician Karl Kautsky, who identified the destructive impacts of agrochemical-intensive farming. There were, indeed, some tantalising signals from the movement's founders that they understood the need for human progress to take place on the basis of an understanding of human interaction with nature. At points, Marx clearly allows for the fact that nature's resources are finite, noting in Volume One of *Capital* that:

> all progress in capitalistic agriculture is a progress in the art, not only of robbing the labourer, but of robbing the soil ... All progress in increasing the fertility of the soil for a given time is a progress towards ruining the lasting sources of that fertility.

Marx also argued, in the context of the absurdity of 'private property of individuals in the earth' that:

even an entire society, a nation, or all simultaneously existing societies taken together, are not *owners* of the earth. They are simply its
possessors, its beneficiaries, and have to bequeath it to succeeding
generations in an improved condition.[5]

Engels recognised that the unintended and perverse consequences
resulting from humanity's acts of 'conquest' over nature, 'only too
often' result in cancelling out the original gains made by our efforts to
'master' and cultivate the natural world. He reflected that:

> at every step we are reminded that we by no means rule over nature
> like a conqueror over a foreign people, like someone standing outside
> nature – but that we, with flesh, blood and brain, belong to nature,
> and exist in its midst, and that all our mastery of it consists in the
> fact that we have the advantage over all other creatures of being able
> to learn its laws and apply them correctly.

Developing this theme, Engels insisted that we should not 'flatter
ourselves too much with our human victories over nature. For every
such victory revenges itself on us'.[6]

Only since the 1970s, however, have there have been any significant efforts to fuse green politics and programmes of the left.[7] In
1979 Herbert Marcuse gave a talk in which he argued that the
ecological movement was 'a political and psychological movement
of liberation'. It was political because it confronted the power of
capital, and psychological in that it sought to 'subordinate destructive energy to erotic energy'. In his response to this talk, Douglas
Kellner noted that Marcuse emphasised the embeddedness of human
beings in nature, and saw reconciliation with nature as an important
component of human liberation.[8] He argued that the movement
must therefore aim at the radical transformation of the institutions
and enterprises responsible for waste and pollution, rather than
focusing on more superficial issues such as the 'beautification' of
existing social settlements.

These arguments built on work by Theodor Adorno and Max
Horkheimer, critical theorists who were central to the Frankfurt
School, a theoretical tradition which Marcuse was also part of. This
tradition had first emerged within Marxism from the early 1920s. In
the 1940s, responding to the development of Nazism, Stalinism and

'managerialist capitalism' during the interwar period, these thinkers strove to understand how people who regarded themselves as heirs to the Enlightenment tradition, one of history's most progressive and productive currents, could be responsible for social practices that were so oppressive. Their understanding of ecological arrogance was framed within this overall theoretical endeavour: it was regarded not simply as another expression of oppressive social behaviour, but as key to understanding its roots and development.[9]

It is often argued that this theoretical tradition is imbued with pessimism, but its stance is better understood as one of reason and insight rather than of despair. And, given the way things ended for the most militantly progressive movement of the twentieth century, who can now say that a profoundly sceptical stance was misplaced, or that concerns about the warping of Enlightenment were unwarranted? The most productive readings of Adorno, Horkheimer and their co-thinkers remember that their work was shaped by progressive intent. As it was for Gramsci, a key starting point for the Frankfurt School was the need to identify the reasons for the failure of attempts at positive social change – precisely to investigate whether these failures could be transcended.

Such work was not a rejection of left-wing goals: it was perhaps the most determined attempt there has yet been to take them seriously. Fredric Jameson, considering the impulses behind the birth of 'Western Marxism' after the failure of world revolution in the 1920s, has also pointed to the ways in which thinkers on the left began to explore possible cultural causes for 'these unexpected ideological developments'.[10] Adorno and Horkheimer's aim was to explore the reasons for irrationalism, rather than an act of 'blindly worshipping at the altar of rationalism'.[11] And they showed how, within the Enlightenment project, 'what men want to learn from nature is how to use it in order wholly to dominate it and other men'.[12]

Laying the basis for a rationalist critique of the difficulties that rationalist politics have got us into, Adorno and Horkheimer consider the psychological costs which humans have paid in the course of acquiring our limited 'control' over nature. On this reading, the problem is not that rationalist political and social projects have gone too far, nor that their unintended and unplanned consequences show the impossibility of rational organisation of social life. The problem is that we have not yet been rationalist enough.

Some of humankind's early social steps led to an alienation from nature, the setting up of an oppositional relationship between people and their world that embedded into our patterns of thinking and behaviour an exploitative approach to the environment. This dynamic of alienation was fuelled by social divisions within the societies that most rapidly developed ways to exploit the natural environment.

When they moved to consider modern times from the standpoint of this theme, Adorno and Horkheimer argued that, 'for all that it broke from religious tradition', the Enlightenment promoted the notion of 'man's mastery over nature' as much as anything in Genesis. The dangerous idea that nature existed to suit human convenience was to shape most modern political movements, including communism. For these exiles from Nazism, 'Enlightenment behaves toward things as a dictator toward men. He knows them in so far as he can manipulate them'.[13]

The idea that reason should be used to bring things under control for the narrow and short-term purposes of humans was a trap rather than a route to real emancipation. Mastery of nature was a myth. The hubris of narrowly 'scientific' outlooks was pushing us towards destruction. Arrogant and distorted forms of rationality would in the end 'spit us out as imbeciles'.[14]

## POLITICS AS IF THERE WAS ONLY ONE EARTH

Developing this kind of thinking, some Marxists have moved towards the position of many within the green movement in rejecting capitalist conceptions of growth. Thus, for example, the Marxist tradition has much to offer in terms of a critique of the desirability of endless consumption, something that will be central to any real fusion of red and green politics.

Sometimes this critique is expressed in terms of longstanding notions about the nature of human labour. Maurice Cornforth, for example, argued that:

Marxists sometimes talk as though continually to produce more and more were the great social aim. But that aim is purely and simply a bourgeois aspiration. If production moves towards 'abundance', that means that we do not need or want to keep producing more and more, but rather that, producing enough, we ... produce it at a minimum cost in human labour-time.[15]

In spite of this potential for red-green convergence, there are still many on the left who do not share this view. As the Green Party's Derek Wall has argued:

> Many anti-capitalists would like to see the economy grow, essentially, forever. Yet for other anti-capitalists inspired by the green critique, such as eco-socialists, economic growth, however measured in a capitalist society, will destroy scarce resources, devastate global ecology and impoverish us in a whole range of ways.[16]

Wall has done much to identify and explore shared principles between socialists and greens; aims to reduce ecologically harmful consumption in the west, for example, are entirely consonant with long-established socialist principles about rectifying global inequalities. Nevertheless, there are still real tensions between the ambitions of the left as they were originally formed in the nineteenth century, and contemporary eco-socialism. Critiques of economic growth and 'productivism' are essentially arguments that we need to accept a form of what some would describe as scarcity, and to repudiate the ambition of creating more and more consumables.

How could such perspectives secure popular acceptance? Communism and social-democracy were both able to connect campaigns for short-term material gains to longer-term visions and values. Promoting the need to reduce the use of natural resources seems a bigger challenge. It is difficult to argue that working for an ecologically sound relationship between people and the rest of nature will in the meantime bring short-term benefits – at least in terms of how 'benefits' are popularly understood in a culture that is hegemonised by consumerism.

Asking people to reduce their standard of living for environmental ends – a kind of progressive, ecological 'austerity' – hardly seems a vote winner. This has meant that some people have questioned whether democratic politics can deliver sustainable economic and social practice. Perhaps, instead, an authoritarian approach, a kind of 'enlightened' green dictatorship, will prove necessary?[17] David Runciman has noted how some people feel that democracy may turn out to be one of the most difficult political problems in the battle to tackle climate change: 'given the reluctance of national electorates to face up to the scale of the challenge, are we going to have to find a way round democracy[?] ... at any given moment, democracy looks more like part of the problem than part of the solution'.[18]

These questions highlight a pesky problem with democracy: that political representatives depend for their access to power on support from voters on a short-term basis – and those voters' views may be based on delusions and misinformation rather than truth. The answer, however, can never be the pessimistic one of dispensing with democracy. The challenge instead is to promote a long-term shift away from the goal of material abundance – defined as having more and more stuff – towards lifestyles in which the good life is defined differently, for example as enabling much greater opportunities for personal, social and cultural development.

In making this shift, there is much to learn from approaches and concepts emerging from the global South and indigenous communities, such as the Buen Vivir movement which has developed in parts of Latin America. This prioritises the importance of community and environmental satisfaction, on the basis that peoples' subjective wellbeing is primarily shaped by factors including positive social relationships and food sovereignty, rather than welfare and *real* prosperity being merely dependent on cash income. Lessons and inspirations from such movements are already proving central to green politics, and these can be connected to the idea of developing counter-hegemonic approaches that will enable the creation of broad alliances for change – an approach that was developed by democratic communists.

We also need the co-ordinated development of an alternative 'ecological economics' that is able to deliver a good life for all without any need for the profligate waste of consumerist capitalism: this should be rolled out during the lifetime of the next two or three generations. This will require changes in our political culture and decision-making systems, which must be based on the recognition that there are finite limits to the world's resources, whether as inputs into human activity or as sinks for the resulting wastes; and on understanding the need to operate on the basis of the 'precautionary principle', so that we can protect 'irreplaceable ecosystems'.[19]

This will not come from simply adding left views to a green agenda, or vice versa. Although effective environmentalism *will* depend on collectivist social policy and economic regulation, there has to date been an insufficient reworking of 'red' socialist politics in the light of 'green' ecological challenges.[20] The compatibility of Marxism with ecology is too often and too easily asserted without the serious rethinking that such a recognition should prompt.

The uneasiness of interaction between left and green thinking is evident in Naomi Klein's 2014 book *This Changes Everything*; and, as Alyssa Battistoni has argued, any gaps and inconsistencies in her work do not indicate 'flaws in her reasoning or research so much as problems that are still being worked out'.[21] Detailed mapping of the varied strands of left and environmental thinking, and serious efforts to 'work things out', are crucial intellectual tasks for the emerging green socialist movement. A resulting progressive politics would reject the particular visions of material abundance which animated the twentieth century left. Environmental responsibility would become central to new conceptions of the common good; such a vision may require less consumption of consumer goods, but the aim would be to share resources equally and promote the wellbeing of everyone, rather than to impose an austerity politics that reserves the right of the powerful to continue to destroy the planet.

Such a shift could be attractive: any restrictions on consumption would be fair in form and distribution; and their popularity would be enhanced if combined with significant measures of redistribution, including better access to all for housing and public services – human needs which do not require the destruction of resources. One condition of such a shift would be widespread cultural reassessment of our 'needs' and 'wants'. Bourgeois economics tends to treat all 'wants' as sacrosanct and deserving of satisfaction. But it is possible to conceive of system in which the satisfaction of particular forms of consumer desire would be judged in the light of its potential effect on the common good, and would be allowed only after prior discussion about what is appropriate. There would be democratic determination of appropriate needs. Judgements about sustainability and equality, taken collectively, would be re-inserted into the dismal science of economics.

This would mean a move forward from today's 'preference-accommodating' politics. This form of politics treats people's raw, unreflective and unchallenged wants and 'false needs' as sovereign, failing to acknowledge that these are shaped by dominant social and cultural forces, or that catering to each individual desire may have harmful consequences for the wider society and the environment. (This is of course to, for the moment, leave to one side the question of whether the current system does in fact meet people's real needs.) Instead, a 'preference-transforming' politics could be developed, promoting awareness of the social and environmental impact of our lifestyle choices, along with a stronger sense of civic responsibility; such an approach could be popularised through the extension of deliberative democracy, the results of which would feed into national and international decision-making.

It is important, too, to identify starting points in this direction: as well as critiques of consumerism and the idea that we need ever more growth, we should be pressing for socialised approaches to issues such as transport, energy and housing. These would be based on the recognition that management of environmental issues on the scale and with the seriousness now required is incompatible with the essential character of a society which 'consecrates private property, or the rights of individuals to pursue their own exclusive interests independently of, and sometimes against, society itself'.[22] These new approaches would absorb the central insight of ecological economics: producing to satisfy all present-day desires and 'wants' as if they are self-evidently justified and should be met must be replaced by a focus on the capacity of the earth to support life indefinitely into the future. Serious efforts to destabilise and undo consumerist ideology will be part of this effort, detaching us from its false promises which pervert and betray our proper desires for a better future.

What we need to establish – in a politics for our generation's great grand-children, rather than one which repeats the errors of our great grand-parents – is a widely held common sense, robust and reproducible for the long term, which will support and apply long-term strategies both for economic justice and ecological sustainability. In the short term, it will be useful to work on issues which can combine at least a partial refusal of consumerism with policies that address people's current frustrations and offer them benefits: incentivising the use of renewable energy and significant investment in public transport are potential examples.

Through measures such as these, increasing progressive and democratic regulation of the economy and social life could be popularised as a basis for popular action to address climate change. Unfortunately, it is possible that widespread interest in such ideas will only come about after further serious environmental incidents with long-lasting effects.

## NOTES

1. Alec Nove, *The Economics of Feasible Socialism*, Allen and Unwin, London 1983, p6.
2. Introduction to Maurice Dobb, *The Development of Socialist Economic Thought*, Lawrence and Wishart, London 2008, p35.
3. Naomi Klein, *This Changes Everything*, Allen Lane, London 2014, p177.
4. Others argue that green agendas are intrinsically at odds with Enlightenment goals of progress. Frank Furedi and his followers have followed the logic of this argument to become, effectively, deniers of ecological risks: an ironic position for people who at the same time supposedly champion the relevance and value of science. Whether or not they have been directly funded by companies whose commercial interests depend on destructive environmental exploitation, as some critics have asserted, the trajectories of these contrarian former Trotskyists have led them to some curious choices. The 'dialectician' Slavoj Zizek, with trademark inconsistency, has found himself able both to attack environmentalism as a middle-class luxury and an indulgent consumer choice, and to present the mounting environmental crisis as proof of the urgent need for his abstract communism.
5. Karl Marx, *Capital, Volume 3*, in *Marx Engels Collected Works, Volume 37*, Lawrence and Wishart, London 1998 [1863-84].
6. Friedrich Engels, *The Dialectics of Nature*, Chapter 9, 'The Part Played by Labour in the Transition from Ape to Man', in *Marx Engels Collected Works, Volume 25*, Lawrence and Wishart, London 1987 [1883].
7. It is important to note that articulation with socialism is not the only possible political pairing for ecology. Links between authoritarian right wingers and the environmental agenda are sketched in Derek Wall's article 'Darker shades of green', which 'traces the thread of ecofascism through the green movement's history', *Red Pepper*, August 2000, available at www.redpepper.org.uk/darker-shades-of-green For many decades, conservationism in Britain had a predominantly upper-class social base; *The Ecologist* magazine's founder, Edward Goldsmith, espoused an extremist conservatism; his nephew Zac Goldsmith, who edited the magazine before entering parliament, has been seen as promoting the perspective of 'leave it to your aristocratic overlords to take care of the land because we know best how to preserve it'. Such realities explain some of the roots of the labour movement's suspicion of environmentalism; but

the evolution of the Green Party in the last ten years or so has seen those who combine ecological outlooks with social conservatism becoming significantly outnumbered by a new, younger and more socialist membership.

8. Herbert Marcuse, 'Ecology and the Critique of Modern Society', talk given in 1979, and first published in *Capitalism Nature Socialism: A Journal of Socialist Ecology*, September 1992. Douglas Kellner's 1982 response, 'Marcuse, Liberation and Radical Ecology', written in 1982, was published in same issue of *Capitalism Nature Socialism*.

9. As Ryan Gunderson states, 'Horkheimer, Adorno, and Marcuse persistently tied the domination of nature to the domination of human beings in the context of two interrelated processes: the instrumentalisation of reason and the development of capitalism'. 'Environmental Sociology and the Frankfurt School', *Journal of Environmental Sociology*, 3, 2015.

10. Fredric Jameson, *Valences of the Dialectic*, Verso, London 2009, p265.

11. Adorno, letter to Horkheimer, 14 February 1965.

12. Theodor Adorno and Max Horkheimer, *The Dialectic of Enlightenment*, Verso, London 1997 [1944], p4.

13. Ibid, p9.

14. Paul Eluard, *A Moral Lesson*, Green Integer, Los Angeles 2005 [1949].

15. Maurice Cornforth, *Communism and Philosophy*, Lawrence and Wishart, London 1980, p272.

16. Derek Wall, *Economics After Capitalism*, Pluto Press, London 2015, p17.

17. In their remarkable dystopian speculation on what might bring about, and happen after, a twenty-first century ecological disaster, Naomi Oreskes and Erik M Conway anticipate that the directive, authoritarian political system now in place in China might enable that country to 'weather disastrous climate change, [vindicating] the necessity of centralised government'. *The Collapse of Western Civilisation*, Columbia University Press, New York 2014, p52. In their 'view from the future', the authors write that 'as the devastating effects of the Great Collapse began to appear [from 2093], the nation states with democratic governments ... were at first unwilling and then unable to deal with the unfolding crisis. As food shortages and disease outbreaks spread and sea-levels rose, these governments found themselves without the infrastructure and organisational ability to quarantine and relocate people'.

18. David Runciman, 'A Tide of Horseshit', *London Review of Books*, 24 September 2015.

19. Pat Devine, *Democracy and Economic Planning*, Polity Press, Cambridge 1988, pix.

20. Important starting points for this ongoing effort included Rudolf Bahro, *Socialism and Survival*, Heretic Books, London 1982; Ted Benton, *The Greening of Marxism*, Guilford Press, New York 1996; John Bellamy Foster, *Marx's Ecology*, Monthly Review Press, New York 2000. A major

recent contribution is Jason Moore, *Capitalism in the Web of Life*, Verso, London 2015. The journal *Capitalism Nature Socialism* carries relevant articles in every issue, aiming to help create a red-green intellectual culture and thus contribute to the development of a red-green politics.

21. Alyssa Battistoni, 'How to Change Everything', www.jacobinmag.com, 11 December 2015.

22. Lucio Colletti, introduction to Karl Marx, *Early Writings*, Penguin Books, Harmondsworth 1975, p37.

# 17. The left since the 1990s

## COMMUNISM AFTER 1991

Vestiges of the communist movement continued after 1991, though, in many cases, their political content changed. In Russia, the communist party in opposition became a haven for nostalgics, upset about change, nurturing hurt national pride. In China, where the Communist Party remains in power, former Maoists took the capitalist road, pursuing industrial and economic development, combined with a focus on political 'order'. Geopolitics has enabled North Korea to cling to its corner as an increasingly paranoid, hurt and defensive state.

In a few atypical contexts, communists could still directly inform successful movements against oppression. Nelson Mandela's release from prison in 1990, and the ending of apartheid, was widely presented as part of the same 'wave of freedom' which saw the fall of the Berlin Wall.[1] But Mandela's identity and strategy was at least partly rooted in his time in the South African Communist Party: he was a central committee member when he was arrested in August 1962.[2]

The SACP played a major role in the anti-apartheid struggle. Alongside non-communists in the African National Congress, its members sustained underground activity inside South Africa; fought in *Umkhonto we Sizwe*; ran ANC structures abroad; promoted international solidarity; and did much to shape the choices and culture which enabled a racially inclusive multi-party democratic system to be put in place following the divisions of apartheid.[3] South African communists had long emphasised that the 'main content' of immediate struggles – class and national – was to defeat apartheid and introduce democracy. SACP members have served in all the ANC governments since 1994, attracting criticism from forces who see themselves as further to the left, but evidencing the positive contribution communists can make during a 'national-democratic revolution'.

In other parts of the world, many long-serving party members put the communist name behind them after 1991 – and some former

Eastern European bureaucrats made a good living for themselves in the process. Across Western Europe, many former communists joined established social-democratic parties, insisting this was now 'the only game in town'. The largest contingent of the Italian party in 1991 refounded itself as the Democratic Party of the Left (PDS), and eventually the majority of the PDS evolved into the avowedly social-democratic Democratic Party (PD). A number of other European communist parties joined left alliance groups and/or parties, such as Die Linke in Germany, United Left (Izquierda Unida) in Spain and Syriza in Greece.

Cuba has been unique as a country in which communists have retained power and also sustained a principled commitment to socialism, expressed through impressive internationalist work. The country which was at the centre of the sharpest moment of nuclear tension to date has managed to survive longer than anyone expected.

## THE RENEWAL OF THE LEFT IN LATIN AMERICA

In his last years, Fidel Castro provided inspiration and friendship to vibrant new left movements across Latin America. Over the last two decades, on the continent which was once regarded as America's backyard, and had suffered under American-backed dictators such as Pinochet, left governments in Venezuela, Bolivia, Ecuador, Brazil, Argentina and Paraguay started to introduce structural reforms designed to improve the living standards of the poor. Shared approaches have included expanded education and welfare; increased public investment; the extension of public ownership; and increasing tax receipts – not only by increasing taxes, but by massively improving collection rates. Such measures appeared ultra-radical because they went against the Washington consensus. As Tariq Ali commented in 2009, 'in reality, the changes amount to a radical version of social-democracy, long forgotten in its homelands'.[4] However, in recent years most have been checked and reversed. The redistribution efforts of the Bolivar revolution in Venezuela, perhaps the most well-known case, were largely made possible because of the income from its oil reserves, but this has been severely damaged by the recent slump in oil prices. In all countries with left governments, right-wing opposition movements have been financed by the US and have had some degree of success.

In southern Mexico, the media-savvy Zapatista movement established 'autonomous' areas, protesting against the devastation wrought
by the North Atlantic Free Trade Agreement between the US, Canada
and Mexico. This was a major inspiration to North Americans and
Europeans who were active in successive phases of the anti-globalisation movement (which many on the left have argued should be called
the anti-neoliberal globalisation movement).

From the mid-1990s, the alter-globalisation movement began to
emerge from a series of direct action campaigns, including demonstrations against symbols of corporate power and ecologically focused
protests against airport extensions and new roads. The Zapatistas were
celebrated for aiming to 'build a new world' directly, without a direct
assault on state power. They were presented as a credible example of
how to gradually undermine the power of capital in such a way that 'at
some point, the state will collapse like a cat hovering over the precipice
in the cartoons'.[5]


## REJECTING THE STRUGGLE FOR HEGEMONY?

The anti-globalisation movement first took widely visible form in
Seattle, during World Trade Organisation talks in December 1999.
A week of spirited protests, some involving attacks on property and
clashes with the police, seriously disrupted the proceedings, while
dissent in the conference hall itself, mainly from developing and underdeveloped countries, succeeding in delaying plans for a new round
of trade liberalisation. This success then fed into a series of protests,
in which large numbers demonstrated outside meetings of other
organisations promoting neoliberal globalisation – the International
Monetary Fund, the World Bank and the G8. At first inchoate –
something many activists saw as a virtue – eventually large sections
of the movement coalesced to become the World Social Forum. Its
slogan, 'another world is possible', recovered and reinstated into the
post-communist landscape the positive sense that current settlements
could be changed.

In the Middle East and North Africa, the Arab Spring of 2010-11
was an inspiration to a new generation of activists, though it too was
ultimately defeated in most countries. Social movements against
'austerity' started to spread across Europe and the US in 2010-11.
The 'movement of the squares' brought millions into diverse protests

across Greece, Spain, Turkey and many other countries. In the US, the Occupy Wall Street protest began in Zucotti Park in New York. These movements of the streets and the squares had a certain affinity with each other, though their forms of organisation vary considerably. Most of these horizontal movements were orientated towards direct action and direct democracy rather than the state. They tended to reject the idea of hegemony as 'intrinsically domineering', and to propose instead an affinity-based politics: 'rather than advocating an appeal to or takeover of the vertical power of the state, horizontalism argues for freely-associating individuals to come together, create their own autonomous communities and govern their own lives'.[6]

Many activists, both in the earlier anti-globalisation movement and in the newer movements, have had a pronounced suspicion of the traditional methods of left organising. Richard Day, in his provocatively named 2005 book *Gramsci is Dead*, was pleased to see that contemporary radical activists were operating '*non*-hegemonically rather than *counter*-hegemonically': 'They seek radical change, but not through taking or influencing state power, and in so doing they challenge the logic of hegemony at its very core'.[7] Occupy activists often disavow any idea of a unified ideology or collective subject: many feel empowered to produce their own critique of capitalism 'in line with their particular identities'.[8]

Such thinking is sustained by writers such as John Holloway, who has argued that capitalism and state power can be undermined through initiatives which repudiate 'old state-centred politics and all that it involves in terms of corruption and boredom and using people as a means to an end';[9] and by Michael Hardt and Toni Negri's notion of 'the Multitude', which is linked to their idea of a new radical agency, organised through lateral relations between its diverse members rather than vertically through political parties.

Many of the thinkers that are linked to these movements see traditional struggles around wages and welfare as outdated. Many of them also draw on the autonomist tradition, the idea that workers should resist capitalism independently – 'autonomously' – of political parties and trade unions. As Fredric Jameson has commented, this kind of response is influenced by a rejection of forms of politics that are marked by 'the authoritarianism and sectarianism of Lenin ... the murderous violence of the Stalin era ... and finally, the corruption of Brezhnev's party'. Instead, activists 'free themselves' from solving the problems which come with the need to organise by believing that 'new times and new historical situations demand new thoughts about political organisation'.[10] And this rejection of traditional models is also fuelled by recognition of the weaknesses of social democracy, and a sense that politics cannot be reduced – as so often with social-democracy – to 'managing a state, as distinct from broader issues of the nature and structure of power in a society'.[11]

But there are problems in a disavowal of organisation and coherence. Thus, for example, Jeremy Gilbert was concerned that debates at a 2002 European Social Forum gathering he attended in Italy almost inevitably concluded with 'vapid calls for co-operation between parties and movements', but with scarcely any discussion of the problems and possibilities inherent in such relationships.[12]

Similarly, the World Social Forum did not countenance activities at state policy level: its 'Charter of Principles' separated social struggles from any sustained attempt to enter the representative political sphere. But, as Emir Sader has commented, this kept activists and campaigners focused on 'denunciation and resistance', while neglecting reflection on political and strategic questions.[13]

Even sympathetic critics have suggested that Occupy's practice has been self-limiting, perhaps self-defeating. Nick Srnicek and Alex Williams have seen Occupy as symptomatic of what they describe as a 'folk politics' – one that fetishes 'local spaces' and 'transient gestures' – when what is needed is 'the difficult labour of expanding and consolidating gains'.[14] Ernesto Laclau, too, saw that 'the horizontal dimension of autonomy' would be incapable, left to itself, of bringing about long-term historical change if it was not complemented by the 'vertical dimension of hegemony' – in other words, a 'radical transformation of the state'.[15]

In the years since the collapse of communism and the rightward drift of social-democracy, the flame of protest has been kept burning by millions of young people in these movements. But these forms of protest are not enough on their own to bring about change. Contemporary left political parties need to learn how to make the links with the movements; and the movements need to look for acceptable and effective strategies for intervention in the state.

In this context, the decentralisation and spontaneity promoted by thinkers such as Holloway, Hardt and Negri can be seen as reflecting a pessimistic viewpoint: it cannot conceive of an appropriately networked and centralised politics of power, widely-supported and accountable through democratic systems and capable of achieving progressive change.

Recently, the need for vertical organisation has begun to be reasserted by voices coming from within the alternative social movements as well as the more traditional left. Thus, for example, Naomi Klein has reflected that:

> I have, in the past, strongly defended the right of young movements to their amorphous structures – whether that means rejecting identifiable leadership or eschewing programmatic demands. And there is no question that old political habits and structures must be reinvented to reflect new realities, as well as past failures. But ... the fetish for structurelessness, the rebellion against any kind of institutionalisation, is not a luxury today's transformative movements can afford.[16]

Jodi Dean's *Crowds and Party* has developed related themes, presenting arguments in favour of the party form.[17] And, recognising the need to combine the energy of social movements with effective governmental policies, Neal Lawson of Compass has proposed '45 degree politics' to focus on the ways that 'the vertical' and 'the horizontal' meet.[18]

Nancy Fraser has argued that, in aiming 'to build counter-hegemonic centres of opinion and will-formation, far removed from circuits of institutionalised power', movements like Occupy effectively 'reject schemes that would democratise global governance by transferring the powers of rogue institutions to transnational parliaments, accountable to transnational publics and electorates, charged with reining in private power and with regulating common affairs':

> the strategy of evading, rather than confronting, the institutions of global governance lets off scot-free the mammoth concentrations of private power whose interests now rule.[19]

In their different ways, these activist-intellectuals highlight the challenge of combining the positives which result from the wide variety of progressive campaigns – with their range of agendas and tactics, and multiple and diverse constituencies – with a capacity to unite for co-ordinated action in order to pursue an agreed-upon aim in agreed-upon ways at an agreed-upon time and place.

## THE 'NEW COMMUNISTS'

While anarchists and autonomists have proposed their abstract conceptions of democracy as a resource for today's counter-systemic movements, another unfortunately influential intellectual current has argued that explicit rejection of democratic norms should be part of any effort to reinstitute effective left politics. Although there are significant differences and debates between Alain Badiou, Slavoj Zizek, Jodi Dean and other 'new communists', there are shared themes in their work which deserve consideration – and critique.

Badiou's purpose is often described as if it were simply about re-inscribing into today's ideological landscape the welcome argument that 'a politics without and against domination is possible'.[20] But the 'communist hypothesis' he promotes is idealist in a negative sense: it combines a grand 'hypothesis' with exhortation to subjective revolutionary commitment. His followers promote a hollow rhetoric of resurrection: 'communism is rising from its grave once again'. As Benjamin Kunkel identifies, the politics is weightless, with neither programme nor organisation, or any suggestion about what political forms or economic models could realise it, or even work towards it.[21]

What Badiou *does* clearly encourage and affirm is impatience with bourgeois democracy. The man practises what he preaches here: he has disdained to vote since 1968, not thinking it proper or useful to make a choice between Giscard d'Estaing and Mitterrand, or between Chirac and Le Pen – thus making his own personal contribution to the 'hollowing out' of representative democracy that 'new communism' presents as one reason for espousing an extreme radical politics.[22]

Zizek has followed Badiou in this, moving away from mere scepticism about claims that democratic practice has intrinsic value. More recently, he has explicitly *rejected* its value, praising Badiou for:

> defining the emancipatory struggle in strictly political terms, as the struggle against (liberal) democracy, today's predominant ideologico-political form ... what, today, prevents the radical questioning of capitalism itself is precisely the belief in the democratic form of struggle against capitalism.[23]

In his call for papers for a conference 'on the idea of communism', Zizek stated that the task of radically rethinking 'the most basic co-ordinates of emancipatory politics' should go well beyond 'the rejection of the Party-State-Left in its "Stalinist" form', and that this rejection should be extended 'to the entire field of the "democratic Left"' as the strategy to 'reform the system from within its representative-democratic state form'.[24] Zizek argues that left-wingers have been mistaken to accept 'the basic coordinates of liberal democracy' and urges that radicals should 'fearlessly ... violate these liberal taboos'. In this mode, Zizek celebrates what he regards as the 'real Leninism' of 'shock effect' calls for violence and proletarian dictatorship.

But, as Simon Critchley notes, Zizek – unlike Lenin – rarely advises his readers as to what they should actually do: instead, 'what we seem to be left with is ... passivity and inertia ... and some rather vague threats of violence'.[25] Zizek often 'solves' the philosophical and political deadlocks he identifies through 'vague apocalyptic allusions to violence and utopian allusions to future structural antagonisms in capitalism that will have possibly dramatic political consequences'.[26] This leads to explicit approval of 'the application of force, or "terror", in support of a policy of egalitarian justice'.[27] There is a real risk here that, in the context of future defeats, such theorising could point radicals down destructive, counter-productive and dead-end paths.

Adopting a somewhat cooler tone than Zizek, Jodi Dean has stated:

> what's wrong with the notion of democracy as even radical democrats have appropriated it is that it leaves capitalism in place. The assumption is that if we have enough democracy the problem of capitalism will either go away or solve itself – and that's clearly false. Take Ernesto Laclau and Chantal Mouffe: their idea of radical democracy is framed specifically to keep class from being a primary political determination.[28]

But Dean's counter-position of democracy to radical change involving class politics is based on a misrepresentation of Laclau and Mouffe. Their key work, *Hegemony and Socialist Strategy*, includes forensic analysis of how the concept of class has been formed and used on the left. Their explanation of why, for example, there cannot be simple and necessary links between anti-sexism and anti-capitalism, and why 'a unity between the two can only be the result of a hegemonic articulation' is guided by genuine interest in how class identities operate in contemporary society, with all its dynamics, conflicts and processes of identity-formation: 'this approach permits us to re-dimension and do justice to workers' struggles themselves'.[29] Overall, Laclau and Mouffe show that relationships between socialism and democracy are crucially important, but that they do not happen automatically, and instead have to be constructed and developed through political work and alliance building.

By contrast, the overall position of Badiou, Dean and Zizek is to reject representative democracy as being part of neoliberal ideology: Badiou refers to 'the capitalo-parliamentarian or "western" order';[30] Dean states that 'for leftists to refer to their goals as a struggle for democracy ... is a defence of the status quo, a call for more of the same'.[31] But these arguments are based on an apparent acceptance that the limited and constrained version of democracy promoted by neoliberals is all that democracy can ever be.

Instead, we should recognise democracy as a complex and contradictory phenomenon, which already does – and could increasingly – involve 'major opportunities for ... ordinary people to participate, through discussion and autonomous organisations, in the shaping ... of public life', in order to tackle today's problems at all levels.[32] Defending, sustaining, improving and using structures of representative democracy are necessary components of authentic change.

One reason for this is that any successful radical movement needs to continually test its support and build its legitimacy. Dean's recent interest in how an actual communist party might be reconstituted, and her welcome arguments on the necessity of political discipline, appear to be leading her to further and detailed consideration of the relationship between building an organisation and the processes that are necessary to secure and maintain support for it.[33]

An objection can easily be made that the critique of Zizek set out here does not give an accurate picture of his thought. This is because he is the 'Buy One Get One Free' philosopher of the left. If you disagree with any of his analyses and arguments, do not worry: he has another, directly contradictory, argument for you in his next book – or even later on in the same book. Zizek's 'various and incompatible' strategic notions include: 'advocating democracy; rejecting parliamentary democracy; arguing for "reinvented" democracy; advocating withdrawal from the system to speed its collapse; making "moderate" demands that can trigger global transformations'.[34]

To define such play with contradictions as 'dialectical' is too charitable: Zizek's work is incoherent. One moment Stalinist repression is being praised as a sign of seriousness in politics: in the next, Edward Snowden and Chelsea Manning are heroes for exposing the pervasive control of information by today's deep state. Setting up 'two opposing points of view' and then urging readers 'to reject both' can at first appear inspirational and radical: but the recurrent use of such stylistic devices betrays a laziness of thought.[35]

Zizek's apparent impatience with democracy and reformism is tied to an overall lack of strategy: his work is in many ways best seen a symptom of the weakness of current theorising about radical politics.

## NEW LEFT-WING PARTIES IN EUROPE

In Spain and Greece, significant new left parties have emerged that seek to combine representative politics with accountability to social movements – Podemos and Syriza.

The roots of Podemos lay in the Indignados mobilisation, which took off from 15 May 2011, when a diverse range of people protesting against the establishment and its anti-popular policies came together to occupy the Puerto del Sol in Madrid. Thereafter city squares across Spain were occupied for weeks, as growing numbers of people expressed their rejection of the regime's policies, socially, politically, economically and culturally. Looking to give political expression to some of this constituency, the founders of Podemos recognised that, however inspired, 'the logic of 15M led to its exhaustion; it didn't achieve the effects desired by its committed activists, who hoped that the social could substitute for the institutional'.[36] Young academics and students in Madrid formed the party in January 2014, after a period of imaginative media work. They aimed to develop an agenda which articulated the views and interests of people in varied campaigns into a 'formal track', in which political institutions could make authorised binding decisions and carry them out.[37]

Podemos grew rapidly. Within four months, using a tiny, crowd-funded budget and promoting anti-corruption and anti-austerity messages, it won 8 per cent of the vote and five seats in the European Parliament. Involving members through participatory 'circles', and tech-savvy internet campaigns, it was 'multi-form', 'socially radical' and 'strategically intelligent'. Consciously drawing from Laclau and Mouffe's suggestions on constructing political agendas, Podemos sought to create a new 'we' through defining a division between 'the people' and Spain's political and economic establishment, which was dubbed 'the caste' ('la casta'). It then re-presented the demands of the street in formal political competition, promoting the value and indispensability of representative democracy alongside participatory processes.

In many ways, the programmes of Podemos have been familiarly social-democratic. Its leading figure Pablo Iglesias stated that:

> in the short term we are limited to using the state to redistribute a little more, have fairer taxes, boost the economy and start building a model that recovers industry and brings back sovereignty. We accept that the euro is inescapable. The change we represent is … about recovering a consensus that twenty years ago would even have included some parts of Christian Democracy.[38]

But twenty years is a very long time in politics. The neoliberal context has rendered Podemos radical and challenging, in seeking for example 'to establish sovereign processes that would limit the power of finance, spur the transformation of production, ensure a wider distribution of wealth and push for a more democratic configuration of European institutions'.[39]

In the December 2015 general election, Podemos won over 20 per cent of the vote, confirming the country's political crisis, and suggesting the potential of radical politics. But realising this potential is never straightforward. In the following June 2016 elections, called after the failure of any party to form a government that could command a majority in parliament, Podemos, now allied with the United Left, found that its momentum had been checked. Debates over appropriate strategy continued. A 2017 leadership contest focused choices on a number of key issues: whether the party should seek conciliation with the socialists or further integrate the communist party; how to achieve a proper balance between consolidating its parliamentary influence and its involvement with popular movements, trade unions and student campaigns; and the extent to which party structures should be centralised. The achievement of a measure of political power at national level continues to raise knotty problems for left parties, particularly when they are strongly connected to social movements.

In Greece, Syriza's achievement of government power has inevitably generated even sharper debates and splits than have been seen in Spain. Becoming a party of government tends to intensify difficult choices rather than to magic them away. As Stathis Gourgouris has described Syriza:

> It is a loose, self-contradictory, and internally antagonistic coalition of leftist thought and practice, very much dependent on the capacity of social movements of all kinds, thoroughly decentralized and driven by the activism of solidarity networks in a broad sphere of action across class lines of conflict, gender and sexuality activism, immigration issues, anti-globalization movements, civil and human rights advocacy, etc.[40]

Syriza began life as a coalition and this continues to shape its structure as a party, while its rapid rise coincided with the Greek political and economic crisis: its life in government has been shaped by that crisis. All this means that its difficulties in government have led to widespread internal criticism from the party's ultra-left, and these in turn have been taken up by the far left outside Greece.

Syriza attracted only around 5 per cent of voters in the 2007 and 2009 general elections. But in 2012, its support shot up to 27 per cent in the second general election of that year. This represented voters' response to the extreme neoliberal measures that the EU was seeking to impose as the price of successive 'bailouts'. The mainstream Greek parties were regarded as giving in too easily to EU pressure.

The European Union's aim had been to enforce fiscal discipline in the aftermath of crash and slump – not just in Greece, but throughout the Eurozone. To this end it had demanded substantial cuts to health provision, education and social services, and reductions in wages and pensions. The result of these measures had been an economy that had contracted by around 30 per cent, and wage levels dropping to two or three Euros per hour.

Syriza fought the 2015 general election on an anti-austerity platform, arguing that the Greek people should not be forced to accept the measures imposed on the country as a condition of the bailout. On this programme it won the largest share of the vote (36 per cent) and formed a government in coalition with the nationalist party ANEL. It also won a second general election in September

2015, although it had made little progress against the EU's hardline stance.

In Alexis Tsipras, the party had found a plain-talking leader who connected to the anger and hurt of ordinary Greeks:

> we are told that 'there is no alternative', by which they mean; 'we'll decide what counts as an alternative and what doesn't' … we are told that 'easy deceptive promises are a threat to stability', and by this they mean: 'democracy is a threat to our power'.[41]

Tsipras's stated aim was to use democratic means to 'achieve the great change we want: to turn the economy around and place it at the service of society and human needs'. In aiming for this classically socialist – and Marxist – objective, Syriza's leaders recognised the difficulties they faced. Their strategy was to act as if they expected that EU leaders would respect their 'democratic mandate' and allow their radical left government to attempt a demand-led recovery in Greece, on the basis that future growth would enable the debt to be paid back.

The government also moved to tackle the widespread corruption in Greek business and public life, including re-establishing processes that had been undermined by previous governments, such as collecting unpaid tax from the many private companies and better off 'entrepreneurs' who had been allowed to avoid it. But, as Gourgouris argues, Syriza's problem was that its internal policies had to be conducted 'under conditions of external institutional assault'.

The Greek debt trap imprisoned the Syriza-led government, as the leaders of the Eurozone refused to make any concessions to the Greek electorate's vote against austerity. The logic of the situation in the end led to Tsipras having to reluctantly accept the need to implement EU-imposed policies that have been described by his leftist critics as 'consistent with the interests of the powerful'.[42]

During 2016, as Syriza implemented a range of 'difficult' measures, Tsipras's approval ratings fell sharply. The options for the country continue to defined by the debt trap, and this means that Syriza's leadership has to try to strike a balance between co-operating with European institutions to repay national debts; seeking to grow the economy in order to generate revenues which could both rebuild living standards and repay the loans and 'bailouts'; and continuing to defy some of the more extreme demands from some Eurozone and

IMF – all the while trying to tackle some of the longer-term problems of Greek society.

## DEMOCRACY AND RADICAL CHANGE

Ongoing debates and difficulties in Greece are of great significance for anyone seeking to pursue radical politics today. And these debates have strong echoes of the discussions around the PCI's historic compromise, and the reformism of the SPD in the years before the First World War: they concern the question of what level of compromise is necessary, or acceptable, when a party of the left becomes, or seeks to become, a party of government. (The situation for Syriza is of course made worse because the Greek debt has been weaponised against them, but any left government today seeking measures of redistribution is likely to encounter serious obstacles because of the entanglements of all countries in the tentacles of globalisation and international finance; this reality confirms the importance of international co-ordination in working for progressive change.)

For some, Syriza's problem was that it wanted to ride two contradic-tory horses: both to resist austerity *and* stay in the EU and Eurozone. The leftists who in 2015 split off into Popular Unity favoured 'Grexit'. There are parallels here with those favouring a 'Lexit' in the UK: there is little sense of the EU as being itself a site of political contestation. Kevin Ovenden notes the impossibility of a short-term strategy based on seeking allies within the institutions of the EU for an alterna-tive. But he does acknowledge that the weight of the explanation for the Syriza government's capitulation is to be found 'in the strategic dilemmas posed by trying to break with austerity capitalism'.[43]

Others have focused on the lesson that democracy is limited by what the European central bankers are prepared to allow. For Yanis Varoufakis, Greek finance minister until September 2015, Frankfurt and Washington are people 'for whom democracy appears ... to be a nuisance'.[44]

Some argue that Syriza underestimated the political antagonism it faced, and had 'counted on the supposed values of the west – of respect for sovereignty, pluralism and democracy – to assure it a fair hearing'.[45] Stathis Kouvelakis judges that Varoufakis's successor, Euclid Tsakalotos, approached negotiations with EU representatives under the illusion that there really could be 'common ground – a "win-win" deal', thus showing not only a lack of 'perception of class antagonism but the elementary realism that any political figure needs'.[46] These judgements are much easier to make, however, than is proposing a serious alternative strategy. The case for Grexit has similar flaws to that of Brexit. As Gourgouris puts it:

> When possible costs of abandoning the Euro are to this day brought up in protest to those who claim that Grexit is the only option, cost estimates are often dismissed as panic-driven, or at the very least, temporary in effect. Rarely are these costs really measured against current costs, and partly this is an obvious methodological issue: the fact that the current costs are known, while the Grexit costs are positively unknown.[47]

Other debates focus on the extent to which left strategy should be based on working within state structures, with governmental action seen as the key agent of progressive change, as opposed to a stronger emphasis on mass social movement activity. This highlights the challenges faced by the left in bringing radical impulses and energies into formal politics, and the need to cohere the energies and concerns of radical mass movements into policies which can be implemented: again, these are precisely the issues faced by Eurocommunists in the 1970s. As Marina Prentoulis observes, experiences in Athens and Madrid demonstrate that 'any decisive assault against neoliberal hegemony has to simultaneously involve a strong grassroots movement and an engagement with parliamentary politics'.[48]

The kind of reactions against neoliberal austerity which won support for Podemos and Syriza have been seen elsewhere. Bernie Sanders's spirited campaign for the 2016 Democratic Presidential nomination is one example; it proved the catalyst for rapid growth by the Democratic Socialists of America, amongst other progressive developments. And the election of Jeremy Corbyn as Labour leader is evidence of some real potential for left populism in Britain. This was expressed through and around the structures of a party whose most experienced parliamentarians have, over a very long period of time, developed an appreciation of established systems and practices. Tensions were perhaps inevitable, but Labour's June 2017 electoral advances may provide the basis for its consolidation as an avowedly left-wing social-democratic party which values its links to social movements with more radical agendas, at the same time as earning and maintaining support from both 'traditional' and new voters.

Another aspect of Corbyn's appeal is worth noting. As with Sanders in the US, Corbyn won support for his evident honesty and straight-talking. Even those opposed to his leadership increasingly came to recognise that Corbyn's justified reputation for saying what he thought and being consistent won a positive response from many voters who had become alienated by the insincere, evasive 'spin' which seemed to characterise 'the political class'.[49]

Developing and translating progressive-populist impulses into electoral success, and then using this as a base to reverse neoliberal culture, is much more difficult than simply stimulating opposition to current realities. Bringing the energy and ambitions of social movements into mainstream politics and thereby changing the mainstream is vital; and this has to be part of a strategy capable of winning the support of a majority.

As movements and parties develop that may be in a position to implement as well as promote policies in different directions from neoliberalism, some of the issues touched on in this chapter will become more important and controversial. Effective practice will connect 'top-down' to 'bottom-up'. Horizontal movements and relationships and organisations of 'vertical' decision-making will have to learn how to work together. Implementing radical agendas will require representatives who take responsibility for governmental processes – but also the grass-roots structures and political culture to hold those representatives to account.

How could this be done? How can preconditions and expectations be put in place so that, when progressive social movements build up and make their push, wide sections of the population support or accept those changes? How could such a scenario be aligned with changes in institutions and among those who currently hold economic power, so that future moments of progressive potential are matched to openings in national states and international institutions, and 'strategic breaks' from current arrangements are achieved? The name of these problems – and of their solution – is democracy.

## NOTES

1. The international context also shaped South African possibilities of course: 'the end of the apartheid regime ... was hastened once the possible implications for the cold war of the assumption of power by the African

National Congress lost their significance'. Michael Rustin and Doreen Massey, *Soundings* 58, Winter 2014-5.

2.  Statement by SACP, 6 December 2013. Mandela participated in the underground SACP conference in December 1960 which determined to begin armed struggle against the apartheid regime.

3.  For example, it was Joe Slovo who convinced Mandela, whilst imprisoned at Robben Island, 'that a free South Africa would have to have a full separation of powers, a constitutional court that could overrule the government, and a bill of rights'. Marshall Berman, *All That is Solid Melts Into Air*, Verso, London 2010, p354.

4.  Tariq Ali, *The Idea of Communism*, Seagull Books, London 2009, p93.

5.  Slavoj Zizek, *In Defence of Lost Causes*, Verso, London 2008, p338.

6.  Nick Srnicek and Alex Williams, *Inventing the Future*, Verso, London 2015, p26.

7.  Richard J F Day, *Gramsci is Dead*, Pluto Press, London 2005, p8.

8.  Jacob Mukherjee, *Soundings* 59, Spring 2015.

9.  John Holloway, *Change the World Without Taking Power*, Pluto Press, London 2010 [2002], pix.

10. Fredric Jameson, in Sebastian Budgen, Stathis Kouvelakis and Slavoj Zizek (eds), *Lenin Reloaded*, Duke University Press, London 2007, p61.

11. Perry Anderson, *Spectrum*, Verso, London 2005, pxv.

12. Jeremy Gilbert, www.signsofthetimes.org.uk, 1 December 2002.

13. Emir Sader, *The New Mole*, Verso, London 2011, p75.

14. Nick Srnicek and Alex Williams, *Inventing the Future*, Verso, London 2015, p3.

15. Ernesto Laclau, *The Rhetorical Foundations of Society*, Verso, London 2014. Quoted in David Slater, 'Ernesto Laclau (1935-2014)', *Soundings* 58, Winter 2014-15.

16. Naomi Klein, *This Changes Everything*, Allen Lane, London 2014, p 158.

17. Jodi Dean, *Crowds and Party*, Verso, London 2016.

18. Neal Lawson, 'Labouring On?' www.opendemocracy.net, 1 July 2016.

19. Nancy Fraser, 'Against Anarchism', www.publicseminar.org, 9 October 2013.

20. Alberto Toscano, *Fanaticism*, Verso, London 2010, p92.

21. Benjamin Kunkel, 'The unbearable lightness of Slavoj Zizek's communism', *New Statesman*, 27 September 2012.

22. Stuart Jeffries, interview with Alain Badiou, *The Guardian*, 18 May 2012.

23. Slavoj Zizek, *In Defence of Lost Causes*, Verso, London 2008, p183.

24. Birkbeck Institute for the Humanities, University of London, 2009.

25. Simon Critchley, foreword to Paul Bowman and Richard Stamp (eds), *The Truth of Zizek*, Continuum, London 2007, pxiv.

26. Critchley, ibid, ppxv-xvi.

27. Geoff Boucher and Matthew Sharpe, 'Introduction' to *International Journal of Zizek Studies*, Volume 4, Number 2, 2010.

28. 'Saying "We" Again: A Conversation with Jodi Dean on Democracy, Occupy and Communism', www.*criticallegalthinking.com*, 6 November 2012.
29. Ernesto Laclau and Chantal Mouffe, *Hegemony and Socialist Strategy*, Verso, London 2001 [1985], pp178,167.
30. Alain Badiou, *The Communist Hypothesis*, Verso, London 2010, p1.
31. Jodi Dean, *The Communist Horizon*, Verso, London 2013, p 57.
32. Colin Crouch, *Coping with Post-democracy*, Fabian Society, London 2000, p 1.
33. Jodi Dean, *Crowds and Party*, Verso, London 2016.
34. Kunkel, op cit.
35. Daniel Trilling, 'Perspectives on the refugee crisis', *Times Literary Supplement*, 24 June 2016.
36. Pablo Iglesias, 'Understanding Podemos', *New Left Review*, May – June 2015.
37. Fraser, op cit.
38. Pablo Iglesias, quoted in Giles Tremlett, 'The Podemos Revolution', *The Guardian*, 31 March 2015.
39. Pablo Iglesias, *Politics in a Time of Crisis*, Verso, London 2015, p 180.
40. Stathis Gourgouris, 'The Syriza problem: radical democracy and left governmentality in Greece', www.opendemocracy.net, 6 August 2015.
41. Alexis Tsipras, 'Foreword' to Pablo Iglesias, *Politics in a Time of Crisis*, Verso, London 2015, p xi.
42. Kevin Ovenden, *Syriza*, Pluto Press, London 2015.
43. Ovenden, ibid, p173.
44. Yanis Varoufakis, 'The lenders are the real winners in Greece – Alexis Tsipras has been set up to fail', *The Guardian*, 21 September 2015.
45. Adam Tooze, 'After the War', *London Review of Books*, 19 November 2015.
46. This quote is from the strong critique of Syriza set out in an interview with Stathis Kouvelakis, 'Syriza's rise and fall', *New Left Review*, January – February 2016.
47. Gourgouris, op cit.
48. Marina Prentoulis, 'From the EU to Latin America: left populism and regional integration', *Soundings*, 63, summer 2016, p 30.
49. For a range of assessments, see Mark Perryman (ed), *The Corbyn Effect*, Lawrence and Wishart, London 2017.

# 18. Prospects for renewal?

## WHERE TO BEGIN?

How could a progressive radical project be successful, and what lessons can be drawn from the efforts covered in this book? At the time of writing, some glimmerings of hope are beginning to emerge after the long winter of neoliberalism that followed the collapse of communism, and the linked ending of the social-democratic consensus. In Britain, the surge in support for the renewed Labour Party in the June 2017 elections is one signal of an emerging break from neoliberalism. It is true that this has so far largely manifested itself in support for reforms that would have looked mild to social-democrats in the mid-twentieth century, let alone communists. Nevertheless, people on the left can now relate to and be part of a sea change in common sense, and here it is the direction of travel that is most important: there is a need to carry forward and build the momentum for change. The question for today's left is the extent to which it can catch and develop the new moods to help shape a stronger rejection of neoliberalism.

Once again we may be facing some of the strategic problems which faced our forebears in the Second International – seeking reforms within current arrangements, but unsure whether these should or could be pushed beyond the limits of the system. The wider left parties within which those still asserting Marxism have recently been most effective – including Syriza, Podemos and, through a totally different trajectory, the African National Congress – have found themselves confronting the familiar choices, responsibilities and constraints of social- democracy. And these have been made even more difficult by the international context, which remains dominated by neoliberal policies; while, at least until recently, the resulting economic and social instabilities have tended to mobilise a dynamic right-wing populism rather than a turn to the left.

One fresh element in the make-up of the new left parties, however, marking an important departure from traditional social-democracy, has been a revived left-wing populism, shaped by rich and fertile links between elected representatives and broadly-based social movements. Most establishment politicians and commentators apply the populist label even-handedly to its 'extreme' right- and left-wing forms, partly so as to discredit the latter. But it is more accurate to see both forms as attempts to build a strong political sense of the people, with the aim of making a challenge to the established elite. For the right this is usually based on an appeal to an exclusively defined national sense of belonging, but for the left it more usually represents a contemporary attempt to establish popular sovereignty. Left populism can be understood as an effort to push back against the way liberal principles are currently being deployed by traditional elites as a defence against the desire for equality by those most affected by neoliberal austerity.[1]

The kinds of dynamics which generated Podemos and Syriza indicate that increasing numbers of people want to see new political movements that are strategic, radical and multi-layered. In Britain, this mood has partly been channelled through the debates and events sponsored by Momentum, a lively movement through which people with varied understandings of left and radical politics have contributed to changes in the Labour Party, drawn many young people into politics, and re-engaged thousands of older activists.

All of this confirms the possibility over the next few years of a growth of movements and parties that are able to inspire and mobilise, but at the same time are capable of being reflexive, focused and historically aware. In such a left, activists would understand the need to work on a step-by-step basis, attempting immediate improvements today, but would pursue these shorter-term aims within a strategic sense of longer-term change, so that they were also working for thoroughly transformed social arrangements. Different groups and networks are likely to focus on different concerns – whether that is reasserting trade unionism; challenging sexism and racism; collectively struggling against precarious working conditions; taking initiatives to tackle the housing crisis; addressing international issues; or focusing on the many other urgent issues that face us. But the aim would be to link these varied efforts in a project that would seek to collectively represent and co-ordinate their energy and potential, in order to establish a new counter-hegemony, and to convince growing numbers of people that the crises of contemporary societies – ecological degradation, financial turmoil, racialised divisions, increasing inequality – are systemic and interlinked, not amenable to legislative reform, and require transformative solutions.

During such developments, one lesson to be learned from the past is that people contribute to progressive change in a wide variety of different ways. Traditional left parties need to acknowledge the debt they owe to social movements and alternative campaigners, and not seek to corral them all into their tent or under their wing. Interplay, dialogue and respect are the appropriate methods and styles, rather than attempts to discipline, control and direct. The connection between Podemos and Syriza and social movements, though not always smooth, has been crucial to their success; in Britain, many in the Labour Party are now looking at ways to relate its parliamentary and municipal socialisms to progressive campaigns and informal movements. In this, there is much to learn from others. The Green Party, for example, has learned better than the rest of the left from feminism.

In working for progressive renewal, it is important to recognise that the road ahead is not in any way straightforward. There *have* been recent advances: but there are as yet no parties and movements with sufficient power or popular enough programmes to be able to resolve current issues in progressive ways. This means that many problems are still likely to be addressed in ways which could further marginalise and crush the left, rather than opening up new possibilities. Being ready and psychologically prepared for such setbacks is important, so that recovery can be as rapid as possible: patience remains a true progressive virtue.

In these challenging times, tasks for radicals include credible criticism of today's social and economic arrangements, in all their complexity; the seeding and nurturing of new social movements and projects; a new purposefulness to research, so that, for example, studies of social movements seek to identify practical ways to realise their progressive intent, as well as producing theories of difference; experiments to pioneer new and socialised approaches to living within the interstices of today's settlements; and political programmes aiming at new, sustainable settlements and positive futures, including through governmental action. It is by no means clear what combination of arguments, initiatives and opportunities will significantly develop and advance such possibilities.

## DEMOCRACY IS FUNDAMENTAL

In this context, is there anything useful to learn from twentieth-century communism? Given how dramatically things have changed over the last thirty years and more, are its histories and debates still relevant? A cautiously affirmative answer to this question of course needs to be tempered by an awareness that current social dynamics – including globalisation, hyper-financialisation, informationalism, demographic change, large-scale migration and the complex connections we establish over distance, through travel and communications – mean that old political cultures and methods cannot be simply recovered and reapplied.

New forms of solidarity and commonality have to be built in today's contexts. And even if the old forms of communist organisation could be recreated, experience suggests that this would be a mistake. Communism's methods did not work. Its failed attempt at long-term social transformation offers little in the way of a realistically different economic structure. Left-wing nostalgics have to accept that future radicalism cannot possibly take the same form as twentieth-century communism. That movement's originating contexts are long gone, and its history highlights fundamental issues to be addressed in future efforts. These would need to succeed across areas in which communism chronically failed, including democracy, ecology and individuality.

Some of the efforts discussed in the previous chapters do, though, suggest aspects of communist practice and thinking which may prove useful in future. These include insights about economic development; experiments in combining the market with socialist planning; and initiatives shaped by progressive internationalism. Wider lessons can also be drawn from the ways communists seeking change in western democracies approached the political process. Within the communist movement serious theoretical and practical efforts were made to understand the relationship between parties and social movements; to comprehend the political dynamics of capitalist societies, and the resulting changes that can be achieved within state structures; to articulate 'horizontal' relationships between people with 'vertical' strategies for running institutions and countries; to build alliances between different forces; and to develop cultural activities to engage substantial numbers of people, enabling them to develop new moral subjectivities that broke with the predominant common sense of their times.

One determinant of any future radical political programme that will necessarily make it different from that of twentieth-century communism is the need to address the rapidly approaching catastrophes resulting from climate disruption. Economic development programmes and regulatory frameworks now need to be ecologically responsible, seeking to reduce and reverse the damage to the ecosphere which industrial development has caused over the last two hundred years. This means developing politics defined by the interests of our future grand-children, great grand-children and generations to come.

Instead, today's political energies on the populist right are largely directed at carrying forward the inherited grievances of our imagined ancestors. Reactionary, sectional, oppressive and self-defeating impulses promote pride in what the forebears of whatever tribe they belong to supposedly said, did or had. Such impulses underpin the desire of European ethno-nationalists to feel in control of a well-defended territory that in their imagination was once peopled by a single and homogeneous group, and is now symbolised by their flag – a totem around which this control could be resummoned; and they also underpin uncompromising state Zionism, with its exclusivist claims on a homeland where large numbers of other people live; as well as extreme Islamist 'jihadism', insistent on a distorted understanding of the faith, with all the horrific and murderous consequences that brings; and the great power chauvinisms emanating from Washington and Moscow.[2]

A consistent theme of this book is that those seeking progressive change should embrace the democratic political process, including in its 'familiar liberal sense of a parliamentary-type system, with party political pluralism and regular elections': working within this system where it exists is a necessary condition of socialist success.[3] The fact that right-wing forces have been prepared to dispense with democracy in developing neoliberalism, as in Chile in 1973, and that neoliberal economic development can take place in non-liberal societies, as in China since the late 1980s, is not evidence of democracy's worthlessness. Nor do these and other examples provide a basis for any polemic against liberal democracy based on exposing the hypocrisy of politicians who only support it when it suits them.

Such contradictions and inconsistencies are instead evidence that democracy is a political form that the left should defend and promote more consistently than the right. It is more, and better, democracy that we need, not less. Democratic principles are crucial for the development of progressive politics: what is needed is their *extension* throughout civil society and the economy, not their rejection as neoliberalism's ideological cover. This is not least because, as the liberal John Stuart Mill recognised, meaningful participation in democratic processes can have positive effects on subjectivities: 'participants come to value their own moral and intellectual worth'. The resulting cultures foster the type of 'personality capable of deferring immediate gratification in favour of longer-term goals', and encourage 'a breadth of vision and sympathy which transcends sectional interests'.[4] Such positive developments are a crucial resource for sustaining progressive change. It is therefore a sign of ongoing confusion and demoralisation when some of the sharpest and most energetic critics of current social arrangements declare that liberal democratic principles are redundant, a sideshow, or a trick.

Radicals need to fully support democratic values, as well as the practices of representation that institutionalise and safeguard them on an enduring basis. 'Liberal' institutions such as modern parliaments – although they first emerged as part of establishing bourgeois class rule, and were used to manage and dissipate opposition to it – do not necessarily or essentially institutionalise the rule of the few. These forms can – and should – be given new political content, and are themselves a terrain of battle. They are not only a space in which ideas are contested and radical programmes are promoted; they are also an important means through which, with majority democratic support, such programmes could be implemented. The practices and freedoms which representative democracy has promised but not always delivered have a crucial role to play in establishing and sustaining long-term settlements based on equality and solidarity. For such settlements cannot be realised without a serious working-through of the issues and debates that express social differences and choices. These need to be negotiated in ways that are engaging and productive. Effective political practice requires a recognition of the inevitability and value of varied opinions and interests, and competition 'on terrains which ... are not of our own choosing'.[5]

## INTERLINKS

Some of the major debates amongst progressive radicals over the last decades have been about the relative merits of different kinds of activity in different locations. But, while some of these debates have been very productive, there needs to be more recognition that there is not always a single answer to these questions. Thus, for example, interstitial activity has been widely celebrated – attempting to live well and prefigure a better future in the spaces that can be occupied and defended from incursion by the currently established powers; this kind of politics helps develop the collectivism and networking that many young people seek in their personal lives. But adherents of this approach often disdain those who opt for governmental and institutional activity through political parties, or campaigning for changes to current policies. Equally, those focused on party political politics often disdain social movement politics.

But there is no need to make these either/or choices. Real change will come through the efforts of transformational agents working in many and varied areas, at all levels. The real prize will come from being able to relate and combine the different forms of activity, in what Italian and Spanish activists call 'transversal politics'. This will not happen simply, or without tension. The multiple connections which are needed between movements, organisations, parties, the state and democratised international bodies will involve negotiation and compromise; and the resulting cultures of dialogue for radical change will anticipate and contribute to the wider democratic processes of the future. The people who succeed in making positive links between the local and the global, and the personal and the political, will constitute twenty-first century examples of the 'organic intellectuals' envisioned by Gramsci in the 1930s. These 'change agents' will learn how to facilitate interlinks across multiple sites of activity, help organise new blocs of social forces, and promote a new common sense about how we should live.

The aim will be to develop and maintain alliances and networks which are both represented in 'the mainstream' *and* active in social movements. The programmatic concern will be to achieve improvements that address current problems, while also asserting an increasingly robust and tried-and-tested vision of a transformed future.

Such a politics cannot be defined in terms of one party. Relationships between actors within different alliances, and the extent to which they 'own' the vision outlined here, will be uneven and unstable. Questions over how to combine the directness and focus of social movements with the disciplines and preparedness to compromise that are inevitably and properly part of representative democracy will provide the material to keep dozens of journals, blogs and conferences going. Nevertheless, such an approach could create and grow a body of organised opinion in mainstream politics that draws on the freshness, energy, anger and frustration of those it represents and is accountable to. Building a new hegemony will require the winning across of many of those who currently support today's settlements, or lend support to right-wing populisms, through the establishment of new frontiers and divisions around which politics can progress.

Such methods would address some of the questions which have not yet been solved by social movement activists, including the question of what activists do on the quiet days, or how to involve people who are sympathetic but do not turn up to demonstrations and occupations. We need to discard any sense that the only moments that matter are the great days of 'direct democracy', and that until those days come there is nothing to do but wait. Rather than echoing the autonomists of the 1970s in their rejection of discipline and strategy, we need to take heed of the lessons from those against whom they were protesting: the Eurocommunist politicians and radicals in social movements who were trying to connect to each other in order to bring about transformative change through deepening democracy in government, municipalities, places of work, cultural spaces and daily life. The context has changed in many ways since the 1970s, of course. But, as Fabien Escalona has argued:

> In spite of these differences, several strategic debates from the Eurocommunist [period] are still relevant today. They concern the capacity of the radical left to escape both marginality and normalisation; in other words, to approach power without its desires for transformation being absorbed or liquidated by existing institutions.[6]

As Syriza and Podemos have found, making such 'approaches to power' is not straightforward, and generates many dilemmas, choices and contradictions.[7] It involves developing ideas, persuading people, effective campaigning, relating different forms of activity and learning, and working to instil new optimism into an expanded democratic politics. None of this is easy: even to begin means attempting to break from the existing consumerist cultures that shape us. In pursuing intellectual and moral reform, we need to begin with ourselves.

Just as the Bolsheviks carried over into their culture elements of the Tsarist context, in ways that proved to be self-defeating, so today's potential agents of change are at risk of reproducing elements of individualism and neoliberalism within radical culture. The resistance to centralisation and co-ordination that has marked successive waves of anti-globalisation protests is in some ways a mirror of 'the pseudo-individualist rhetoric of contemporary capitalism'.[8] Then there is the tendency for oppositional politics to take the form of individual dissent connected to personal issues, or 'micro' claims for personal recognition. Such concerns can be all too easily consoled and assimilated by consumerism.

Thinking through these issues will be key for future progressive movements. It is important to recognise that power is dispersed and complex, and that the old lefts neglected many important forms and dynamics of oppression that people experience subjectively. But this insight needs to be articulated to a politics that also addresses objective aspects of power. The goal is to go beyond recognition for and understanding of our particular oppressions: to work for the transformation of social relations so that those oppressions no longer exist.

The counter-positioning of direct democracy to the disciplines and requirements of organising in accountable hierarchies should be dropped. On the one hand this generates a self-denying ordinance through which many radicals refuse to engage in representative politics and the reform and development of current institutions. On the other it prevents many mainstream politicians from understanding the wider drivers of social change. This results in a great withholding of potential by people who could effectively match 'lateral' and 'horizontal' efforts to 'vertical' structures and struggles.

Such an approach would enable the reassertion of an effective and modernised class politics. This cannot be done abstractly: any such reconstitution must be based on the practical, lived forms in which class is now experienced, and connect to the many ways in which people see themselves and others – in terms of their economic position, their diverse cultural and social identities and their aspirations. Our gender, race, age and many other aspects of our identity necessarily shape our understanding of current issues and possibilities. But we can also look for generalisable lessons. The way forward is through seeking commonalities while respecting difference, and developing a political logic which is able to knit people together and respond to different issues, through defining shared opponents and embodying a shared vision of new ways of living.

A more complex understanding of class would help make sense of the varied and fragmented ways in which people experience exploitation and disadvantage, and unnecessary barriers to the realisation of their potential and ambitions. This will mean that we stop thinking of ourselves as individual consumers, let down by the system's failure to deliver on its promises, and facing our own personal difficulties in housing, finance, education and work. Instead, we will be able to think of ourselves as members of a group – a collective – whose interests require new social arrangements.

The strategy and tasks sketched here will require continuous learning, and thousands of little steps to build confidence and develop skills. The pioneers of new, socialised, approaches to living and working will need to be practical when addressing immediate issues, but at the same time capable of generating big ambitions. The way ahead will also mean successfully challenging – and defeating – those currently powerful forces who want us to live in ways which meet their own interests, rather than realise the potential of the many.

## ALTERNATIVES FOR THE FUTURE

In looking forward from the defining moments of twentieth-century communism, what are the prospects we face over the next decades and centuries? I would argue that there are three broad possibilities.

The first is that there will soon be the total destruction of human life, resulting from a series of environmental disasters of our own making, linked to highly destructive conflicts, and perhaps nuclear disasters. These may stretch over decades – or last only moments. Many will see this statement as pessimistic and alarmist, a science fiction script. But we have already put all the elements in place for such a scenario. We need to become better at imagining what could happen as a result.[9]

The second possibility is that there will be a series of social, economic and environmental shocks and disasters, with associated conflicts, wars, large-scale chaotic migrations and health crises, that seriously reverse human achievement.[10] Most people's quality of life and cultural standards will be severely degraded, and large parts of the planet rendered uninhabitable. The means of subsistence will be available to only a fraction of the numbers of humans alive today, and uncountable fatalities will result, as well as intense miseries for the survivors. The resulting political dislocations will make the 'turmoil' following 2016's Brexit vote look like a mill pond on a calm summer day.

For those who do not recognise this possibility, some information. We are already living in the early stages of this scenario. The symptoms of our descent include: sudden economic collapses; ongoing increases in poverty and gross inequality; the plundering of public assets and pension funds, sometimes through 'corruption', sometimes legally sanctioned; the subjection of the poor to multiple coercive controls, alongside an ongoing erosion of real social order; precarious work, as automation threatens our livelihoods rather than liberating us from drudgery; multiple indications of global warming, including damage beyond any safe level to the key processes on which life depends; the rise of extremism, which grows in the soil of despair; the proliferation of conflicts and wars. In every direction, divisions and problems feed regression and barbarism. There are many reasons to be pessimistic.[11]

But we can also assert a third possibility – one that depends on sustaining an 'optimism of the will', and recognising the positive potentials still held in today's social structures. In this version of the future we will achieve transformed social arrangements, through new waves of change in culture and politics, and these will enable us to rebuild the ideals of freedom, equality and social solidarity. This scenario will depend on the left – and many others – inter-acting with, learning from, and adding to the revolts, reactions and movements that are arising in response to current dangers. Through such engagement, dialogue and development, a range of positive and practical projects could be built. Arguments and strategies would be constructed, and rational proposals implemented, opening up routes to new ways of living. Alliances would be brought together around critiques of current realities, and would work together for alternative social models.

A long-term 'war of position' would succeed in generating popular support for alternative economic, environmental and social settlements. Agents for change would show that radical politics can be the emergency brake on the runaway train currently speeding us to catastrophe.[12] Developing social movements and new institutions could lead to a series of sharp breaks and ruptures with current systems – or they could work through a cumulative series of reforms, blocks and controls, 'making capitalism human, until, maybe, it isn't capitalism any more, a progressive project which would perhaps last two hundred years'.[13] Success in this battle would mean recovering, expanding and institutionalising a generous conception of democracy and establishing ecologically sustainable forms of consumption, work and resource management.

Unfortunately, our best efforts to avert the next major events on the road to regressive barbarism may well fail: it may take a disaster at least as desperate as the first world war to galvanise any effective level of support for a future progressive radical politics. In that case, the usefulness of all current campaigns, movements, initiatives and small steps forward will be judged on their ability to contribute, at that point, to putting in place the organisations, understandings and cultures that could shape and positively develop popular responses to disaster.

In the context of these three broad possibilities, many people – perhaps most people – continue acting as if there were a fourth. But the idea that this 'fourth option' points the way to a possible future is so preposterous, delusional and fantastic that it is hardly worth considering: and that is the notion that this world, as it is, will last – that we can carry on as we are.

## NOTES

1. See Inigo Errejon, in Errejon and Chantal Mouffe, *Podemos: in the name of the people*, Lawrence and Wishart, London 2016, p91; also Paolo Gerbaudo, 'The populist era'; and Kevin Morgan, Marina Prentoulis, Sirio Canós and Jeremy Gilbert, 'Alliances, fronts, parties and populism', both in *Soundings* 65, spring 2017.
2. It should, however, be noted that not all Jews are Zionists, and that not all Zionists refuse the possibility of compromise; Islamism is not Islam; and there is a demoralised class politics within right-wing populism which liberals and left-wingers would do well to attend to.
3. See Pat Devine, *Democracy and Economic Planning*, Polity Press, Cambridge 1988, p130. As Devine argues, 'the dismissal of this immensely important historical achievement on the grounds that it constitutes mere

"bourgeois" democracy is, at best, an unthought through legacy from an earlier historical period or, at worst, active dogmatic fundamentalism'.

4. See the discussion by David Purdy of Mill's *Considerations on Representative Government* (1861) in 'Keywords: Democracy', *Perspectives*, Democratic Left Scotland, Dundee Autumn 2007.

5. Pablo Iglesias, *Politics in a Time of Crisis*, Verso, London 2015, p170.

6. Fabien Escalona, 'The Heritage of Eurocommunism in the Contemporary Radical Left' in *Socialist Register 2017*, Merlin Press, London 2016, p104.

7. Costas Douzinas, 'The Left in Power?', www.nearfuturesonline.org, March 2016. The observation that '"contradiction" is the name of the left in power' is explored further in Costas Douzinas, *Syriza in Power*, Polity, Cambridge 2017.

8. Benedict Seymour, 'Nationalise This! What Next for Anti-Globalization Protests?', *Radical Philosophy*, May-June 2001.

9. This is so even though, as Fredric Jameson has said, it has already become easier to envisage a total catastrophe which ends all life on earth than it is to imagine the changes that could be made in capitalist economic and social structures so as to remove the risk of catastrophic man-made threats.

10. For an assessment of one of these prospects, see John R. Wennersten and Denise Robbins, *Rising Tides: climate refugees in the twenty-first century*, Indiana University Press, Bloomington IN 2017.

11. Fernando Claudin closed his book *Eurocommunism and Socialism* (New Left Books/Verso, London 1978) as follows: 'There are many reasons to be pessimistic. But was it not always so on the eve of some great historical upheaval?'.

12. This sentence reworks Walter Benjamin's characterisation of socialism.

13. Judith Shapiro, speaking at the 'Are We Powerless?' event, Manchester International Festival, July 2013.

# Reading on ...

## JOURNALS

The ongoing, 'real time' assessments and provisional analyses in a number of journals produced every few months offer a good way of 'reading on' from this book.

*Soundings*, published by Lawrence and Wishart, has articles and debate in every issue, in different registers, on problems and prospects covered here.

*Socialist History* and *Twentieth Century Communism*, also published by Lawrence and Wishart, provide high quality material on left history.

*New Left Review*, *Radical Philosophy* and the journal *Capitalism Nature Socialism* always carry valuable articles.

*Socialist Register*, the annual put out jointly by the Merlin Press and Monthly Review Press, is another excellent journal.

The long-established *Monthly Review* is a useful read from the USA, as is the upstart *Jacobin*.

For important online material, see www.opendemocracy.net

## SUGGESTED BOOKS FOR FURTHER READING

For overviews of the record of the left across the last 150 years:

Eric Hobsbawm, *Age of Extremes*, Michael Joseph, London 1994
Lucio Magri, *The Tailor of Ulm*, Verso, London 2011
Donald Sassoon, *One Hundred Years of Socialism*, Fontana, London 1997
Willie Thompson, *The Left in History*, Pluto, London 1997

On Marxism:

Terry Eagleton, *Why Marx Was Right*, Yale University Press,
London 2011
Eric Hobsbawm, *How to Change the World*, Little, Brown, London
2011
Leszek Kolakowski, *Main Currents of Marxism*, WW Norton and
company, New York, (single volume edition) 2004 [originally
published in three volumes in 1978]

On the Soviet experience:

Fedor Il'ich Dan, *Two Years of Wandering*, Lawrence and Wishart,
London 2016
Sheila Fitzgerald, *Everyday Stalinism*, Oxford University Press,
Oxford 1999
Sheila Fitzgerald, *On Stalin's Team*, Princeton University Press,
Princeton NJ 2015
Kristen Ghodsee, *Lost in Transition*, Duke University Press,
Durham NC 2011 (on post-communist nostalgia)
Moshe Lewin, *The Gorbachev Phenomenon*, Radius/Century
Hutchinson, London 1988
Moshe Lewin, *The Soviet Century*, Verso, London 2005

On some political leaders:

Aldo Agosti, *Palmiro Togliatti*, I B Tauris, London 2008
Stephen Cohen, *Bukharin and the Bolshevik Revolution*, Oxford
University Press 1971
Israel Getzler, *Martov*, Cambridge University Press, Cambridge,
1967
Lars T Lih, *Lenin*, Reaktion, London 2011
Massimo Salvadori, *Karl Kautsky and the Socialist Revolution 1880-
1938*, New Left Books/Verso, London 1979
William Taubman, *Khrushchev*, Simon and Schuster, New York
2003

Antonio Gramsci's key writings are available in various volumes from
Lawrence and Wishart.

The most useful commentaries include:

Kate Crehan, *Gramsci's Common Sense*, Duke University Press, Durham NC 2016

Antonio A. Santucci, *Antonio Gramsci*, Monthly Review Press, New York 2010

Roger Simon, *Gramsci's Political Thought*, Lawrence and Wishart, London (third edition) 2015

Palmiro Togliatti, *On Gramsci and Other Writings*, Lawrence and Wishart, London 1979

On some political parties and movements:

Geoff Andrews, *Endgames and New Times*, Lawrence and Wishart, London 2004 (on the Communist Party of Great Britain from 1964 to 1991)

John Callaghan, *Cold War, Crisis and Conflict*, Lawrence and Wishart, London 2004 (on the CPGB from 1951 to 1968)

Costas Douzinas, *Syriza in Power*, Polity, Cambridge 2017

Inigo Errejon and Chantal Mouffe, *Podemos: in the name of the people*, Lawrence and Wishart, London 2016

William F. Fisher and Thomas Ponniah (eds), *Another World is Possible*, Zed Books, London 2003 (documents from the World Social Forum).

Pablo Iglesias, *Politics in a Time of Crisis*, Verso, London 2015 (perspectives from a key figure in Podemos)

Andre Liebich, *From the Other Shore*, Harvard University Press, Cambridge, MT 1997 (on the Mensheviks in exile)

Rossana Rosssanda, *The Comrade From Milan*, Verso, London 2010 (memoir of an Italian communist and new leftist)

On the ecological fundamental:

John Bellamy Foster, *Marx's Ecology*, Monthly Review Press, New York 2000

Naomi Klein, *This Changes Everything*, Allen Lane, London 2014

Jason Moore, *Capitalism in the Web of Life*, Verso, London 2015

Naomi Oreskes and Erik M Conway, *The Collapse of Western Civilisation*, Columbia University Press, New York 2014

Some theory:

Theodor Adorno and Max Horkheimer, *The Dialectic of Enlightenment*, Verso, London 1997 [1944]

Jodi Dean, *Crowds and Party*, Verso, London 2016

Pat Devine, *Democracy and Economic Planning*, Polity Press, Cambridge 1988

Nancy Fraser, *Adding Insult to Injury*, Verso, London 2008

Stuart Hall, *Selected Political Writings*, Lawrence and Wishart, London 2017

Ernesto Laclau and Chantal Mouffe, *Hegemony and Socialist Strategy*, Verso, London 2001 [1985]

Ernesto Laclau, *New Reflections on the Revolution of Our Time*, Verso, London 1990

Herbert Marcuse, *One Dimensional Man*, Routledge, Abingdon 2002 [1964]

James Martin (ed), *The Poulantzas Reader*, Verso, London 2008

Nicos Poulantzas, *State, Power, Socialism*, Verso, London 2014 [1978]

Jacques Ranciere, *Hatred of Democracy*, Verso, London 2014

Nick Srnicek and Alex Williams, *Inventing the Future*, Verso, London 2015

The best books on the issues covered here are, hopefully, still to be written. They would be histories showing how people organised through campaigns, social movements, parties and governments to promote and implement ecologically sound politics, reducing and reversing the environmental damage our systems have caused over the last two hundred years; how neoliberalism was overcome; how the ideologies of consumerism and individualism were broken down in the course of finding better ways to live; how oppressive and exploitative social and economic relationships were dismantled, through processes of change achieved without terrible wars and conflicts, and involving the extension and consolidation of real democracy; and how the promise of modernity was recovered, refocused and realised for future generations.

# Index